Language Perspectives

Language Perspectives
Papers from the *Educational Review*

Edited by Barrie Wade

Heinemann Educational Books
London

Heinemann Educational Books Ltd
22 Bedford Square, London WC1B 3HH

LONDON   EDINBURGH   MELBOURNE   AUCKLAND
HONG KONG   SINGAPORE   KUALA LUMPUR   NEW DELHI
IBADAN   NAIROBI   JOHANNESBURG
EXETER (NH)   KINGSTON   PORT OF SPAIN

First published 1982

British Library Cataloguing in Publication Data

Language perspectives.
   1. Language and Languages
   I. Wade, Barrie
   400   P106

   ISBN 0-435-10910-3

Printed and bound in Great Britain by
Biddles Ltd, Guildford and King's Lynn

Contents

Foreword

IN recent years perspectives on language in education have undergone change. To begin with more people have concentrated on language and on the relationship between language and learning. Linguists and psychologists have continued their traditional interests but have been joined by others who have added to and widened existing perspectives. For example, sociologists have begun to explore the ways in which language controls the teaching, beliefs and practices of groups as well as the part that language plays in constructing reality as we perceive it. At the same time, the emphases within traditional fields have altered. While some linguists have continued their preoccupations with the nature of language and its description, others have turned to actualities of situations in which an individual may, or may not, be communicating effectively.

These changes and emphases have been recorded and in many cases initiated by many important papers which have appeared in *Educational Review* over the last decade or so. In particular, the special issues devoted to the state, context, functions, developments and assessment of language have made an important contribution to our knowledge of the rôle of language in education. The selection of papers here, draws from this fund of material and presents the perspectives in such a way that they will be useful to anyone working to gain insights into language and learning.

I should particularly like to acknowledge the help and advice I have been given in compiling this selection by the secretary to the editors of *Educational Review*, Margaret Hier.

BARRIE WADE
Faculty of Education
University of Birmingham

Language: Advantage and Disadvantage

Barrie Wade

THIS introductory chapter to the present collection can hardly do justice to the viewpoints and insights contained in the rich variety of influential papers that follow. The editorial matter which precedes each paper can introduce them more appropriately, and thus leave this chapter to make its own perspective.

One overarching concern of both the recent past and the present is the relationship of language to culture in general and to educational success and failure in particular. Since most of the following chapters touch on these issues it is appropriate to present a general review here. Terms such as 'deficit', 'deprivation', and 'disadvantage' have too often been used synonymously and, together with fixed attitudes to language, have led to some research papers and curriculum development projects having unwarranted underlying assumptions.

The term 'culture' here denotes patterns of behaviour which an individual develops through interaction with his or her environment. Cultures therefore vary – depending upon their environments – and within cultures there will be variations also – depending upon the values and beliefs of subcultural groups and upon the affective and cognitive functioning typical of such groups. Immediately one notion of 'cultural deprivation' can be rejected since no one is *without* culture in the way it has now been defined.

The notion of disadvantage introduces the idea of comparison across cultures or subcultures. When such a comparative view enables us to be more critical of our accepted parochial ideas or to obtain a deeper understanding of human behaviour then it is likely to be beneficial. For example, Margaret Mead's studies of initiation and trial marriage in New Guinea and Samoa and of 'dating' in North America give insights into patterns of human courtship. These adaptations to environment are presented as differences and without ethnocentric valuations.

The problem comes when the researchers, seeing things from their own point of view, evaluate all cultures exclusively according to the standards of a single one. It is one thing to note that ancient Egyptian drawings included perspectives from different viewpoints; it is quite another to say that because Constable painted Flatford Mill from one spot, then Egyptian art is inferior. Hudson (1960, 1967) has shown that the act of perception includes interpretation and that different people may see the same representation in different ways depending upon their knowledge, experience and values. Early family-planning posters in India were ineffective since the smiling, well-dressed couple with two children provoked typical responses of sympathy that they were 'unlucky' compared with the sombre family of six children. Values and beliefs do not change overnight and we should always consider whether it is responsible to insist on particular changes. The North American Indians' association with the buffalo was ecologically well-balanced and the interference with their culture is well documented. We should also consider whether the changes we seek are trivial. It is easy to become modern Victorian missionaries giving our main effort to covering nakedness in hot climates.

A further problem is that of relying upon extreme views about deficit or difference when discussing cultural disadvantage. Bernstein, for example, certainly contributed to the deficit theory in his early work when he used terms such as 'poor' and 'inaccurate' to describe the structure of 'public' language. In the same way, Raph (1967) wrote of working-class speech:

> Sentences are largely incomplete, short, and made up of a simple clause, or of a string of simple clauses linked by 'and' . . . (pp. 205–6)

This way of reporting differences makes them into deficits, but the notion that there is no systematic structure in lower class language is not supported by evidence.

Firstly, one cannot assume that 'primitive' people speak primitive languages. The dictionary of Yoruba, compiled by Dr Abraham, contains 40,000 words, and Kambari, a North Nigerian language, has 30 tenses in the verb. Some 'primitive' languages are extremely subtle and capable of precise differentiation at both morphological and syntactical levels. Sapir (1921) has argued that:

> the lowliest South African Bushman speaks in the forms of a rich symbolic system that is in essence perfectly comparable to the speech of the cultivated Frenchman: (pp. 22–23)

Secondly, differences that occur within varieties of a single language depend more upon geography than deficit. The same edible item is called 'crumpet' or 'pikelet' according to where it is sold. A Jamaican creole speaker who says:

Im sell me de mangodem yeside. (She sold me mangoes yesterday.)

is not 'ignorant of English grammar', but following a system, similarly rule-governed, in which gender, tense and plurals are indicated in ways *different from* Standard English. Wight (1971) argues for the grammatical equality of dialects and therefore acceptance in speech of varieties such as:

he had went (Belfast)
shall us have us dinners (S. Yorks)

Thirdly, at the phonological level Giles (1970) has stressed the equality of accents. However, his research shows that people assign high-status to some accents (e.g. Received standard pronunciation or lowland Scots), and low status to others (Birmingham especially).

We can summarize this evidence by saying that there is no *linguistic* foundation for any notion of deficit. However, as Giles points out, evaluations are made by people. Even if these are made on social grounds they cannot be dismissed or ignored; it is useful, however, to expose their underlying assumptions.

It is difficult to expose the causes of disadvantage when much depends upon how the term is defined and the viewpoint of the definer. When the *Plowden Report* wrote:

The educational disadvantage of being born the child of an unskilled worker is both financial and psychological,

it omitted reference to language. It also makes assumptions about class and causality.

Assumptions about class are common and tarnish many interpretations of Bernstein's work. Bernstein himself was always careful to refer to *lower* working class and Roberts (1971) in a thorough analysis of working-class cultures shows that the working class is itself a hierarchy of discrete classes:

Division in our own society ranged from an 'elite' at the peak, composed of the leading families, through recognized strata to a social base whose members one damned as the 'lowest of the low'. (p. 17)

Defining class by father's occupation is as crude a procedure as class is a measure.

There is evidence to show the association of educational failure with social conditions and situations. Davie, *et al.* (1972) compute the chances of a child of a manual worker being a poor reader at seven years-old as three times greater than if he were born in other families. Morris (1966) also showed that of her poor readers 80 per cent had manual worker fathers, half of whom were unskilled.

This kind of research makes real correlations between performance and socioeconomic status, but it is important to remember that correlations do not explain the *causes* of a relationship, only its association. They say nothing, for example, about relationships inside the school, although these will be explored here.

The problem with the deficit theory is that it is easy to accept it (even when arguing against the fundamental importance of language) and then to rush on and design compensatory programmes. Blank and Solomon (1969) do this without even evaluating the meaning of deficit:

> the deprived child's verbal weakness is so overwhelming but it blinds one to his more subtle but basic deficiency. This deficiency is the lack of a symbolic system for thinking. (p. 47)

The implication here is that many programmes may be designed to repair deficits that simply do not exist.

When it is a matter of conflict within a system – say, a recent immigrant – then the issue is somewhat different. Cultural and linguistic shocks are inevitable and pain can be caused in ways that the DES (1971) has mentioned:

> Some may have a form of English so divergent from the standard form as to be almost unintelligible – a fact that they resent and find difficult to accept. (p. 10)

Here again it depends whether the intention is to *assimilate* immigrants into the main cultural stream or to *accommodate* to their differences – at least by recognizing the positive worth of the culture and language they possess.

It is perhaps worth mentioning that it is equally dangerous to be too optimistic about attitudes to differences and to overshoot available evidence. In a mainly sound and seminal paper Labov (1969) is guilty of these faults when he claims 'negro children in the urban ghettoes . . . hear more well-informed sentences than middle-class children . . .; they have the same basic vocabulary, possess the same capacity for conceptual learning, and use the same logic as anyone else' (p. 198). Labov's paper suggests that middle-class speech can be lacking logic and that given a favourable context a negro child *can* argue logically; however, his case study is not proof of the generalizations he makes. The implication of Labov's position (though taken somewhat out of context) would be that no extra investigation or assistance is necessary for negro ghetto children. A more fruitful concept is that of 'equality with difference' and by emphasizing 'same' Labov perhaps obscures this. It may well be necessary firstly to investigate rigorously just what these differences in language and behaviour are. I agree with Baratz and Baratz (1970) that:

then and only then can programs be created that utilize the child's difference as a means of furthering his acculturation to the mainstream while maintaining his individual identity and cultural heritage. (p. 49)

At this point it is clear that the deficit and difference perspectives both have deficiencies when stated in their extreme forms, although on the whole it seems sensible to recognize and foster children's differences while helping them (simultaneously) to extend their range. However, up to this point both perspectives have been focused on the child. Context and the role of educational institutions (including relationships with teachers) play an important part and these aspects will now be explored.

It is well known that the context of an experiment can affect its results. Greenfield (1966) found that Wolof children gave more than twice the number of conserving responses when they poured the liquid than when she, the experimenter, did and Vernon (1969) also shows how performance can be affected by the test situation. It is hardly surprising that Bernstein's messenger boys performed badly when asked to discuss corporal punishment compared with public school boys used to formal debate.

The teacher as well as the experimenter, can affect the course of the child's learning – especially if guided by assumptions such as those underlying the deficit theory. If the child is seen as an empty vessel to be filled with concepts and bits of language (the 'vacuum ideology' referred to by Wax and Wax (1971)), emphasis will be placed on ethnocentric standards. Bereiter and Engelmann (p. 70) assume that the standards of American schools are to be reached by drills and repetitions. One of the model lessons they analyse shows the teacher encouraging chanting such as 'this is a gun', 'this is a weapon'. When one of the boys begins to talk about the cannon he has seen, the teacher reaches his hand forward to within a few inches of the child's mouth and the child stops talking. Amazingly Bereiter's commentary refers to this as a 'useful technique'. Certainly what could have been a complex, lengthy initiation was stopped short. The rest of the children's utterances are short, often monosyllabic *because the situation* (chanted responses) *makes them so.*

Cazden (1970) draws attention to the crucial importance of recognizing the situational variables which affect performance. One of these is the function of language. Joan Tough has shown how not all children will have equal facility in using language for imaginative play, for predicting, or for hypothesizing. Much depends upon socialization and in particular experience of interaction with parents and according to Labov (1968), for example, the child's own interest in the topic is highly significant in producing more complex responses. Cazden (p. 159) reports that when great care was taken by Francis Palmer:

> to insure that the child comprehended the nature of the test questions and felt at ease with the examiner

social class differences in performance disappeared.

Labov's (1969) evidence shows that complex language performance can result when the *situation* (sitting eating potato crisps) and *audience* (presence of peer group friend) are conducive to setting the speaker at ease. Much of the work on language codes was done in experimental situations not natural ones (Bernstein's early work), and it is worth looking at one of these experiments in detail.

Referring to the work of Hawkins (1969) which considers 'context bound' and 'context free' language and claims that 'the middle-class child can be understood outside the immediate context' whilst the speech of a working-class child 'is therefore tied to the context in which it occurs' (Hawkins, 1969, p. 134), Bernstein concludes:

> Because a code is restricted it does not mean that a speaker will not in some contexts, and under specific conditions use a range of modifiers or subordinations, or whatever. But it does mean that where such choices are made they will be highly context-specific. (1970, p. 347).

There are two aspects concerning this conclusion and Hawkins' study which could be misleading and which illustrate the need for empirical work based on speech contexts with some reference to individual scores. Firstly, Bernstein does not convey the same meaning as Hawkins by 'context-specific' which, for Bernstein, means a particular context stimulates more elaborated speech appropriate to the speaker's understanding of the situation but such a mode of speech will be limited to that context. Hawkins, on the other hand, is concerned with communication which requires references to items in the context to complete the meaning ('He kicked *it*' – referring to a ball in a picture).

Secondly, Hawkins' study does not contribute much to the development of Bernstein's theory, but also includes some of the worst features of the early work, notably the crude class division and results reported solely in total numbers per group of averages per child. The method of presentation leads Hawkins to conclusions which are as exaggerated as his examples of speech. Rates of usage of exophoric pronouns (referring to something in the speaker's environment) are compared with anaphoric pronouns (referring to something in the sentence) in two tests, as shown:

	Anaphoric pronouns (average number per child)		Exophoric pronouns (average number per child)	
	W.C.	M.C.	W.C.	M.C.
Picture Cards	16.0	14.3	4.12	2.84
Trotin Cards	9.6	5.9	4.59	2.44

Hawkins' Comparison of Pronoun Usage

Hawkins claims that 'in the use of exophoric pronouns the two classes differ enormously. The average middle-class child uses 2.84, the working class 4.12, half as many again' (1969, p. 132).

Apart from the slight mathematical exaggeration here, it will be seen that the table says nothing about the average length of speech samples for the classes, clearly of paramount importance if the rate of one particular usage is to be compared. Did the working class produce longer samples? In any case, to discover whether the classes are using pronouns 'in a different kind of way, for a different purpose' (p. 131) requires a comparison of the two rates of usage on each task. The results would then be presented as ratios as in

	W.C.	M.C.
Picture Stories	1.4	1.5
Trotin Cards	1.2	1.2½

Ratio of Exophoric to Anaphoric Pronouns (Hawkins' Results)

My conclusion is different from Hawkins' exaggerated statement for the table shows that in these *specific* tasks the middle-class group as a whole performs in a *slightly* different way from the working-class group as a whole. There is no 'enormous' difference. Sometimes the researcher pursues his interest in counting exophoric pronouns, say, totally ignoring the fact that the child is inexplicit because he knows the experimenter can also see the pictures he is supposed to describe. Attention is thus drawn to the folly of proceeding to generalize about competence from one performance in one context. The implications are as Cole and Bruner (1971) state:

> One must inquire, first, whether a competence is expressed in a particular situation and, second, what the significance of that situation is for the person's ability to cope with life in his own milieu. (p. 177)

The importance of these arguments (which undermine the deficit theory) must not be underrated since they place the blame not on the child and his home, but also (or instead) upon the school. As Labov argued succinctly:

The myth of verbal deprivation is particularly dangerous, because it diverts attention from real defects of our educational system to imaginary defects of the child. (1969, p. 198)

Barnes (1971) has shown how teachers frequently force pupils into the role of passive recipients of instruction. Midwinter (1969) has argued for the kind of community school which will take advantage of pupils' existing skills and encourage development while also preserving positive attitudes to their cultural background. So personal relationships and organizational structure are two of several school variables which facilitate (or impede) learning and in recent years they have received more attention.

This review has therefore dismissed the deficit theory and has accepted with reservations the difference perspective (i.e. provided the differences are given equal status). Finally, it has drawn attention to the need to look for some of the complex causes of failure not in the child or particular social groups, but in the school, its organization, content and attitudes. Cultural dis-advantage (unlike poets!) may be made not born!

Lâbov's argument that differences in language use between social groups are merely stylistic does not negate the work of Bernstein or Joan Tough since their developed theories and empirical work emphasize functions and the different kinds of meaning that are communicated. Whereas Bereiter's programme is based upon a simplistic notion of deficit, Joan Tough's communication skills project accepts that schools may need to change by emphasizing that teachers must become more aware of the way young children use language. If children can be helped to use language as a way of learning, to question, to solve problems, to organize experience, and to investigate meaning in specific contexts, they are likely to extend their abilities. If at the same time their own skills and culture are fostered they may learn better with no damage to their self-concept and motivation.

Finally, this chapter has shown how language differences and educational failure must be seen in the context of social conditions and social relationships and not treated separately. It matters crucially how teachers respond to characteristics in the child and whether they perceive acceptable variation or inadequacy. It has explored how deficits may be caused by the way they are measured, and it has revealed assumptions about imposing fixed standards. Attitudes do change: it is no longer thought necessary to force left-handed children to write with their right hand or to force RP accents on all Bradford school children. At the same time many people do need to acquire skills to benefit from new challenges, new jobs, and new environments. At the beginning of this chapter culture was defined not as a static thing but as changing with people's own changes in adaptation. Individuals need to have the flexibility of attitude and skill to change within a culture or sub-culture and to adapt easily to others. If they remain static their experience of life is likely to be limited. Lord Boyle once said with regret that his education had made him unable to talk with working men. This kind of disadvantage has yet to be explored.

Should Traditional Grammar be Ended or Mended?
By Noam Chomsky

Editor's Introduction

Whatever else generations of school-children have thought grammar to be, it is essentially a system which gives us rules which govern the relationships between words and groups of words. For Chomsky, a grammar must explain the way the words in a sentence like 'The headmistress kissed the caretaker' are related. So a diagram can represent by its branches the way each unit is part of a group.

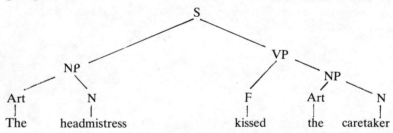

So we see that here a sentence is composed of a Noun Phrase plus a Verb Phrase and that these groups consist of other smaller groups and units (noun phrase, verb, article, noun). However, a description of a sentence's 'phrase structure' is not enough for Chomsky who also seeks to examine the relationship between such sentences as:

Did the headmistress kiss the caretaker?
The headmistress did not kiss the caretaker.
Was the caretaker kissed by the headmistress?
Wasn't the caretaker kissed by the headmistress?
Will the headmistress kiss the caretaker (again)?

An edited version of Professor Chomsky's main statement delivered informally in a debate with Professor Peter Geach at the University of Birmingham, 1969.

Such transformations give us rules for adapting our sentences in a variety of ways.

It is important to remember that grammatical statements tell us not so much about a particular sentence but describe the general ways in which sentences may be constructed and adapted. One of Chomsky's contributions to education has been to suggest that young children who start by learning simple constructions and patterns of transformation from conversations with adults acquire a set of rules which enable them to *create* original sentences that they have not heard before.

In the article that follows Chomsky shows that his concern is to build a theory of language and thereby obtain insights into 'human mental processes'. He sees that the crux of the problem of grammatical description is the importance of specifying precisely a person's knowledge about language. So his main interest is in the knowledge that speakers/hearers have of their language – what he calls *competence*. Chomsky admits that the descriptions of 'competence', 'transformations', 'deep structure' and 'surface structure' are oversimplified. However, these notions are important to an understanding of his theory and his article introduces and illustrates them particularly well. He argues that the categories of traditional grammar (noun, verb, adjective, sentence, noun phrase, verb phrase, etc.) can be usefully employed to describe the structures which are the bases of English sentences.

B.W.

WHAT I would like to do is to sketch in the high points of a framework for studying problems of language, a framework, which I think raises very interesting problems and leads to quite surprising and in many ways deep results:

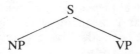

And then I will suggest that within that framework a good bit of traditional grammar finds a very natural place, in particular the traditional categories – noun, verb and adjective, but also more generally the categories that were traditionally regarded as being in a sense projected from noun, verb and adjective, namely such categories as noun phrase, verb phrase and adjective phrase and so on and so forth. In a sense there has been very little debate about this whole issue in modern linguistics. To my knowledge there has never been an alternative presented to this point of view and as a result I will merely describe the kinds of questions that I want to raise, and what I think are approaches to answering them, concerning how the traditional categories fit into this framework.

The central problem of grammatical description, as I see it, is the problem of giving a recursive characterization or precise specification of the various aspects of a person's knowledge of his language; and, more specifically, to give a recursive specification of the particular form-meaning connexion that constitutes a particular natural language, the fact that a certain noise has a certain meaning in English, let us say. And evidently this form-meaning connexion ranges over an infinite set of sentences, so some kind of recursive mechanism is going to be necessary to constitute the central core of the grammar. Well, what kind of recursive mechanism exists in a particular language or in arbitrary languages to specify the form-meaning connexions? To answer that kind of question, of course, one has to do the appropriate empirical research, and all the work, at least that I know of, that attempts to meet this problem and deals with the actual sentences of language as they exist, works roughly in the following fashion. It assumes that a grammar consists of rules which I will call a base, some class of rules which specifies some rather abstract structures that underlie – in a sense to which I will return – the sentences of a language; and it also consists of a set of operations which I will call grammatical transformations, which operate upon these underlying structures, turn them into other structures and ultimately turn them into something which I will call surface structures.

By the surface structure of an utterance I mean that characterization of the phrasing of the utterance, breaking of an utterance up into its sub-parts, its bigger sub-parts and so on, and the identification of those sub-parts as being of particular types. By the surface structure of an utterance I mean the phrasing of an utterance which directly underlies its phonetic form, that is from which the physical form, the perceived form, is determined by some set of phonological principles. Let me just give an example and you can see what I mean more clearly than from a very abstract description. If I consider, say, the sentence:

John is certain to see the boy

and I ask what is the phonetic form of this utterance, well, of course, it consists of certain sounds and certain intonational structures and certain stress patterns. And I think we can demonstrate easily that in order to account for its perceived physical form, we have to analyse it into phrases such as the phrase *certain to see the boy*, the phrase *see the boy*, the phrase *the boy*, the phrase *John,* the phrase *John is certain to see the boy,* and maybe some others that one might argue about. One might argue about the details but roughly some phrasing of that sort which seems intuitive enough, and has always been assumed in traditional grammar, can, I think, be shown to underlie the perceived physical form of the utterance. That is, the stress contour and the intonational structure associated with it, can be predicted by rules of considerable generality from that form. There is a good deal of literature about this and I will simply refer you to it. There is a long book, for example, called *Sound Pattern of English* by my colleague Morris Halle and me that came out about a year ago, which goes through this in detail.

In order to account for the perceived physical form, one needs not only the phrasing but also the assignment of phrases to particular types. For example, in order to ask how the rules operate to produce a certain physical form, one has to know that *John* and *the boy* are phrases of the same type, that is the same type of rules apply to them. It doesn't matter too much in this case because *John* is so simple that nothing applies to it. If I had selected a longer phrase, say, *elevator operator,* I would have to know, to get the perceived perceptual form, that *the elevator operator* is a phrase of the same type as *the Secretary General of the Party,* let's say, and not a phrase of the same type as *see the boy.* So one needs a characterization of these types. It seems to me from the empirical work that I am familiar with, that the traditional characterization of the types is approximately what we need. That is, we want to say that *John* and *the boy* are items of the same type, let's call it a Noun Phrase, which is a moderately traditional name, or at least close to it. We want to say that *see the boy* and *is certain to see the boy* are also phrases of the same type. Let's give them the name Verb Phrase. We want to say then that *certain to see the boy* is a phrase of a different type, let's call it an Adjective Phrase. And we want to say the whole sentence is a phrase of a certain type, let's call it Sentence. Now such a characterization again, one might argue about in detail (for example, does 'is' belong in a separate phrase, is there a tripartite division instead of a bipartite division and so on?). But something roughly of that form is what I mean by the surface structure, and I think if you gave a person the task of breaking up a sentence into parts, he would come out with approximately that even if he knew nothing, had never gone to grammar school. He might have chosen different names in that case but it would not occur to him that *John* is a phrase of the type *certain to see the boy* let's say, and so on. Furthermore, I think there is strong empirical evidence that this characterization into a surface structure underlies the perceived physical form and in fact the produced form of the utterance.

Well every sentence of the language has a surface structure of that type as a properly bracketed expression. Hence the grammar must, in particular, generate an infinite set of surface structures, and what I propose, and what I think the empirical evidence supports, is that the way in which a grammar generates surface structures is as follows. It contains base rules of an extremely restricted but recursive sort which generate an infinite class of underlying structures. In the case of *John is certain to see the boy* it would generate the underlying structure, which is also a bracketed expression, that would be approximately like this: First it would indicate that the whole thing is a Sentence, so we would have big brackets inside of which we are going to put the abstract underlying structure. And then we will discover, empirically, I am asserting, that if we want to construct appropriate generalizations to explain the generation of surface structures of this infinite class we would be led to assign to *is certain* the category Verb Phrase which contains the Adjective Phrase *certain* or perhaps *is certain*. Then we would call *John see the boy* a Phrase which is of the form of a Sentence, where the Noun Phrase would be *John* and the Verb Phrase would be *see the boy*, where *the boy* is again a Noun Phrase. Thus:

(s (np (s (np *John*) (vp *see* (np *the boy*))))) (ap *is certain*))

or

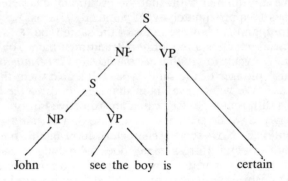

Now note once again that one has a bracketing of an underlying structure which is of the form *John see the boy is certain*. Now that underlying structure which I would like to call a base structure or a deep structure has the interesting property that it in a sense expresses the grammatical relations that are appropriate for understanding the meaning of a sentence. That is, when I hear the sentence *John is certain to see the boy* I know that I am not attributing to John a psychological property of certainty. It is not a sentence like *John is certain the boy will leave* let's say, which attributes to John the prospects of being certain about something. It doesn't attribute anything to John; it attributes to the proposition that John will see the boy, a certain roughly logical property of certainty and that is about what is expressed in the underlying deep structure; or to put it differently, it would not be very difficult to relate the underlying deep structure to a characterization of the meaning of the utterance. On the other hand, the surface structure doesn't tell us very much at all in this case, and that is characteristic, about the meaning of the utterance. *John is certain to see the boy* and *John is certain that he will see the boy* are very similar in surface structure in their bracketing and their form but entirely different in their interpretation and what's predicted of what, and so on.

Now what are the properties of this formal underlying object, the deep structure, and this superficial object, the surface structure? A number of kinds of properties can be specified. First of all the base structures themselves are of a very narrow type. This is not just true of English vernacular but of every language that has been looked at from this point of view. It seems to me that there is a very restricted and limited class of possible base structures and this class is very much determined by notions like noun, verb and adjective. In fact, roughly speaking, if you look at the simplest underlying structure of English, the ones to which we are led if we try to make precise this notion of specifying an infinite class of surface structures, then really, schematically speaking, they are approximately like this. There are nouns, verbs and adjectives; and there are structures containing nouns, verbs and adjectives as their central core, adding on to these nouns, verbs and adjectives possible things which are called complements. For example, in English, say, a verb can have as a complement nothing (an intransitive verb), an object (a transitive verb), a double object as in *Give John the book* or *Give the book to John* if you want. It can have an object in a sentence like *Persuade Bill that so and so* and maybe a dozen or so other possibilities for the complement system. Furthermore, these complements are roughly the ones we find for nouns and adjectives. So just as we can have verbs being either intransitive or transitive or taking sentential complements, let's say, so one can find adjectives like *sad* that are intransitive, to extend the term; adjectives like 'proud' that are transitive, to extend the term (*proud of John* let's say) and adjectives that take sentential complements like, say, *certain that Bill will leave* which is like *believe that Bill will leave* and so on. And exactly the same is true if we look at a set of nouns; we find that they too fall into phrases which are in a sense a projection of the basic categories and have approximately the same complement system.

Base Phrase Structures

I Noun	without complement	*John*	(NP)
		walked	(VP)
		sad	(AP)
II Verb	with Noun Phrase complement	*Secretary-General of the Party*	(NP)
		saw the boy	(VP)
		proud of John	(AP)
III Adjective	with Sentence complement	*fact that I was tired*	(NP)
		saw that I was tired	(VP)
		certain that I was tired	(AP)

Then we also discover that there are sub-phrases, things like auxiliaries, determiners of nouns, elements that specify the degree of adjectives and so on and so forth, and that these go with these kind of phrases. For example, nouns have associated with them a determiner system. Along with the complex noun phrase *message from John to Bill* let's say, which is a noun phrase with two prepositional phrases just like a verb with two prepositional phrases, one can have a determiner system which might include things like *some of those messages from John to Bill.* Associated with verbs there is a system of auxiliaries which includes tense and aspect; and associated with adjectives there is a system of specifications of degree and intensity and so on and so forth. There are some internal similarities among these.

Sub-phrases

I Determiner, Noun   :   some of these boys
II Auxiliary, Verb   :   will have been feeling
III Specifier, Adjective :   rather sad

And then underlying this we discover that the full structure of a sentence is something of the form Noun Phrase, that is a phrase containing a noun as its basic element; Verb Phrase, that is a phrase containing a verb as its basic element, with the Verb Phrase. Or it may be Noun Phrase; Adjective Phrase with a copula; and that's about all there is.

Deep Structure

$$S \longrightarrow \begin{Bmatrix} NP & VP \\ NP & Cop & AP \end{Bmatrix}$$

I've left a lot of details out but it seems to me one could say that the structure of the base for English, and in fact for every language that I have any evidence of, is roughly constituted out of notions of this sort in a very restricted sense.

Now let me introduce a technical notion, the notion 'context-free grammar'. Basically a context-free grammar is a finite set of rules which characterizes properly bracketed expressions where the brackets identify items of certain types, and it is in fact the appropriate system for generating a set of structures of this base type. Now let me just refer to the Adjukiewicz system. The Adjukiewicz system is essentially a notation for one type of context-free grammar, that is as far as I know what it comes down to, and it is not too unreasonable a notation for base systems. It is a good notation for certain kinds of context-free grammar. In fact it is a notation for context-free grammars which basically contain only endocentric constructions. One can extend it of course to other things and I have no objection to it as one notation for context-free grammar. In fact there has been some formal investigation of Adjukiewicz-type systems as compared with more general context-free grammars, concerned with what they can generate and so on. It's an amusing sub-domain of the field of mathematical linguistics. In any event one can use various kinds of notation for describing these base grammars but it seems to me that approximately this is the structure that they have.

Then to complete this very brief and absurdly over-simplified description of what a grammar would be like, I assume then that the base generates an infinite class of such structures – for example this one, *John see the boy is certain* – and that there really is a very restricted class of such cases. And then the grammar will contain a set of formal operations of which I will illustrate only two, that convert these base structures ultimately into surface structures. For example, one of the operations in the grammar will be something which I will call extraposition, which takes the bracketed structure *John see the boy be certain* and converts it into a bracketed structure which will be something like *It be certain for John to see the boy*. Now notice that that could be just about a surface structure in itself. It could be, *It is certain that John will see the boy* let's say. So that process could end at that point. But I have picked a slightly more complicated one to illustrate. To get the surface structure *John is certain to see the boy* one would need a further operation which I will call 'it replacement' which takes *It is certain for John to see the boy,* an operation determined by taking *for John to see the boy* and attaching it to the right hand of the bracketed structure that I had as deep structure. So we take that and we look at the subject. Notice that there will then be an embedded proposition over here, namely *for John to see the boy* which will have a Noun Phrase Subject. And the operation of 'it replacement' takes that Noun Phrase Subject and puts it back into the subject position of the full sentence, where we had the word 'it'. And that will give *John is certain to see the boy*.

Now notice that the same operation would have applied if I had an arbitrarily complex noun phrase there. Suppose I had *The elevator operator who I told you about yesterday while you were in England*. Well in that case the operation of 'it replacement' would have taken that whole huge mess and put it in front of *see the boy* and similarly for any one of the infinite number of Noun Phrases. But notice that in order to apply each of these operations we have to know something quite precise about the bracketing of this sentence, and in fact, what we have to know in all the cases that I am aware of, is precisely what is determined by the class of base structures, and then recursively generated by repeated application to them of transformations. Transformations, and this is the crucial point, are operations on bracketed structures. They care only about where the brackets are, and what the labels of the brackets are. Some operations will apply to Noun Phrases but entirely different ones will apply to a Sentence, for example extra-position; 'it replacement' will apply to a Noun Phrase, but it requires that the rest of the sentence has a certain bracketing and so on.

Now a very strong empirical hypothesis that has been proposed and I think is roughly right, is the following: begin with the categories, noun, verb and adjective, consider the projections of these categories into bigger categories based on nouns, verbs and adjectives, add a few other modifying items like auxiliary, determiner and degree and then say that the whole business is of the form 'phrase which has a noun as its centre', Noun Phrase, and 'phrase which has an adjective or a verb as its centre'. In roughly this way we characterize base structures. Notice that these constitute a set that is infinite in scope (though highly restricted in form), because of the recursive property of the categories. Thus a Noun Phrase can contain a Sentence which contains a further Noun Phrase, and so on. The hypothesis further says there is a very restricted and highly general class of formal operations, gram-matical transformations which, operating on those base structures in a certain well-defined fashion, generate all and only the class of surface structures, which then turn into physical form. Now you know there isn't the slightest reason, logically speaking, why this should be true. If it is true it is very remarkable and I think there is quite a lot of evidence that it is true. And it is the evidence that it is true that ultimately leads back to tell us that noun, verb and adjective are basic categories, and the phrases containing them are basic categories and so on and so forth, because it is precisely with these notions that one can characterize the full class of surface structures, and also on the way generate an underlying set of structures which express the meanings of utterances rather closely as in the case that I mentioned. And there are many similar examples.

Now I don't want to over-state. There are plenty of areas of language where there is no satisfactory explanation of the phenomena in these or in any other terms. Within the framework of the questions that I am asking, namely how does one find the finite set of rules that generate the infinite class of surface structures and associated form-meaning pairs, there are large areas of language where nobody has any idea what the proper rules are of whether one has to look in a different direction or whether there are new concepts required and so on and so forth. Well, those areas at the moment then are empirically irrelevant to the question of whether noun, verb and adjective are basic categories because they don't support this theory but they also don't support any other theory that attempts to answer that question. And in so far as I see it, where we have an attempt to answer that question which I described, and I repeat that is a fundamental and perfectly appropriate question, not the only one, but a central and appropriate one, it seems to me roughly fair to say that a structure essentially of this form does meet whatever empirical evidence is available and explain a good deal of it.

Now just let me indicate one small point about the kind of thing that could be explained by an approach of this sort which I would take to be characteristic of the kind of evidence that supports the whole picture. I mentioned two sentences, namely *John is certain to see the boy* and *John is certain that he will see the boy*, and observed that in the sentence *John is certain to see the boy* the surface structure is rather remote from its deep structure. It involves two rather complicated formal operations to convert the deep structure into the surface structure. On the other hand, the sentence *John is certain that he will see the boy* could very well be derived exactly as it stands from a base structure of the kind I have already specified. That is, it could have the subject Noun Phrase *John*, the Verb Phrase *is certain that Sentence* where *certain that Sentence* is one of the types of Adjectives plus Sentence just like *Believe that so and so* and *fact that so and so* which would be Verb plus Sentence and Noun plus Sentence, respectively. So in fact there is a structure which contains Noun Phrase, Verb Phrase, or Noun Phrase Adjective Phrase if you like, where the adjective phrase contains an adjective *certain* plus its sentential complement and where the sentential complement again would be of this form, ultimately, *he will see the boy*. So in fact it would be appropriate to regard *John is certain that he will see the boy* as in fact just having a deep structure that is very much like its surface structure, with only minor differences.

Now that distinction between these two sentences correlates with a difference of meaning as I have already noted. In one case we have certain things predicated of a proposition, of a coherent unit *John see boy* which of course does not appear in the sentence at all. It's scattered all over the sentence and we could get cases where it is much more scattered. But nevertheless there is a coherent semantic unit *John see the boy* of which certainty is predicated and that is expressed in the deep structure. On the other hand we had a sentence in which the coherent units of the surface structure are also the coherent units from a semantic point of view. They are the things that appear in the deep structure itself approximately.

Now that distinction between the sentence which is virtually the same in its deep and surface form, and a sentence like this which is very different in its deep and surface form, happens to correlate not only with the semantic distinction that I talked about, but also with certain formal properties of English of great generality and it is here that interesting and surprising explanations begin to be developed. For example, consider the process of forming nominal expressions in English, expressions like *John's refusal to leave* or *John's belief that so and so* which, of course, are nominal expressions; that is the transformations will deal with them the way they deal with *John,* not the way they deal with *read the book* or something of that sort, otherwise things will go haywire in generating structures. These nominal expressions are formed basically from sentences, or structures like sentences, but in a very restricted fashion. For example, corresponding to the sentence *John is certain that he will see the boy* we have the nominal expression *John's certainty that he will see the boy.* Perfectly all right. But corresponding to *John is certain to see the boy* we do not have the nominal expression *John's certainty to see the boy* as we can't say *John's certainty to see the boy* referring by it to the fact that for John to see the boy is certain. It doesn't mean that; there is no such phrase. That is a very general property of English: wherever a sentence differs in its deep and surface structure in a precisely specifiable fashion, it does not have a corresponding nominal. Let me just run through a couple of cases to illustrate this. A sentence such as *John believes Harry to be a fool* does not have the nominal expression *John's belief of Harry to be a fool.* But *John believes that he will leave,* does have the nominal expression *John's belief that he will leave. John is difficult to please* does not have the corresponding nominal expression *John's difficulty to please.* In this case the deep structure is very different from the surface structure. You are not predicating difficulty of

John, you are predicating difficulty of pleasing John. But *John is eager to please* has the nominalization *John's eagerness to please* and that is quite on a par with *John is certain that so and so.* And so it goes for a large class of cases.

Well how can we explain this? We could explain it very simply in terms of this framework by saying that there is no process of forming nominalization from sentences in English; rather there are nominalizations expressible directly in the deep structure. In fact just as we have phrases of the form 'verb plus complement', so we have things that are of the form 'noun plus complement'. In fact there are also some things of the form 'adjective plus complement', as already noted. Furthermore, we can have certain items which happen by accident to be in the category of both noun and verb, like the item *refuse* which appears as the verb *refuse* and appears as the noun *refusal* with its complement system. Hence we have *John's refusal to take the offer* and *John refused to take the offer.* Similarly we might have something which is both, let's say, a noun and adjective because the categories in general overlap, intersect. An example would be *certain. Certain* appears as an adjective with its complement in *John is certain that something will happen* and it similarly appears as a noun with exactly the same complement in *John's certainty that something will happen,* and so in many other cases. But if we make that proposal which is the simplest possible proposal, namely that there is no real process of forming nominals at all, that the only thing that happens is that some items happen to fall in intersection of the categories noun and verb, or verb and adjective, or noun, verb and adjective, and so on, then it follows from that assumption, which is certainly the simplest assumption that could be formulated, that there will be no nominal expression corresponding to anything that is derived by transformations. For example there will be no nominal expression corresponding to *John is certain to see the boy* or corresponding to *John is easy to please* or corresponding to *John believes Harry to be a fool,* and so on in a very large number of cases. And of course all of that is true; there is no such nominal expression corresponding to any of those forms. Rather there are nominal expressions corresponding precisely to the deep structures and that means that we can characterize a certain class of possible surface structures directly in terms of a certain very elementary and simple property of deep structures, which in turn is based on the notions noun, verb and adjective; and that exhausts the cases and characterizes all the cases.

Now I think I will mention this as my last example. One could mention lots of other things, but this is a typical example of the kind of evidence that leads one to believe that this approach is capturing a good part of the central core of natural language, maybe all of it, maybe not all. There is no logical reason why grammars should have the general form that I have described. Hence if they do it is an empirically interesting discovery. There is no logical reason why there should not be a sentence in English such as *John's difficulty to please*. If there was such a phrase we would know exactly what it means. It is perfectly sensible meaning. It is just that you cannot say it. There is something in English that makes that a non-formulable phrase, and what I have outlined is, I think, explanation of what it is that makes it a non-formulable phrase. We have evidence about how the language works and we can explain that evidence on the basis of some very general properties of English grammar, and even more so on the basis of a very general schematism that characterizes possible grammars and universal grammar, a schematism that says this is what base structures are like and these are the possible transformations and they have to act in a certain fashion and so on. It is when we have such a configuration of evidence and hypotheses explaining it that we have the beginnings of a science. Then we have results that are empirically confirmed and carry explanatory power and stand as something that has to be taken seriously as one step towards a theory that will undoubtedly change through time, a theory of language and, presumably, of the nature of human mental processes.

A very marginal part of everything I have said has to do with the role of the categories noun, verb and adjective. But it seems to me that nevertheless these categories are playing a very definite role. Without them we would not have built up this projection and we would not have the operations working the way they are supposed to work, and we would not have the surface structures that we observe and we would not have the explanations that we have. And it is because of that very indirect argument that I think the traditional grammar was quite right in so far as it established these three categories as its basic categories, maybe one more or something of that sort, and maybe some interaction among the three or four basic categories. It seems to me that all of this structure with the basic categories, the phrases containing them, the mappings of bracketed expressions onto others, has roots in traditional grammar. This conception of language achieves its justification in terms of the large explanatory framework that I have tried to outline.

What is Correctness?
By W. H. Mittins

Editor's Introduction

It is likely that die-hard traditionalists will continue to expend much wit and scorn in written protests to newspapers about terms such as 'skyjack', 'sexist', 'telecon' and 'no way'. Linguistic evidence that language is constantly changing and readapting to satisfy new purposes is not likely to change their view that it should be static and that there is (or should be) a correct form of language which must be adhered to on all occasions.

As teachers, we may feel it is unprofitable to battle Canute-like against the tide of linguistic change, haggling over the 'correct' use of 'due to' or warning against split infinitives and ending sentences with prepositions. If so, we shall probably regard our major task as helping pupils to use the actual language that they have learned. Chomsky's discussion of 'competence' suggests that normal children naturally acquire rules about their language which enable them to distinguish well-formed sentences from fragments and 'incorrect' sentences. There are two points which follow from this: firstly, there are likely, in many cases, to be considerable discrepancies between what children intuitively know about their language and their abilities *to put that language to use*. As we have already suggested the teacher will need to find ways of translating some of this 'competence' into 'performance'. Secondly, although Chomsky's concern is with syntax it must not be supposed that 'correctness' is purely a matter of grammar or even of vocabulary. The two-year-old child who one morning said to her father as he left for work, 'Bye-bye, Daddy. Thank you for coming to see us', was using grammar and vocabulary that no-one could object to. Yet her form of farewell was more appropriate to a guest than to her father. As well as learning the grammar and vocabulary she had still to learn from the context in which the language was used

This paper was given at the Annual Conference of the National Association for the Teaching of English, 1969.

those aspects which would determine how *appropriate* her valediction was.

This example is enough to suggest that 'correctness' needs to be carefully defined if it is to be a useful term. In the following article Bill Mittins examines various criteria for correctness and shows how crucial it is that as teachers we should distinguish 'helping a pupil to say what he means to say from inducing him to say what (we) think he ought to mean to say.' Mittins shows how many 'correctness' rules are traditional, conventional or even invented. Many are taken from 'authoritative' languages other than English. He exposes the assumption that Latin and English work in the same way and shows the unreliability of analogy and logic as criteria. Mittins discusses the implications of his conclusion that 'there is and can be no external standard of correctness in usage', noting at the same time that if we accept any usage *simply because it is used* we are left without the guidance that pupils need to help them use language as an adaptable tool. This is similar to the dilemma in which the compilers of the *Bullock Report* (1975) found many secondary teachers:

> A substantial number considered that the express teaching of prescriptive language forms had been discredited, but that nothing had been put in its place. They could no longer subscribe to the weekly period of exercises, but they felt uneasy because they were not giving language any regular attention. It seems to us that this uncertainty is fairly widespread, and that what many teachers now require is a readiness to develop fresh approaches to the teaching of language.

Helpful recent guides to teaching *about* language exist, for example *Language in Use* (Doughty, Pearce and Thornton, 1971) and Chapter 4 of *Patterns of Language* (Stratta, Dixon and Wilkinson, 1973). Mittins prefers the term 'appropriateness' for the act of conforming through use of language to the various registers and media demanded by particular situations within a particular speech community. So as teachers we need awareness of both the linguistic and social criteria which affect the *use* of language and we shall be concerned with the business of helping pupils to understand that 'Shall us have us dinners?' is appropriate within a restricted context and in the spoken medium, but less so in certain kinds of written communication and to larger and more varied audiences.

Achieving this understanding may be a more complex task than attempting to fashion a simple notion of prescriptiveness, but ultimately it is more worthwhile and helpful to a pupil.

B.W.

WHATEVER correctness is or is not, it has something to do with usage, and – as an American recently wrote – 'there are few touchier subjects in this world than English usage. . . . There is no more effective way of losing friends and alienating people than by knowing more about language than they do, particularly the language they themselves speak and write. It is the better part of wisdom under such circumstances to avoid the subject as one would avoid religion, politics, and the cozier aspects of sex.' But, of course, teachers of English cannot avoid it; they are paid, among other things, to help learners in their use of language. At the York Conference last year, Michael Marland recognized this very clearly. In his admirable talk on the needs and contributions of the schools to the making of teachers, he gave an important place to the teacher's need of a theory of correctness.

What, then, is 'correctness'? The term and its cognates (correct, incorrect, correction, etc.) are used in various fields of discourse. For example, we hear of houses of *correction* where *corrective* measures are taken against undesirable tendencies. In personal relationships we recognize *correct* as distinct from *incorrect* behaviour in situations ranging from the trivial (e.g. table-manners) to the serious (doubtless, Russian troops in Prague are behaving with scrupulous *correctness* towards the civilian population). The language of mathematics uses *correct* in the sense of accurately obeying certain laws prescribed by the subject-discipline. In the territory of verbal language, we are familiar outside school with the *correcting* of proofs and inside school with the *correcting* of pupils' errors in speech and writing. The common thread running through all these senses is that of conformity to some standard. In most of these spheres, the standard is fairly easy to define; it involves conformity to the laws of the land, or to convention, or to the principles of a subject-discipline. The proof-reading instance is a little more complicated. The proof-reader is concerned in general with matching his proofs to the approved script, and in detail with conforming to the practices approved in standard reference books (such as the *Authors' and Printers' Dictionary*). In a limited number of matters he may also apply the rules of his publishing-house; if he works for the OUP, for example, he will insert an *e* in the middle of *judg(e)ment*.

Pedagogic practices – as reflected in attitudes to dialectal speech, in essay-marking routines, in error-spotting examination questions, and in text-book prescriptions and proscriptions – may have the same flavour as some or all of these analogues. There is a long penal tradition in English-teaching, nowadays referred to as preaching the doctrine of original linguistic sin. Less punitive and more rational is the concept of verbal correctness as acceptance of convention, though the particular conventions may be arbitrarily selected and ferociously insisted upon. Some teachers, too, seem to want to teach the language as if its parts of speech and other categories constituted a system as logically closed as that of number. And these penal, conventional and mathematical notions may all find expression in processes and attitudes reminiscent of proof-reading. Some of you will recall an article in which Andrew Wilkinson described some of the dubious roles adopted by teachers of English and found the proof-reading one the most pernicious of all.

There is, I suppose, a limited area of common ground between English language teaching and proof-reading – the area of those arbitrary house-rules for deciding borderline issues. But the similarities are dwarfed by the differences. Whereas, for instance, the proof-reader starts from an approved text, the teacher is only working towards one. And whereas proof-reading is by definition confined to the written code, teaching is very much concerned with speech as well. It might, of course, make life easier for the teacher if the analogy were closer, if there were a tangible and generally accepted model with which to compare pupils' utterances. Such a situation might go some way towards satisfying the learner's lust for certainty and the teacher's preference for time-saving dogmatism. But not only would such a state of affairs be more dull; it would also be self-defeating, in that in the event the alleged certainties would prove spurious.

I am not saying that there is no situation in which a teacher may reasonably arbitrate between linguistic rightness and wrongness, but that these situations are comparatively rare and special in character. Perhaps the clearest examples might be found in relation to the usage of non-native English speakers. When, years ago, I rashly invited a young Belgian boy living with us to do something that apparently my wife had forbidden, he gleefully retorted: 'But missus said I don't may do that!' I would call that incorrect English, on the ground that it failed to conform to the speaker's obvious intention to speak our sort of English. Similarly, in a television programme in which Malcolm Muggeridge revisited India and watched an English lesson, the Indian teacher whose sophisticated discourse on Shakespeare included references to the *so'lilo'quies* was probably speaking incorrectly. Even if this pronunciation is a feature of some Indian English dialect, he was demonstrably attempting (mostly with success) to speak a kind of British English to which that pronunciation is alien. Parallel examples to these can be found among native English-speakers. I dare say I'm not the only veteran who long ago misread a famous advertisement as 'Don't be *mizzled*. Buy so-and-so.' Nor probably was my wife's one-time 'help' unique in remarking that 'Grandma is a wonderful old woman; she still has all her *facilities*.' The fact that I now say *misled* while she may not have acquired *faculties* does not affect the case. We both spoke incorrectly in the sense that we would have spoken otherwise if we had known better. The difficulty for the teacher is in distinguishing between mistakes of this sort and usages that are fully intended but seem to him to be sub-standard. It is only too easy to slip over the invisible line that separates helping a pupil to say what he means to say from inducing him to say what you think he ought to mean to say.

I have perhaps laboured this point, because I want it to represent one end of a theoretical scale. I can then contrast this zone, in which 'correctness' is legitimately invoked to change a usage because the user doesn't know any better, with the zone at the opposite end, where there is no better to be known. An obvious occupant of this latter area is the publishing-house rule I have already referred to. Given consistency within one stretch of writing, it does not matter whether *acknowledg(e)ment* has two *e*'s or three, or whether certain words (e.g. motor-car) are hyphenated. Similarly in speech, the pronunciations *eether* and *eye-ther* seem equally acceptable, and one may stress the first or second syllable of *controversy* indifferently.

In my view, this last area might well be extended, but I doubt whether I should get very far even with such an enlightened audience as this with a catalogue of free-choice items beginning, say, with *each other/one another*, or *if it was/were*. Certainly, it seems unrealistic to advocate a return of Elizabethan free-trade in spelling. Perhaps our energies might more profitably be directed to the other end of my scale, but there in the interests of restriction rather than expansion. We need to guard against the tendency to multiply the number of usage-situations in which one form is asserted as the only correct one. Only too easily can this tendency make the use of language a tiresome business of avoiding booby-traps, of suspecting that the next corner conceals a rule lying in wait like a speed-cop or traffic warden, armed with a little book of prohibitions. Whatever has education done to the student-teacher who, asked to judge the acceptability of 'the data *is*', answered: 'If *data is* sounds ignorant, *data are* is apt to sound pedantic and affected'?

Let me offer a sample of some of the kinds of 'rule' that can make using one's own language as difficult and frustrating an exercise as using a car in a busy city. I will start with a fairly extreme example, from my own remote schooling. I was taught, when using abbreviations in addresses and the like, always to put a dot after *Esq.* or *Hon.*, but never after *Rd* or *Dr*; I was allowed free choice with forms like *St*, because there it is impossible to tell whether the *t* represents the medial or the final *t* of *Street*. The headmaster who vouchsafed this law to me had not made it up himself – I have met others who have been similarly taught – but he probably inherited it at second or longer hand from some ingenious inventor. It represents a class of rules that have been called 'ipsedixitisms'. It was so merely because he said so. In the long tradition of 'school-mastered' English there have been many other *'ipse*'s'. There was, for example, in the seventeenth century, the famous Dr Wallis, who devised the *shall/will* fantasy that has dogged grammarians ever since; in the eighteenth century Bishop Lowth decided that *than* was always a conjunction and never a preposition (hence She is taller than *I*, not *me*); and someone unknown in the early nineteenth century thought up the split infinitive bogey.

It takes courage to 'ipsedixit'. One needs, perhaps, to be as convinced as Lowth was that, compared with the superior classical languages, English suffers from a simplicity and facility which 'occasion its being frequently written and spoken with less accuracy', even by the most distinguished writers. Frailer mortals than the Bishop, seeking rules to endorse their preferences, tend to look for support to some outside authority, usually institutional rather than personal. Of the range of possible authorities, the oldest and most respected is that of the classical languages. In turn the Greek writings of the Attic period and the Latin works of Virgil, Cicero and Horace were taken as exemplars, providing a standard which subsequent users invariably failed to attain. As early as the third century BC, colloquial Greek speech was condemned as much less 'correct' than the literature of a couple of centuries earlier. The Tower of Babel incident precluded the setting up of a single Christian model on the same lines. Instead, the classical models, especially that of Latin, were taken over as yardsticks for assessing Western European vernaculars. Early grammars of English, many of them actually written in Latin, regularly adopted the Latin definition of grammar as 'ars recte loquendi et scribendi', the art of speaking and writing correctly. In consequence, these grammars and their successors would, as someone has said, be excellent for any ancient Roman wishing to learn modern English.

But the effect on the native English of this Latinate bias was less encouraging. We all know how Dryden became aware, from study of the Latin model, of his own and others' transgressions. Ben Jonson, for instance, had written 'The bodies that those souls were frighted from.' On this, Dryden comments severely: 'The preposition in the end of the sentence; a common fault with him, and which I have but lately observed in my own writings.' He expiated his offence by 'correcting' many of his own sentences, introducing the stiff pedantries of *to whom, for which*, and the like. In so doing he satisfied the myth that English prepositions, like Latin ones, should be pre-posed, but seriously damaged the naturalness and effectiveness of his writing. Sadder still than this particular fetish is Dryden's more general confession of guilt. In dedicating his *Troilus and Cressida* to the Earl of Sunderland, he observes:

> How barbarously we yet write and speak, your lordship knows, and I am sensible in my own English. For I am often put to a stand, in considering whether I write the idiom of the tongue or false grammar. . . . I am desirous, if it were possible, that we might all write with the same certainty of words, and purity of phrase, to which the Italians first arrived, and after them the French; at least we might advance so far, as our tongue is capable of such a standard.

Clearly he has in mind that instrument of linguistic correctness, the national academy. The Italian Academia della Crusca had been operating since 1582, and Richelieu had founded the French Académie in 1635. That of the third major Romance language was not to follow until 1713, in the shape of the Real Academia Española. Meanwhile, proposals for similar attempts at language control were being made in England. A year or two before Dryden's death, Defoe advocated the founding of an English Academy, and the suggestion was taken up some years later by Swift in his 'Proposal for Correcting and Ascertaining the English Tongue' (1712). For the failure of the enterprise, some credit has been given to Dr Johnson's sturdy common sense; this might be rated a measure of compensation for the Doctor's attempts to regulate usage by eliminating such vulgarisms as *budge, fun, clever,* and *mob*. The academy movement is not just a historical curiosity. As recently as 1965, Roger Fowler quoted from the *Radio Times* a letter claiming that 'What is needed in this country is an institution on the lines of the Spanish Academy, a body of eminent and authoritarian men whose duty it is to maintain the purity of the language'. I would guess that one of the purification procedures would surely be the expulsion of alleged Americanisms. If so, it is virtually certain that a British Academy would be no more successful in this than the Continental ones have been in preventing contamination of their languages by Anglicisms. The French Académie has notoriously failed to prohibit 'le weekend' and a whole range of technical sporting terms, according to which one may hear at a Rugby football match how 'il a drop-kické un goal' or see a boxer receive 'un knockout par un uppercut'. Worse still, those tiresome French students recently extended the contamination from lexicon to syntax. Presumably echoing Louis XIV's 'l'état c'est moi!' they declared on their banners that 'l'anarchie c'est je!'.

Seekers after uniformity and 'correctness' in English who are frustrated by the lack of a linguistic academy often appeal for support to one or other of the various criteria that an academy, if there were one, would presumably apply. The commonest such criterion is the one I have already mentioned – the model of Latin. Latin usage offers a basis for ostracizing, not only the final preposition, but also 'different *to*' and 'different *than*', '*under* the circumstances', 'if it *was*', 'it's *me*', and a host of other very common locutions. The Latin influence operates both semantically (*a*verse *from*, not averse *to*, because the *a*-prefix means 'away from') and grammatically (a past participle must not be modified by an intensifier – we are not *very*, but *much* amused; nor must adverbs be allowed to qualify nouns, as in 'He was *quite* a character').

In a sense the appeal to Latin is an act of analogy, based on the assumption, quite unwarranted, that the two languages work in much the same way. But analogy also operates more generally, as when the London Passenger Transport Board, according to report, insisted on their trainee-clippies calling out 'Hold tight*ly*!' (The underlying fallacy here is that, because English has many adjective-adverb pairs distinguished solely by the adverbial suffix *-ly*, all adverbs with corresponding adjectives must be so marked.) Of course, analogical levelling is always going on. We have long since added that *-ly* to our ancestors' 'flat' adverb 'uncommon' in 'It's uncommon civil of you'. What is more, we would regard attempts to restore forms that have been analogized out of existence (e.g. *clomb* for *climbed*) as no less absurd than William Barnes's efforts to de-Latinize our language by renaming an *omnibus* a *folkwain*. But it is one thing to recognize the inevitability of analogy after the event, and quite another to try and impose analogy on language as a principle. To do the latter would mean, for example, insisting on *hisself* and *theirselves* to parallel *myself, ourselves* and *yourselves*. Not that such a move would be unprecedented. Nothing is so unlikely in language as not to be urged by someone. The great Sanskrit scholar, Sir William Jones, in his *Grammar of the Persian Language* (1771), writes:

> I here use *his self* and *their selves* instead of the corrupted words *himself* and *themselves*; in which use I am justified by the authority of Sidney, and of other writers in the reign of Elizabeth.

Again, if analogy were pressed, we might follow Bishop Lowth in writing *Her's, Our's, Your's,* and *Their's* all with *'s*, and even join him in taking *His* to be equivalent to *Hee's*. But though our pupils may use some of these forms (and incidentally get chastised for it), we ourselves abhor them. As with other criteria, we accept analogy when it suits us, but ignore or defy it when it doesn't. As Fries points out, we accept 'The sun had *shone*' but condemn 'He had *wrote*'. Instead of the latter we demand 'He had *written*', but we cannot tolerate 'The sun had *shinnen*'.

Another possible criterion is logic, but that is no more reliable than analogy. Not only would it too favour *hisself* (what more logical than 'He couldn't bear the sight of his self'?), but it would prefer 'This book of *me*' to 'This book of *mine*'. Alternatively, if, as some of the text-books do, it defended 'This book of *mine*' as equivalent to 'This one of *my books*', it would fall foul of analogy, which would make 'This wife of *mine*' similarly equivalent to 'This one of *my wives*'. Logic would also support a writer to *The Times* in 1961, quoted by Jeremy Warburg. He insisted with impeccable reasoning that the so-called *postgraduate* students in a photograph, since they were neither *undergraduates* reading for degrees nor *graduates* who had obtained degrees, must either have lost their degrees or be dead.

Another criterion that deserves mention is that of alleged 'real meaning', usually indicated by derivation. Evelyn Waugh, in his autobiography, associates this with two of the previous criteria by arguing that only by classical studies can a boy 'fully understand that a sentence is a logical construction and that words have basic inalienable meanings, departure from which is either conscious metaphor or inexcusable vulgarity'. For many teachers, the *bête noire* in this class is the use of *aggravate* in the sense of *annoy*. They argue that *aggravate*, since it incorporates Latin *gravis*, has long meant *make worse*, and ought to go on meaning that. They don't go back beyond the figurative meaning to the primary sense of *gravis*, namely 'physically heavy' or 'burdensome'. If they did, they would perhaps recognize as 'correct' only a use such as in 'The water soaked through the container and *aggravated* the contents'. But they would probably think such literalness as unreal as to demand that *silly* should still mean *blessed*, that *horrid* can only mean *bristling*, and that *dilapidated* must be applied only to stone houses.

The last criterion I will mention, and that briefly, is the aesthetic one. Opposite to the poeticizer who applauds the union of sound and sense in Tennyson's 'murmuring of innumerable bees' (incidentally, as someone has ironically remarked, so much more musical than the almost identical 'murdering of innumerable beeves') is the purist who finds *subsi'dence* (rhyming with *tridents)* as ugly as *cali'bre* (rhyming with *fibre*) or who, more generally, thinks certain dialects (e.g. Cockney and Scouse) repulsive or comic compared with others (e.g. R.P. or Edinburgh Scots). This is no more reasonable or defensible than the old view of the whole English spoken language as vastly inferior to the classical languages – a view expressed, for example, as late as 1774 by Lord Monboddo, who found that, compared with the excellence of Greek, English was a language

> composed almost entirely of hard inflexible words, mono-syllables for the greater part, and crouded with consonants that do not easily coalesce in sound, and [that] these words are unskilfully tacked together by ill-favoured particles constantly recurring, and fatiguing the ear, without either melody or rhythm to soften the harshness of so rude an articulation.

I hope that I have given sufficient of a catalogue to show that the correctness-monger looking for rules is not short of possible sources; on the contrary, he suffers from 'embarras de choix'. There are precedents for saying that a certain usage is wrong because it defies Latin, or because it is ugly, or because it flaunts analogy, or because it contradicts logic, or just because. These criteria are such a mixed bag that it is quite impossible to arrange them in any systematic order. In any case, they tend to inter-penetrate each other in a variety of ways. In the end the linguistic legislator has no option but to choose that criterion which suits his purpose. If he writes a text-book, he will, as L. M. Myers puts it, interpret 'correct' usage as that which 'our best authors would no doubt have observed if they had had the opportunity to read this book and follow all its rules'. This circularity drives one to the conclusion that there is and can be no external standard of correctness in usage. The alternative is to take usage itself as the arbiter. This answer has its tradition, too, dating at least from Horace and Quintilian. By its very nature, however, it can hardly be taken as conclusive. An immediate problem it raises is that of whose usage. The growth of population and the spread of literacy has made this problem infinitely more complex than it was in Roman times.

There have been and are those who advocate as a standard some notion of the *best* usage, the usage of the best speakers and writers. But the famous users of the language are notoriously indifferent to rules. Many of them can't spell or punctuate, and all the usages outlawed by the text-books are represented in their works. That alleged non-word *alright* occurs in the *Ancren Riwle* in the early thirteenth century. Lily's *Euphues* talks of '*less* faults' instead of '*fewer* faults'. Shakespeare is constantly offending, with his '*These kind* of knaves' and – worse still – 'All debts are cleared between you and *I*'. Donne is addicted to the split infinitive. Milton knew no better than to confuse *infer* and *imply* ('Consider, first, that great or high *infers* not excellence') and to perpetrate 'At least try *and* teach the erring soul'. The death of Little Nell provoked Dickens to record that 'Nobody will miss her *like* I shall'. As for the nineteenth-century women novelists, they betrayed the educational handicap (or perhaps advantage) of their sex with 'A *very* unique child' (C. Brontë), 'How different *to* your brother and mine' (Jane Austen), and 'I am becoming *very* hurried' (George Eliot). Nearer to our own times, Hardy asked '*Who* are you speaking *of?*'. As Shaw said of something else, 'It's enough to drive every*one* out of *their* senses'.

If those whose professional business is language cannot be relied on, and if – as you will surely agree – it would be unthinkable to entrust the job to the grammarians, we are hardly likely to find any other section of the educated public to provide the model. Hence we are left with usage in general, and this exposes us to the 'anything goes' accusation and to the logical absurdity of granting every man the right to his own standard. Even if this would do in the adult world, it would not do in schools. There, some direction and guidance must be given, some consensus must be established. Furthermore, such guidance must take into account not only linguistic but also social considerations. A teacher may find it advisable on the one hand to defend the linguistic status of a controversial usage (e.g. the split infinitive), on the other hand to advise applicants for jobs to avoid splitting.

This complexity makes the question 'What is correctness?' seem an absurdly naïve formulation. If we accept that the simplistic right/wrong conception of correctness is applicable only in the very limited sector characteristically (but not exclusively) inhabited by the lapses of the second-language learner – so that, in R. A. Hall's words, 'The only time we can call any usage totally incorrect is when it would never be used by any native speaker of the language, no matter what his social or intellectual standing' – we must accept the corollary that what native speakers *do* normally say or write is correct. As Henry Sweet said long before Fries and other modern linguists got into trouble for saying it, 'whatever is in general use in language is for that very reason grammatically correct'. Of course, 'general use in language' is a pluralistic notion; language is a manifold phenomenon, and each sub-language, dialect and register has its own norm. What is 'correct' in one linguistic situation or community is not so in another, and we all belong to a number of speech-communities. Barbara Strang perhaps sums this up best in a definition of correctness as 'conformity to the usage required of one's speech-community in relation to a given medium, "style", and "register"'.

Many people would prefer to call this 'appropriateness'. In my view it would be convenient to do this, so that 'correctness' may be reserved for the notion – however mythical it may be – of conformity to a uniform general standard. Such a terminological distinction makes sense of Fitzedward Hall's wise observation (in 1873) that 'language may be at once perfectly correct and ludicrously inappropriate'. It also illuminates Trollope's dilemma in writing dialogue; he found that a character may either speak real and sound funny or speak correct and sound unreal.

Having played the usual academic trick of taking a simple-seeming concept and making it complex, and perhaps having undermined an area of security (though I would say *false* security), I must not leave the topic without asking why, if the simplistic notion of correctness is so untenable, it is so persistent. One possible cause I have already referred to as a lust for certainty. The child, especially the young child, has this lust, at least at the absolutist stage described by Piaget and others; and the teacher would often like to satisfy it simply and directly, thereby saving time and living up to the child's expectations of him. Such a motive, though unrealistic, is creditable. A less desirable factor might be reluctance in face of the alternative practice; ascertaining the facts, linguistic and social, and determining a policy involve what somebody called 'the insupportable fatigue of thought'. The American R. A. Hall goes much further than this. He accuses the prescriptivist of much more than intellectual laziness. He suggests that 'there are only three psychological bases for purism: sadism, masochism, and desire for personal aggrandizement. Authoritarianism in any field (including language matters) is based primarily on sadism, the desire to force one's will on others and to cause unhappiness while doing so; most purists are, consciously or unconsciously, sadists.' I think he is exaggerating, and in any case my own strain of pedantry prevents me from agreeing whole-heartedly. Nevertheless, I have heard arguments about trivialities of usage pursued with a degree of self-righteous passion that lends a little colour to the charge.

It brings me, in any case, to the first of my final remarks, on the implications of all this for teachers. My first recommendation would be to try and lower the temperature in which differences about usage are discussed. We need to beware of confusing linguistic non-conformity with moral degeneration. If not, we may fail to avoid the alleged American situation in which, according to Hayakawa, most people suffer from more or less grave linguistic neuroses. This, too, may be a bit exaggerated, but in a delicate and intimate matter such as one's personal language behaviour damage is possible at the hands of the dogmatist, however well-intentioned. Certainly, prejudice abounds in the territory of usage. We are too often willing to dismiss the usage of others as less educated and literate than our own. We are over-ready to stigmatize, usually as Americanisms, locutions we don't like (the current proliferation of words with the suffix *-wise*, e.g. money-wise, profit-wise, may be a revival of the form used respectably in this country centuries ago rather than or as well as an importation). This is no better than the tribalism that has long bedevilled the *shall/will* debate, from Dean Alford (1869), who 'never knew an Englishman who misplaced *shall* and *will*, but had hardly known an Irishman or Scotchman who did not do so sometimes', to the American Grant White (1899), who thought it presented difficulties only to 'persons who have not had the advantage of early inter-course with educated people' (i.e. Scotchmen, Irishmen and 'the great mass of the people of the Western and Southwestern States'), and to our own Fowler brothers, who found that there was no problem for southern Englishmen, to whom mastery of the *shall/will* usage 'comes by nature'.

Having freed the mind of prejudice, it remains to face up to the facts, the general facts about the multifarious character of language and the particular facts about specific utterances. This means consulting the records of the past and noting the practice of the present. It means defending clarity and precision to an appropriate degree but not to excess. It means not fighting battles that have already been lost, against, for instance, adverbial *due to* or the singular *data*. It means recognizing that the job is to encourage a confident and resourceful flow of words, not to inhibit it. It means acknowledging that over-insistence on one allegedly 'correct' form may have unforeseen consequences elsewhere, as when 'you and *me*' in the position of subject is so energetically attacked that it feels wrong everywhere and we all end up saying 'Between you and *I*'. It means reasonable tolerance of alternative usages where no issue of comprehensibility is involved, with perhaps an enlargement of the area of what Fowler called the 'sturdy indefensibles'; even the French Academy's grammar now suffers a category of 'toléré'. Above all, it means accepting that language changes and that change is not corruption. I like a recent American way of putting this:

> The living language is like a cowpath: it is the creation of the cows themselves, who, having created it, follow it or depart from it according to their whims or their needs.

What is more, the young have a right to a share in the process. One of the flood of recent American books on linguistics reports an interesting experiment which might well be replicated over here in our schools and colleges. Two groups of people, one adults, the other children, were invited to comment on a piece of idiosyncratic English speech. It went:

> Lawd, we ain't what we wanna be; we ain't what we oughta be; we sho' nuff ain't what we lak to be; but thank the Lawd, we ain't what we was.

The teachers' responses varied from depressing condemnation ('grammatically this is terrible') to self-conscious literary applause

('I think it is good English. We should teach this in class, along with Shakespeare, and Chaucer and perhaps E. E. Cummings'). None of them rivalled the sense and sensibility of the young secondary-school child who wrote:

I'll bet God will listen to this man better than to a lot of others.

Relevant Models of Language
By M. A. K. Halliday

Editor's Introduction

A good deal of the work in language done in the 1950s and 60s concentrated on form. Even sociological accounts such as Bernstein's attempts to explain the differences between 'restricted' and 'elaborated' codes did so in terms of quantities of syntactical and lexical items. Halliday makes an important contribution in this seminal article by drawing attention to the functions of language. He shows that children acquire the *uses* of language not merely the vocabulary, structures, sounds, and meanings that previously had received the attention of those interested in language acquisition.

'Relevant Models of Language' distinguishes seven functions – language to get things done, to exercise control over other people, to interact with others, to express one's own individuality, to find out about things, to create an imaginative world, and to convey a message. There may be other uses, for example to order events or to clarify one's thinking: Halliday does not claim the list is totally comprehensive and there is still a good deal of work to be done on the theory of language functions. The main point, however, which the article makes clearly is that even very young children have had experience of these functions in actual use and so recognize them intuitively.

The educational implications become clear when we consider that some adults have a restricted view of the function of language. Halliday suggests that many see language only as a means of communicating information and the *Bullock Report*'s brief summary of some of the findings on classroom interaction points the same way:

This is a revised version of a paper presented to the Conference of Teachers in Approved Schools on 'Language, life and learning', organized by the Home Office Children's Department Development Group and the Programme in Linguistics and English Teaching (University College London) at Sunningdale, May 1969. I am much indebted to Professor Basil Bernstein for his very helpful comments on the paper, which already owes a lot to the inspiration of his work.

> There is research evidence to suggest that on average the teacher talks for three-quarters of the time in the usual teacher-class situation. It has been calculated from this that in a 45-minute period the amount of time left for a class of 30 to contribute is an average of some 20 seconds per pupil. (10.4, p. 142)

The language that teachers use and the expectations of the school situation clearly affect and constrain the language that pupils themselves use. Interesting accounts of some of these processes are given by Douglas Barnes, notably in *Language Learner and the School* and *From Communication to Curriculum*. Despite talk about extending and developing the range and variety of children's language, pupils may come to reduce the number of models available to them as their knowledge of language becomes more consciously formulated and schools may restrict opportunities for pupils to develop some of the linguistic functions that they have acquired. If teaching is to be adapted to a pupil's needs, the teacher must take into account the range of language functions a pupil possesses. It is not helpful merely to impose a stereotype of language as Halliday shows is done, for example, in some reading schemes. It is far more profitable for the teacher to examine his own conception of language functions and to ensure that they are adequate for meeting the needs of the child. Halliday's paper rightly directs us to examine our own and our pupils' uses of language as they interact, for it is unlikely that we will otherwise be able to ensure a steady development of pupils' abilities. As the *Bullock Report* stresses:

> If a teacher is to control the growth of competence he must be able to examine the verbal interaction of a class or group in terms of an explicit understanding of the operation of language. (1.11, p. 8)

'Relevant Models' is an important contribution towards such explicit understanding.

B.W.

———————————

THE teacher of English who, when seeking an adequate definition of language to guide him in his work, meets with a cautious 'well, it depends on how you look at it' is likely to share the natural impatience felt by anyone who finds himself unable to elicit 'a straight answer to a straight question'. But the very frequency of this complaint may suggest that, perhaps, questions are seldom as straight as they seem. The question 'what is language?', in whatever guise it appears, is as diffuse and, at times, disingenuous as other formulations of its kind, for example 'what is literature?' Such questions, which are wisely excluded from examinations, demand the privilege of a qualified and perhaps circuitous answer.

In a sense the only satisfactory response is 'why do you want to know?', since unless we know what lies beneath the question we cannot hope to answer it in a way which will suit the questioner. Is he interested in language planning in multilingual communities? Or in aphasia and language disorders? Or in words and their histories? Or in dialects and those who speak them? Or in how one language differs from another? Or in the formal properties of language as a system? Or in the functions of language and the demands that we make on it? Or in language as an art medium? Or in the information and redundancy of writing systems? Each one of these and other such questions is a possible context for a definition of language. In each case language 'is' something different.

The criterion is one of relevance; we want to understand, and to highlight, those facets of language which bear on the investigation or the task in hand. In an educational context the problem for linguistics is to elaborate some account of language that is relevant to the work of the English teacher. What constitutes a relevant notion of language from his point of view, and by what criteria can this be decided? Much of what has recently been objected to, among the attitudes and approaches to language that are current in the profession, arouses criticism not so much because it is false as because it is irrelevant. When, for example, the authors of *The Linguistic Sciences and Language Teaching* suggested that teaching the do's and don'ts of grammar to a child who is linguistically unsuccessful is like teaching a starving man how to hold a knife and fork, they were not denying that there is a ritual element in our use of language, with rules of conduct to which everyone is expected to conform; they were simply asserting that the view of language as primarily good manners was of little relevance to educational needs. Probably very few people ever held this view explicitly; but it was implicit in a substantial body of teaching practices, and if it has now largely been discarded this is because its irrelevance became obvious in the course of some rather unhappy experiences.

It is not necessary, however, to sacrifice a generation of children, or even one classroomful, in order to demonstrate that particular preconceptions of language are inadequate or irrelevant. In place of a negative and somewhat hit-and-miss approach, a more fruitful procedure is to seek to establish certain general, positive criteria of relevance. These will relate, ultimately, to the demands that we make of language in the course of our lives. We need therefore to have some idea of the nature of these demands; and we shall try to consider them here from the point of view of the child. We shall ask, in effect, about the child's image of language: what is the 'model' of language that he internalizes as a result of his own experience? This will help us to decide what is relevant to the teacher, since the teacher's own view of language must at the very least encompass all that the child knows language to be.

The child knows what language is because he knows what language does. The determining elements in the young child's experience are the successful demands on language that he himself has made, the particular needs that have been satisfied by language for him. He has used language in many ways – for the satisfaction of material and intellectual needs, for the mediation of personal relationships, the expression of feelings and so on. Language in all these uses has come within his own direct experience, and because of this he is subconsciously aware that language has many functions that affect him personally. Language is, for the child, a rich and adaptable instrument for the realization of his intentions; there is hardly any limit to what he can do with it.

As a result, the child's internal 'model' of language is a highly complex one; and most adult notions of language fail to match up to it. The adult's ideas about language may be externalized and consciously formulated, but they are nearly always much too simple. In fact it may be more helpful, in this connexion, to speak of the child's 'models' of language, in the plural, in order to emphasize the many-sidedness of his linguistic experience. We shall try to identify the models of language with which the normal child is endowed by the time he comes to school at the age of five; the assumption being that if the teacher's own 'received' conception of language is in some ways less rich or less diversified it will be irrelevant to the educational task.

We tend to underestimate both the total extent and the functional diversity of the part played by language in the life of the child. His interaction with others, which begins at birth, is gradually given form by language, through the process whereby at a very early age language already begins to mediate in every aspect of his experience. It is not only as the child comes to act on and to learn about his environment that language comes in; it is there from the start in his achievement of intimacy and in the expression of his individuality. The rhythmic recitation of nursery rhymes and jingles is still language, as we can see from the fact that children's spells and chants differ from one language to another: English nonsense is quite distinct from French nonsense, because the one is English and the other French. All these contribute to the child's total picture of language 'at work'.

Through such experiences, the child builds up a very positive impression – one that cannot be verbalized, but is none the less real for that – of what language is and what it is for. Much of his difficulty with language in school arises because he is required to accept a stereotype of language that is contrary to the insights he has gained from his own experience. The traditional first 'reading and writing' tasks are a case in point, since they fail to coincide with his own convictions about the nature and uses of language.

*   *   *

Perhaps the simplest of the child's models of language, and one of the first to be evolved, is what we may call the INSTRUMENTAL model. The child becomes aware that language is used as a means of getting things done. About a generation ago, zoologists were finding out about the highly developed mental powers of chimpanzees; and one of the observations described was of the animal that constructed a long stick out of three short ones and used it to dislodge a bunch of bananas from the roof of its cage. The human child, faced with the same problem, constructs a sentence. He says 'I want a banana'; and the effect is the more impressive because it does not depend on the immediate presence of the bananas. Language is brought in to serve the function of 'I want', the satisfaction of material needs. Success in this use of language does not in any way depend on the production of well-formed adult sentences; a carefully contextualized yell may have substantially the same effect, and although this may not be language there is no very clear dividing line between, say, a noise made on a commanding tone and a full-dress imperative clause.

The old *See Spot run. Run, Spot, run!* type of first reader bore no relation whatsoever to this instrumental function of language. This by itself does not condemn it, since language has many other functions besides that of manipulating and controlling the environment. But it bore little apparent relation to any use of language, at least to any with which the young child is familiar. It is not recognizable as language in terms of the child's own intentions, of the meanings that he has reason to express and to understand. Children have a very broad concept of the meaningfulness of language, in addition to their immense tolerance of inexplicable tasks; but they are not accustomed to being faced with language which, in their own functional terms, has no meaning at all, and the old-style reader was not seen by them as language. It made no connexion with language in use.

Language as an instrument of control has another side to it, since the child is well aware that language is also a means whereby others exercise control over him. Closely related to the instrumental model, therefore, is the REGULATORY model of language. This refers to the use of language to regulate the behaviour of others. Bernstein and his colleagues have studied different types of regulatory behaviour by parents in relation to the process of socialization of the child, and their work provides important clues concerning what the child may be expected to derive from this experience in constructing his own model of language. To adapt one of Bernstein's examples, as described by Turner, the mother who finds that her small child has carried out of the supermarket, unnoticed by herself or by the cashier, some object that was not paid for, may exploit the power of language in various ways, each of which will leave a slightly different trace or after-image of this role of language in the mind of the child. For example, she may say *you mustn't take things that don't belong to you* (control through conditional prohibition based on a categorization of objects in terms of a particular social institution, that of ownership); *that was very naughty* (control through categorization of behaviour in terms of opposition approved/disapproved); *if you do that again I'll smack you* (control through threat of reprisal linked to repetition of behaviour); *you'll make Mummy very unhappy if you do that* (control through emotional blackmail); *that's not allowed* (control through categorization of behaviour as governed by rule), and so on. A single incident of this type by itself has little significance; but such general types of regulatory behaviour, through repetition and reinforcement, determine the child's specific awareness of language as a means of behavioural control.

The child applies this awareness, in his own attempts to control his peers and siblings; and this in turn provides the basis for an essential component in his range of linguistic skills, the language of rules and instructions. Whereas at first he can make only simple unstructured demands, he learns as time goes on to give ordered sequences of instructions, and then progresses to the further stage where he can convert sets of instructions into rules, including conditional rules, as in explaining the principles of a game. Thus his regulatory model of language continues to be elaborated, and his experience of the potentialities of language in this use further increases the value of the model.

Closely related to the regulatory function of language is its function in social interaction, and the third of the models that we may postulate as forming part of the child's image of language is the INTERACTIONAL model. This refers to the use of language in the interaction between the self and others. Even the closest of the child's personal relationships, that with his mother, is partly and, in time, largely mediated through language; his interaction with other people, adults and children, is very obviously maintained linguistically. (Those who come nearest to achieving a personal relationship that is not linguistically mediated, apparently, are twins.)

Aside, however, from his experience of language in the maintenance of permanent relationships, the neighbourhood and the activities of the peer group provide the context for complex and rapidly changing interactional patterns which make extensive and subtle demands on the individual's linguistic resources. Language is used to define and consolidate the group, to include and to exclude, showing who is 'one of us' and who is not; to impose status, and to contest status that is imposed; and humour, ridicule, deception, persuasion, all the forensic and theatrical arts of language are brought into play. Moreover, the young child, still primarily a learner, can do what very few adults can do in such situations: he can be internalizing language while listening and talking. He can be, effectively, both a participant and an observer at the same time, so that his own critical involvement in this complex interaction does not prevent him from profiting linguistically from it.

Again there is a natural link here with another use of language, from which the child derives what we may call the PERSONAL model. This refers to his awareness of language as a form of his own individuality. In the process whereby the child becomes aware of himself, and in particular in the higher stages of that process, the development of his personality, language plays an essential role. We are not talking here merely of 'expressive' language – language used for the direct expression of feelings and attitudes – but also of the personal element in the interactional function of language, since the shaping of the self through interaction with others is very much a language-mediated process. The child is enabled to offer to someone else that which is unique to himself, to make public his own individuality; and this in turn reinforces and creates this individuality. With the normal child, his awareness of himself is closely bound up with speech: both with hearing himself speak, and with having at his disposal the range of behavioural options that constitute language. Within the concept of the self as an actor, having discretion, or freedom of choice, the 'self as a speaker' is an important component.

Thus for the child language is very much a part of himself, and the 'personal' model is his intuitive awareness of this, and of the way in which his individuality is identified and realized through language. The other side of the coin, in this process, is the child's growing understanding of his environment, since the environment is, first of all, the 'non-self', that which is separated out in the course of establishing where he himself begins and ends. So, fifthly, the child has a HEURISTIC model of language, derived from his knowledge of how language has enabled him to explore his environment.

The heuristic model refers to language as a means of investigating reality, a way of learning about things. This scarcely needs comment, since every child makes it quite obvious that this is what language is for by his habit of constantly asking questions. When he is questioning, he is seeking not merely facts but explanations of facts, the generalizations about reality that language makes it possible to explore. Again, Bernstein has shown the importance of the question-and-answer routine in the total setting of parent–child communication and the significance of the latter, in turn, in relation to the child's success in formal education: his research has demonstrated a significant correlation between the mother's linguistic attention to the child and the teacher's assessment of the child's success in the first year of school.

The young child is very well aware of how to use language to learn, and may be quite conscious of this aspect of language before he reaches school; many children already control a metalanguage for the heuristic function of language, in that they know what a 'question' is, what an 'answer' is, what 'knowing' and 'understanding' mean, and they can talk about these things without difficulty. Mackay and Thompson have shown the importance of helping the child who is learning to read and write to build up a language for talking about language; and it is the heuristic function which provides one of the foundations for this, since the child can readily conceptualize and verbalize the basic categories of the heuristic model. To put this more concretely, the normal five-year-old either already uses words such as *question, answer* in their correct meanings or, if he does not, is capable of learning to do so.

The other foundation for the child's 'language about language' is to be found in the imaginative function. This also relates the child to his environment, but in a rather different way. Here, the child is using language to create his own environment; not to learn about how things are but to make them as he feels inclined. From his ability to create, through language, a world of his own making he derives the IMAGINATIVE model of language; and this provides some further elements of the metalanguage, with words like *story, make up* and *pretend.*

Language in its imaginative function is not necessarily 'about' anything at all: the child's linguistically created environment does not have to be a make-believe copy of the world of experience, occupied by people and things and events. It may be a world of pure sound, made up of rhythmic sequences of rhyming or chiming syllables; or an edifice of words in which semantics has no part, like a house built of playing cards in which face values are irrelevant. Poems, rhymes, riddles and much of the child's own linguistic play reinforce this model of language, and here too the meaning of what is said is not primarily a matter of content. In stories and dramatic games, the imaginative function is, to a large extent, based on content; but the ability to express such content is still, for the child, only one of the interesting facets of language, one which for many purposes is no more than an optional extra.

So we come finally to the REPRESENTATIONAL model. Language is, in addition to all its other guises, a means of communicating about something, of expressing propositions. The child is aware that he can convey a message in language, a message which has specific reference to the processes, persons, objects, abstractions,qualities, states and relations of the real world around him.

This is the only model of language that many adults have; and a very inadequate model it is, from the point of view of the child. There is no need to go so far as to suggest that the transmission of content is, for the child, the least important function of language; we have no way of evaluating the various functions relatively to one another. It is certainly not, however, one of the earliest to come into prominence: and it does not become a dominant function until a much later stage in the development towards maturity. Perhaps it never becomes in any real sense the dominant function; but it does, in later years, tend to become the dominant *model*. It is very easy for the adult, when he attempts to formulate his ideas about the nature of language, to be simply unaware of most of what language means to the child; this is not because he no longer uses language in the same variety of different functions (one or two may have atrophied, but not all), but because only one of these functions, in general, is the subject of conscious attention, so that the corresponding model is the only one to be externalized. But this presents what is, for the child, a quite unrealistic picture of language, since it accounts for only a small fragment of his total awareness of what language is about.

The representational model at least does not conflict with the child's experience. It relates to one significant part of it; rather a small part, at first, but nevertheless real. In this it contrasts sharply with another view of language which we have not mentioned because it plays no part in the child's experience at all, but which might be called the 'ritual' model of language. This is the image of language internalized by those for whom language is a means of showing how well one was brought up; it downgrades language to the level of table-manners. The ritual element in the use of language is probably derived from the interactional, since language in its ritual function also serves to define and delimit a social group; but it has none of the positive aspects of linguistic interaction, those which impinge on the child, and is thus very partial and one-sided. The view of language as manners is a needless complication, in the present context, since this function of language has no counterpart in the child's experience.

Our conception of language, if it is to be adequate for meeting the needs of the child, will need to be exhaustive. It must incorporate all the child's own 'models', to take account of the varied demands on language that he himself makes. The child's understanding of what language is is derived from his own experience of language in situations of use. It thus embodies all of the images we have described: the instrumental, the regulatory, the interactional, the personal, the heuristic, the imaginative and the representational. Each of these is his interpretation of a function of language with which he is familiar. Doughty has shown, in a very suggestive paper, how different concepts of the role of the English teacher tend to incorporate and to emphasize different functions, or groups of functions, from among those here enumerated.

*   *   *

Let us summarize the models in terms of the child's intentions, since different uses of language may be seen as realizing different intentions. In its instrumental function, language is used for the satisfaction of material needs; this is the 'I want' function. The regulatory is the 'do as I tell you' function, language in the control of behaviour. The interactional function is that of getting along with others, the 'me and him' function (including 'me and my mummy'). The personal is related to this: it is the expression of identity, of the self, which develops largely *through* linguistic interaction; the 'here I come' function, perhaps. The heuristic is the use of language to learn, to explore reality: the function of 'tell me why'. The imaginative is that of 'let's pretend', whereby the reality is created, and what is being explored is the child's own mind, including language itself. The representational is the 'I've got something to tell you' function, that of the communication of content.

What we have called 'models' are the images that we have of language arising out of these functions. Language is 'defined' for the child by its uses; it is something that serves this set of needs. These are not models of language acquisition; they are not procedures whereby the child learns his language, nor do they define the part played by different types of linguistic activity in the learning process. Hence no mention has been made of the chanting and repeating and rehearsing by which the child practises his language. The techniques of mastering language do not constitute a 'use', nor do they enter into the making of the image of language; a child, at least, does not learn for the luxury of being a learner. For the child, all language is doing something: in other words, it has meaning. It has meaning in a very broad sense, including here a range of functions which the adult does not normally think of as meaningful, such as the personal and the interactional and probably most of those listed above – all except the last, in fact. But it is precisely in relation to the child's conception of language that it is most vital for us to redefine our notion of meaning; not restricting it to the narrow limits of representational meaning (that is, 'content') but including within it all the functions that language has as purposive, non-random, contextualized activity.

Bernstein has shown that educational failure is often, in a very general and rather deep sense, language failure. The child who does not succeed in the school system is one who has not mastered certain essential aspects of language ability. In its immediate interpretation, this could refer to the simple fact that a child cannot read or write or express himself adequately in speech. But these are as it were the externals of linguistic success, and it is likely that underlying the failure to master these skills is a deeper and more general failure of language, some fundamental gap in the child's linguistic capabilities.

This is not a lack of words; vocabulary seems to be learnt very easily in response to opportunity combined with motivation. Nor is it, by and large, an impoverishment of the grammar: there is no real evidence to show that the unsuccessful child uses or disposes of a narrower range of syntactic options. (I hope it is unnecessary to add that it has also nothing to do with dialect or accent.) Rather it would appear that the child who, in Bernstein's terms, has only a 'restricted code' is one who is deficient in respect of the set of linguistic models that we have outlined above, because some of the functions of language have not been accessible to him. The 'restriction' is a restriction on the range of uses of language. In particular, it is likely that he has not learnt to operate with language in the two functions which are crucial to his success in school: the personal function, and the heuristic function.

In order to be taught successfully, it is necessary to know how to use language to learn; and also, how to use language to participate *as an individual* in the learning situation. These requirements are probably not a feature of any particular school system, but rather are inherent in the very concept of education. The ability to operate effectively in the personal and heuristic modes is, however, something that has to be learnt; it does not follow automatically from the acquisition of the grammar and vocabulary of the mother tongue. It is not, that is to say, a question of which words and structures the child knows or uses, but of their functional significance and interpretation. In Bernstein's formulation, the child may not be oriented towards the meanings realized by the personal and heuristic functions of language. Restricted and elaborated code are in effect, as Ruqaiya Hasan suggests, varieties of language function, determining the meanings that the syntactic patterns and the lexical items have for the child who hears or uses them.

To say that educational failure is linguistic failure is merely to take the first step in explaining it: it means that the most immediately accessible cause of educational failure is to be sought in language. Beyond this, and underlying the linguistic failure, is a complex pattern of social and familial factors whose significance has been revealed by Bernstein's work. But while the limitations of a child's linguistic experience may ultimately be ascribed – though not in any simple or obvious way – to features of the social background, the problem as it faces the teacher is essentially a linguistic problem. It is a failure in the child's effective mastery of the use of language, in his adaptation of language to meet certain basic demands. Whether one calls it a failure in language or a failure in the use of language is immaterial; the distinction between knowing language and knowing how to use it is merely one of terminology. This situation is not easy even to diagnose; it is much more difficult to treat. We have tried here to shed some light on it by relating it to the total set of demands, in terms of the needs of the child, that language is called upon to serve.

The implication for a teacher is that his own model of language should at least not fall short of that of the child. If the teacher's image of language is narrower and less rich than that which is already present in the minds of those he is teaching (or which needs to be present, if they are to succeed), it will be irrelevant to him as a teacher. A minimum requirement for an educationally relevant approach to language is that it take account of the child's own linguistic experience, defining this experience in terms of its richest potential and noting where there may be gaps, with certain children, which could be educationally and developmentally harmful. This is one component. The other component of relevance is the relevance to the experiences that the child will have later on: to the linguistic demands that society will eventually make of him, and, in the intermediate stage, to the demands on language which the school is going to make and which he must meet if he is to succeed in the classroom.

We are still very ignorant of many aspects of the part language plays in our lives. But it is clear that language serves a wide range of human needs, and the richness and variety of its functions is reflected in the nature of language itself, in its organization as a system: within the grammatical structure of a language, certain arcas are primarily associated with the heuristic and representational functions, others with the personal and interactional functions. Different bits of the system, as it were, do different jobs; and this in turn helps us to interpret and make more precise the notion of uses of language. What is common to every use of language is that it is meaningful, contextualized, and in the broadest sense social; this is brought home very clearly to the child, in the course of his day-to-day experience. The child is surrounded by language, but not in the form of grammars and dictionaries, or of randomly chosen words and sentences, or of undirected monologue. What he encounters is 'text', or language in use: sequences of language articulated each within itself and with the situation in which it occurs. Such sequences are purposive – though very varied in purpose – and have an evident social significance. The child's awareness of language cannot be isolated from his awareness of language function, and this conceptual unity offers a useful vantage point from which language may be seen in a perspective that is educationally relevant.

Children's Use of Language
By Joan Tough

Editor's Introduction

A considerable amount of interest has been shown in the language of young children ranging from studies of how individuals acquire their language (e.g. Brown, 1974) to programmes for remediation (e.g. Bereiter and Engelmann, 1966). Some studies have taken a naïve position by suggesting that the early language acquired is of little value or, more dangerously, that some 'deprived' groups have little or no language. Labov (1970), on the other hand, has exposed the weakness of this extreme view. It is equally dangerous to misunderstand and to overstate the view that children have acquired *all* their language structures by the age of four or five and Carol Chomsky (1969), for example, produces contrary evidence. More worthwhile studies have begun to categorize the speech of children in naturalistic situations and to place emphasis on the purposes for which children use language.

Joan Tough, for instance, examines other category systems and examples of language in use in her attempt to specify the ways children use language to order and organize their world. She describes the *relational* function which provides both a framework for the child to organize his/her meaning and choices of showing his/her relationship with others. What she classifies as *content* functions include language used by the child: to look after his/her own interests (self maintaining); to organize his/her own actions (directing); to interpret experience and to order meaning (interpretive); and to go beyond actual or remembered experience (projective). This notion of language function gives an important place to children's perception of their relationships with other people and to the strategies they use for learning and for expressing thoughts and feelings.

So Joan Tough provides a naturalistic study of children's language and a classification system to compare different groups of children. Above all she provides insights into language as a powerful tool in the learning process and provides a framework for encouraging various kinds of cognitive ordering. A teacher who wishes to encourage, for example, predicting, hypothesizing, collaborating, forecasting and the recognizing of sequences, causes and effects will need to give thoughtful attention to children's use of language.

B.W.

Abstract

It is important to consider the ways in which language functions for the child in order to say what he achieves by using language and to discover what meanings he attaches to his experiences. The language of three-year-old children is examined to discover whether existing classifications of language functions account for all the ways in which language is used. One mode of classification is used to compare the language used by three-year-olds from different groups.

1. Introduction

SOME of the earliest studies of children's language, notably those of Piaget (1926) and Vygotsky (1962), attempted to develop a theory which would explain the way in which language functioned in the social and intellectual development of the child. With the development of a number of linguistic indices, however, more recent studies of children's language have tended to centre on the examination of the linguistic structures which occur in children's speech, and have been relatively unconcerned with the purposes for which children use language.

The development of a generative grammar which provides a ready tool for examining the sequence in which the child acquires speech structures, has created a new interest in the language of young children. The research which has followed, however, has been mainly concerned with testing hypotheses about the developing system of rules by which the child proceeds towards the adult form of speech, and with testing the young child's knowledge of language structures. We now have some evidence about the order in which particular structures will be used and understood, about the structures which are not likely to be produced by the young child, about the errors which children are likely to make and the age at which such errors are likely to be overcome.

We are, then, in a better position than formerly for describing the language used by children, and for making comparisons between the language used by different children, between the same children at different ages and between children at the same age who have had substantially different opportunities for learning to use language. Studies which have set out to make comparisons of this kind have usually relied entirely on such methods for describing the differences; that is they have set out to discover differences in syntax or in the verbal elements of the language used by children. But there has been little attempt to relate the differences which have been found in the structures of children's language to the differences in the purposes for which the language is being used.

Until quite recently the study of the functions of children's language appears to have been neglected: the development of methods of describing what children actually *do* with language has not kept pace with the development of methods for describing what children's language is *like*. If we know little about the purposes for which children use language, we do know that their interest lies not in the language itself: language is used because it helps them to achieve particular goals: language serves their purposes, and in doing so fulfils certain functions in their social and cognitive development.

Halliday (1973) has recently contributed a series of papers to the discussion which take a functional approach and which has opened up a new phase in the study of children's language. His socio-linguistic view of the functions of language however, leads to a study of the principles which relate the functions of language to language itself. The question that Halliday is asking is whether the social functions of language are reflected in linguistic structure, that is in the internal organization of language.

But we have different questions in mind. The first is concerned with what the child achieves by using language: the second is concerned with discovering the range of meanings that the child attaches to his experiences. A final question which might then be asked would be concerned with discovering the extent to which the expression of particular kinds of meaning was dependent on the use of particular syntactic structures.

In considering the way in which language functions for the child it seems to be generally assumed that functions must be inferred only from the evidence of the syntactic structures, but this is the relationship we seek to examine. Piaget's approach (Piaget op. cit.) presents us with this kind of problem since his classification is also based on the identification of categories of use by their particular linguistic form, for example, demand, request and questions.

In order to illustrate the kind of problem that a functional analysis must meet, a short extract from the talk of two three-and-a-half-year-old boys is given below. This example is taken from a collection of the talk of groups of three-year-old children, all of whom were friendly and above average intelligence.

This example is by no means typical of the talk of all the three-year-olds in the sample. Stretches of talk which show a similar range of uses of language are to be found in the recordings of all the children who came from professional families but only some of the uses to be identified in this passage were found in the talk of children from lower working-class families. Although girls usually chose doll play materials the same range of uses of language are to be found in their talk.

For any classification to be useful for our purposes it must not only be able to accommodate data of this kind but it must also differentiate the uses on some recognizable criteria which are not dependent on statements about linguistic structure, but about the purposes for which language is used by children.

2. What children do with language: an example

Tommy and John are both three-and-a-half years old. They are playing with a collection of toy vehicles. The teacher is nearby but rarely intervenes. Tom picks up a car which John has put down a few minutes ago.

1. John: Hey – give me it – it's mine.
2. Tom: It's not – I got it first.
3. John: Will you give me it – 'cos it's mine.
4. Tom: I want it – that's not yours.
5. John: I bringed it with me. I did – from my house.
   J.T. I think it really is his, Tom.
6. Tom: (Gives car to John and pulls a face.) You're a meany. (He picks up a lorry and begins to push it round on the floor.) It's a lorry this. Br-brr – round the corner – fast – like this. (John watches for a moment then goes over to other side of room.)
7. Tom: Pip – pip – a big bus coming – coming on the road – down the road – pip – pip – out of the way – and it's got big wheels – pip – pip. (He becomes aware of John again. He sits back and calls to John.) Hey look – look what I'm doing.
8. Hey – you know – I saw an accident. The car – and it had gone – it had gone on to the grass – at the side – it had gone off the road – and it banged – right on to the wall – and it was an accident.
9. John: Well – and I've seen one as well – and a man got hurt – very bad.
10. Tom: Yes and I did – I saw one – and the ambulance came – to help.
11. John: I'm driving a bus – br – br – down the road.
12. Tom: And I'm going to – that's a baddy, a baddy coming – and this is a policeman coming – er-er-er-er.
13. John: Here's another policeman coming in his car – er-er.
14. Tom: He's going to shoot him. This baddy's going to shoot.
15. John: Hey – don't shoot me – shoot the bus.

16. Tom: He's shooting all the bus up – bang – bang – the people are getting hurt – he shot the driver.
17. John: We'll have to fetch the doctor – where's the doctor – that's not the doctor.
18. Tom: If there isn't a doctor he might die – 'cos he'll bleed all away – that's how you die.
19. John: If it's an accident you do. My grannie died – but she didn't bleed all up – she just died. She was poorly and she was very old – so she died – in hospital she died. And now I've only grannie T.
20. Tom: I want a hospital here.
21. John: Let's make the policeman shoot the baddy.
22. Tom: Yes – let's shoot him now, – bang – bang. Is he dead John? Is he dead now? Will you let the doctor come?
23. John: Make the ambulance come – make it come to take the people to the hospital.
24. Tom: And I've been to hospital – with my arm I went. And if you break your arm, or your leg – you've to go to hospital – and then they put something on it – all round.
25. John: Yes – I know – they do. What a mess – all in the road – like a bomb.
26. Tom: All on fire – it's all on fire.

We can summarize the purposes for which Tom and John used language here to be the following:

   (i) The first six utterances are concerned with gaining or maintaining possession of the car. (1 to 6).
  (ii) Tom uses language as an accompaniment to his manipulative play – guiding his action. (6 and 7).
 (iii) Language is used to attract the attention of the other. (7 and 8).
 (iv) Tom and John recall incidents they have witnessed. They give accounts or reports of it. (8 to 10).
  (v) The two boys together build up an imaginative scene for their play. (11 to 26).
 (vi) In amongst the imaginative play the children return to reality and they show their ability to reason, to see causal relationships, to indicate possibilities.
     18. Tom – 'If there isn't a doctor he might die – 'cos he'll bleed all away – that's how you die.'
     24. Tom – 'And if you break your arm, or your leg – you've to go to hospital – and then they put something on it – all round.'
(vii) And perhaps we see the early indication of the recognition of abstract concepts or principles.
     19. John – 'If it's an accident you do. My grannie died – but she didn't bleed all up – she just died. She was poorly and she was very old – so she died – in hospital she died. And now I've only grannie T.'

3. Some problems of classification

If we look at this extract we can see that neither Piaget's nor Halliday's (1969) classification meets our purpose. Piaget's examination of the talk of two six-year-old children led him to propose a broad classification of functions which has provided a model for most later work that takes a functional approach (Piaget op. cit.). A major section of the young child's language is described as *egocentric*, fulfilling self needs and failing to accommodate the needs or viewpoint of others: in Piaget's classification the ego-centric function is realized in monologue, or collected monologue, that is speech which is addressed to the self. In the above episode Tom's utterances beginning (7) 'Pip – pip – a big bus coming – . . .' would be an example of monologue, serving the egocentric function: his speech parallels his action and he is clearly talking for himself alone.

The rest of the child's speech in the extract would be classified by Piaget as *socialized*, and would be realized in demands, requests, answers, criticisms and adapted information.

From the episode above we pick out the demands:

(1) John: Hey – give me it – it's mine.
(4) Tom: I want it – that's not yours.
(15) John: Hey – don't shoot me – shoot the bus.
(20) Tom: I want a hospital here.
(23) John: Make the ambulance come – make it come to take the people to the hospital.

It is clear that using a category like 'demand' sets up linguistic structures as criteria for classifying. It is also clear that the demands that Tom and John make serve very different purposes. One purpose is to retrieve the child's property and another is to pursue an imaginary play sequence in which he projects into experiences through his imagination. Speech in the same form can be directed towards very different goals.

Halliday's classification does not resolve the problems of giving an account of the uses of language in the above episode either. He argues that the functions present in the earliest stages of language development later become systematized in the grammar so that as the child selects language a particular function is served by those grammatical features which express his meaning. The functions are realized in the grammatical structure of the child's language (Halliday, 1970). So the uses of language which are identified (the instrumental, the regulative, the interactional, the personal, the heuristic, the imaginative and the representational or informative) form a classification which is based on the recognition of syntactic structures (Halliday, 1973). We recognize the usefulness of this approach but it does not help us to solve the problem of analysing the language used by Tom and John above.

There are two main problems to resolve. The first is to deal with uses of language which are different in linguistic structure but serve the same purpose, for example:

'Give me that car – it's mine.'
and
'Would you please give me my car because it belongs to me?'

in both cases the child's goal is to retrieve his possession.

The second problem is concerned with language uses which are classified by Piaget as 'adapted information' and by Halliday as 'representational' or 'informative'. In the episode we have quoted the major part of the children's talk would fall into these categories, and would remain undifferentiated although it can be seen to include uses as different as:

(5) John: I bringed it with me. I did – from my house.
(19) John: If it's an accident you do. My grannie died – but she didn't bleed all up – she just died. She was poorly and she was very old – so she died – in hospital she died. And now I've only grannie T.

But this seems likely to be the kind of difference which might provide a means of distinguishing between the language used by different children. Statements like the first are made frequently by our three year olds and explanations like the second occur much less frequently, and are clearly different in quality and not just in length. Some means of differentiating within this large class of 'informative' use is essential for a satisfactory method of classifying our data. We need a classification which will accommodate and differentiate the purposes for which children can and do use language.

We are not here trying to put forward a complete classification of the uses or purposes for which children use language, but we are trying to examine what we can infer about the functions of children's language from the evidence of language in use. We regard functions as being the characteristic modes in which language is used to organize or order experiences and intentions. These modes may be seen to be fulfilling more general functions in the child's cognitive and social development but the modes can only be inferred from the evidence of the particular strategies which are selected by the child for conveying his meaning. From the examination of a great amount of data from the same sixty children at the ages of three, five and seven years we have been led to some conclusions about what these functions might be.

Clearly the problem of analyzing functions, as Halliday (1975) has indicated, is the multifunctional nature of most of the language we use. Not only will different kinds of content be conveyed, but the language used may be directed towards more than one goal. It is clear that even within a single utterance at least two purposes are served, one is concerned with establishing or maintaining relationships and the other with the kind of content to be conveyed – the purpose of the talk. So we first distinguish two different kinds of functions, the *relational* function and a range of 'content' or *ideational* functions.

4. The relational function

What we say to another generally has some indication of the relationship in which we view the other. Usually we select our language without giving much thought to our relationship with the other: the relationship is so familiar to us that we intuitively select a form of language that expresses it. Only when there is some reason for being very much aware of the relationship being a crucial one, perhaps because of the status or power of the one to whom we speak, do we choose our approach very deliberately.

In the case of a child this forms a major part of his learning: through relationships into which he is drawn, by continuous exposure to the expression of the relationships in which members of his family hold him, he will learn to assume similar relationships with others. He may be formally instructed in the use of phrases which imply respect to older people or people in authority, but as they are assimilated they, too, become an habitual means of expressing such relationships.

In this short extract the relationship between the two boys can be inferred by the way each approaches and responds to the other. For the most part there is an assumed equality, a friendly, informal basis for their talk, although in the first few utterances we see the relationship under strain and a renegotiation of the relationship has to be made later.

John (1) first demands his property and takes a self assertive position 'Hey – give me it – it's mine.' Tom (2) takes a similar position, but recognizes the conflict and offers a justification for his claim 'It's not – I got it first.' John (3), perhaps becoming aware of the difference between ownership and possession, tries to set the relationship on a different foot, appealing to Tom's reason 'Will you give me it – 'cos it's mine.' Tom (4), however, maintains his own self assertive claim 'I want it – that's not yours.' Which presses John (5) into producing further evidence that the car belongs to him, 'I bringed it with me. I did – from my house.'

Only the teacher's intervention perhaps prevents a quarrel, and even so Tom (6) expresses his anger by accusing John 'You're a meany.' There is a consequent withdrawal in which Tom uses language only for himself as he directs his own play.

However, Tom (7) restores the friendly equality and then we have a mutually supportive relationship emerging with (17) 'We'll have to fetch the doctor – . . .' (21) 'Let's make the policeman shoot the baddy.' (22) 'Let's shoot him now . . .'

The different uses here, which range from *self-assertive* to *other recognizing* and *mutual concern* reflect choices that have been made which indicate the relationship in which the other is being held at the time of speaking. We would describe this function as the *relational function* and the strategies which indicate the choice of the relationship we see as strategies which provide a framework which then contributes to the organization of the 'content'. These strategies are of two kinds, those which *assert the self* and are *closed* to negotiation and those which *recognize the other* and formally leave negotiation open to the other.

The remaining functions are those which are concerned with the 'content' of the language, that is they are the *ideational* functions.

5. The self-maintaining function

The relational function is not likely to operate separately from others except, perhaps, in some greetings and exclamations: it is necessarily integrated with other functions. A function which is a dominant one in the young child's use of language is one which is *self maintaining,* that is it is concerned with the welfare, comfort, feelings, and success and status of the self, and with preventing trespass on one's person, property and rights.

The self-maintaining function is served by a number of strategies which include *identification of self-interest, justification, the setting of a condition* and *surveying alternative possibilities.*

Since maintenance of the self necessarily involves trying to control others and is often realized in reaction to others it may not at first seem clear that these are two functions to be distinguished and not one. To regard the *relational* and the *self-maintaining* functions as separate means that judgements can be made about the relationship in which the speaker holds the listener and also allows a separate judgement to be made about the content. Two separate strategies can be identified in the message given by John in the effort to retrieve his property:

'Hey – give me it – it's mine.'

The *self-maintaining* strategy here is the *identification of self-interest.* The relationship strategy is *self-assertive* but not so strongly as if he had been speaking to a child towards whom he was particularly hostile. The *self-maintaining* strategy might then have included a condition for example:

'That's mine – give it back, or I'll hit you.'

Had John been speaking to an adult known to require politeness and respect for status he might have said:

'Could I have my car please?'

But to the teacher, who had picked up his car he might have been much more tentative saying,

'I think that might be my car.'

In these last two examples we see the *relational* function being served by two different *other recognizing* strategies, but the message remains the same – 'the car is mine I want it.' This 'content' reflects John's appraisal of the situation, that Tom has taken his car and he wants to reclaim it. But an older child's appraisal of the same situation might have been different, that Tom was only playing with the car and knew that it was not his and that there was no cause for alarm. This appraisal of the situation would have produced a different message, though still self maintaining, perhaps one of the following:

'When you're finished with my car I'll have it back if you don't mind.'
or
'I see you've borrowed my car. You won't forget to give me it back before you go, will you?'
or
'Put my car back when you've finished playing with it.'

Any of these responses would have suggested that the speaker had made a very different appraisal from that made by John. The 'content' shows a different organization of meaning: there is a statement of conditions. But a relational strategy has also been chosen: in the case of the first two they show different degrees of *recognition of the other* and leave negotiation open; in the third, the strategy is *self-assertive*, that is, closed to negotiation.

We are not saying that every child has such an awareness of the range of possible relationships on the one hand, or that he would be aware of other possible interpretations. Whether he will or not will depend both upon his view of his relationship with others, and his orientation towards the cognitive ordering of his experiences. There is no doubt that the two functions are closely related and that the orientation the child has towards relationships with others will have a strong influence on the way in which he appraises his experiences.

Much of the work that has examined the relationship and linguistic interaction between mother and child has been mainly concerned with these two functions – the *relational* and the *self-maintaining* functions.

6. The directive function

This function is concerned with directing one's *own* actions, although often in conjunction with the actions of others. In the episode quoted earlier Tom talks to himself as he pushes the car along, almost as though he is *monitoring* his own actions, and sometimes using speech to concentrate his action.

Later on in the episode we see Tom and John using language to pace their play, together *collaborating* in their actions to achieve mutually agreed ends. Frequently in this kind of activity, the *relational function* will be served by instructions and commands, a self-assertive strategy will be used. But in this episode we also see *mutual concern,* a strategy of the *relational function.* The *directive function* itself appears to be served by a number of strategies which will include the *monitoring* of action, *collaboration,* and *forward planning* of action.

7. The interpretive function

This function relates to immediate and recalled experiences and is concerned with organizing the experience at different levels of meaning. Recalled experience may be inspected as though it were an ongoing scene, that is the image of the experience can be regarded as an immediate experience so the various strategies which deal with recalled experience are considered to be within the *interpretive* function. The uses range from the limited purpose of *identification* of elements of experience, for example Tom (8), 'It's a lorry this', the *recognition of causes and effect,* as Tom (24) 'If you break your arm you've to go to hospital', and the *recognition of principles and abstract concepts,* for example John (9) 'She was poorly and she was very old – so she died'. It can be seen from this that there are a number of different strategies by which interpretation of experience is achieved: they include *analysing, recognizing sequence, relationships and causes* and the *abstraction of central meaning.* These might be considered to be cognitive strategies which are a reflection of the child's attempts to organize the meaning of his experience.

8. The projective functions

Sometimes the three-year-old, and often the five-year-old, uses language in a way that shows that his thinking extends beyond the actual concrete present or recalled experience: he projects in thought and through language beyond his own experience. Although recalled and present experience inform such uses the essential quality of the projective function is its dependence upon the imagination for its realization. There appear to be three different kinds of projection here and perhaps we should distinguish three different functions accordingly.

(i) *The predictive function*
In the talk of three-year-olds there is some evidence of the *predictive* function. More can be found in the talk of five-year-olds. This function is concerned with the cognitive ordering of events that have not yet happened, projecting beyond the present experience: it is based on anticipation and prediction and a number of strategies are used, including *forecasting,* the *surveying of possible alternatives,* the *setting up of hypotheses,* the *anticipation of consequences,* the *recognition of problems* and the *prediction of solutions.*

(ii) *The imaginative function*
Projection leads to the imagined scene, the creation of an imagined situation as, for example, in the quoted extract. We can see here different strategies. First at a *representational* level where the material used is just renamed, John (11) 'I'm driving a bus down the road', or a scene is built up with language as the sole representation to which the children react as though it were a reality, for example (15) John – 'Hey don't shoot me – shoot the bus.' (16) 'He's shooting all the bus up – the people are getting hurt – he shot the driver.' (17) 'We'll have to fetch the doctor – where's the doctor – that's not the doctor.' There is nothing here to represent people, or guns, or the doctor, except the language which places them in the imagined scene.

(iii) *The 'empathetic' function*
Lastly, we distinguish the *empathetic* function through which the child projects into the feelings and life of others. This may include the role he takes in his imaginative play, or projection into the feelings and experiences of others. These he can never know, except by projecting from his own experiences and feelings into theirs. Through the imagination, based on first hand and second hand knowledge that he has acquired, he projects into the feelings and lives of other people.

9. Conclusion
We have not intended here to set up an exhaustive classification of functions and strategies, but merely to indicate one which could be inferred from the examination of the talk of our groups of three-year-old children. Uses of language vary considerably from context to context, so that all we can say is that our classification, based on the functions outlined above, accounted for the language of our three-year-olds which had all been collected in similar play situations, and their language at five and seven years old which was collected in task oriented contexts.

The classification was used to compare the language of the three-year-old children drawn from the homes of unskilled or semi-skilled manual workers and of professional workers. Our results indicated that children from these different social environments had already, at the age of three years, established markedly different dispositions to use language.

Bernstein (1971) has shown how different social contexts, which provide the early experiences through which children develop language, result in different orientations both in social relationships and towards the use of language. From our study of children's language it would seem that not only have children by the age of three established particular social orientations, but at the same time they have acquired markedly different cognitive orientation towards their experiences and set markedly different meanings on them.

The differences in the incidence of uses of language, which distinguished the groups at the age of three, became more marked at the ages of five and seven. Differences are then seen, both in the frequency with which language serving particular functions is used, and in the organization of the meaning conveyed. We infer from the incidence of particular strategies, which the child persistently employs to achieve his purposes, the nature of his developing frame of reference. The differences between the groups seem to lie in the different models of reality through which the child processes his experiences. (Tough, 1973).

> The children of professional workers used language five times as often as the other group for predicting and for collaborating in action with others, three times as often for the interpretive use of language beyond the level of the monitoring of their experiences, and five times as often for projecting through the imagination to a scene not present except through the use of language. The children from the homes of unskilled and semi-skilled manual workers used speech almost three times as often to secure attention for their own needs and to maintain their own status by defending or asserting themselves in the face of the needs and actions of others, and twice as often to parallel or monitor their own actions, as the children of professional workers. (Tough, 1969).

The Implications of Oracy

By Andrew M. Wilkinson

Editor's Introduction

Listening and talking are two activities important in the education of children. Firstly, they are means by which a pupil can learn through receiving and representing experiences and information to himself and to others. In group discussion, for example, a pupil listens to make sense of another viewpoint which he relates to his present view of the world. His own spoken utterances can be worked on by both himself and others and ideas can be explored, modified and restructured with the immediate feedback that face to face talk provides. Secondly, they are important ways in which people learn about their language and how to use it appropriately: through listening we learn the particular registers necessary for many different speech situations; through talk we put these into practice.

The word 'oracy' was coined to stand for the abilities of listening and talking. The term emphasizes the close connection between listening and talking referred to in the previous paragraph. In the paper which follows Andrew Wilkinson discusses some reasons for the neglect of talk by schools and argues for a 'productive' role for the pupil in school learning. It is, after all, through being in speech situations that we learn about relationships between talkers and listeners as well as about feelings and ideas and the language used to communicate them. Wilkinson explores various aspects of a model of speech situations and outlines the implications for teachers and the school curriculum.

The survey of schools reported in the *Bullock Report* showed that the amount of attention given explicitly to oral English declines between six and nine years old (p. 390). With 12- and 14-year-olds, even in English lessons, the time spent on writing substantially exceeds that spent on talking (p. 434). In many other subjects the time spent on writing is likely to be much greater than in English lessons. Wilkinson's argument and its implications clearly still have a good deal of relevance.

B.W.

I

THE term oracy first appeared in print in 1965 (Wilkinson *et al.*, 1965). Since then it has often appeared in print and occurs in the conversation of teachers of English. It has even been attacked by a correspondent in the *Times Educational Supplement* as a 'vulgar, nasty word' (28 April 1967, p. 1429). Reactions to new words would themselves provide an interesting study: as another correspondent pointed out in reply it is the associations of words that determines such reactions to them. A new word can have gathered no relevant associations; it might call to mind irrelevant ones like 'idiocy' which would be unfortunate – but why should it not call up words with romantic associations such as 'sourcery' or 'tracery'? In other words the criticism exposes its own prejudices.

Of themselves such comments are not really worth refuting, but there is often much more serious linguistic misunderstanding behind them. The correspondent makes this clear when he asserts 'neologism is becoming to a true student and lover of the language'. (Significantly enough he also objects to 'numeracy'.) Such a lover of the language would find it impossible to study chemistry beyond the alchemical stage, or any other posited stage. In fact he would be thinking of language as static. He would not recognize that words come into use or fall away as ideas change and develop and that the one does not take place without the other. Not to have words for a concept is not to think about that concept.

This was one consideration which prompted the coinage of oracy (inoracy), orate (inorate). The neglect of the spoken word is forced upon them when one comes to consider the terms in which to describe an ability to use it. *Eloquence, the gift of the gab*, even *fluency* are suspect nowadays. Conversely one may describe a poor speaker as 'illiterate' – yet his literacy or otherwise is not the point of issue. T. H. Pear in 1930 noted that a word was needed for 'deliberate adequate verbal expression', and coined *euphasic*. However this only describes one part of oral skill – speaking. One needs a word for skill in both speaking and listening. For this *oracy* was suggested.

Again, the features of the spoken language lack adequate descriptive terms. In western culture for over 2,000 years grammarians have done their work on the written language. Their definitions of a sentence have been based on ideal written sentences. These definitions, never very satisfactory, are exposed as even less adequate when applied to the variety of utterances which pass for single units in the written language. Again, common features of speech like 'you know' when it signals 'are you receiving me?' or 'come into this conversation' or 'you are an intelligent being like myself: I don't really need to tell you this' have gone unmarked and unnamed, because they do not occur in the written language. They have been classed as faults. Pause phenomena like 'er' have been classed as faults, regardless of how they are used. It is clear that a whole new vocabulary is required. Much of this vocabulary will take the form of neologisms. These, whilst not, of course, acceptable to a 'true student and lover of the language' will be necessary if we are to think meaningfully about speech.

II

The spoken language has been neglected in English education. The concern of the educator has been literacy. This is not in itself sufficient reason for paying attention to it now. It might have been neglected for good reasons. Now these reasons appear to be of three kinds. One is certainly practical – that it is much more difficult to teach oracy than literacy. These difficulties are connected with such matters as the size of classes, the problem of control, the thinness of walls and the absence of teaching patterns. The second is connected with the structure of society – its attitudes, assumptions and rewards. The third is psychological – lack of knowledge until comparatively recently of the relationships between language and thought.

The first set of reasons are very real ones: one would not wish to minimize their importance, but they are largely dependent on the second and third set, for social and psychological beliefs and pressures must have a large influence on what goes on in the classroom.

Let us therefore consider the second set. Society has given large rewards to literacy: one of its measures of educational success has been examinations in reading and writing, in whatever subject – the candidate has taken 'papers'. This has obviously had a considerable effect, what is fashionably called 'washback', on the preceding teaching. But the problem goes deeper than this – to the hierarchical structure of English society. Was Oliver Twist disgraced because he asked for more, or because he asked? The children of a governing class attended a few select schools and were not taught to speak because there was no need – their linguistic background was good. The children of others received universal education and they were not taught to speak, also because there was no need – their place was to listen. Had they been encouraged to speak, they might have answered back. Their linguistic roles were intended to be receptive rather than productive. Things have, of course, changed since Dickens, but the point still has relevance and will be returned to later. Firth in *The Tongues of Men* (1937) says, 'speech is the telephone network, the nervous system of our society, much more than the vehicle for the lyrical outbursts of the individual soul. It is a network of bonds and obligations.' Of course, not everybody has a telephone.

Thirdly, the spoken language has been neglected because its importance in mental development has not, until recently, been appreciated. Now, however, the relationship between the two has been amply demonstrated. Negatively the point is sharply made by studies of deaf children whose 'progress in conceptual thinking is slowed down by the poverty of the verbal instruments at their command' (Lewis, 1963, p. 75). The Newsom Report speaks of our ignorance of how many (normal) children 'never develop intellectually because they lack the words with which to think and reason' (1963, para. 43). From the linguistic standpoint Sapir (1921) and Whorf (reprint 1966) drew our attention to the linguistic relativity of our cosmic perceptions. For instance, to think of an atom as a noun, a finite thing, might have delayed insights into its nature, as compared with a language in which it could be a verb implying a continual process. In the socio-linguistic field this kind of thinking has been brilliantly developed by Bernstein. Bernstein regards a certain type of language which he terms a 'restricted code' as excluding from its users types of perceptions, and ability to handle certain types of relationships. To take just one aspect of this language use – on the grammatical level the sentence structures of such speakers are simple, and where conjunctions are used they tend to be *and, so, then, because*: other conjunctions, implying more complex relationships and subordinations, being rare. Such structures are clearly important in logical thought, and are a characteristic of a more generally useful language which Bernstein calls an 'elaborated code' (Bernstein, 1959). Further work, for instance by Lawton (1966) seems to confirm these and other differences in language use even where IQ (as measured by conventional verbal and non-verbal tests) is held constant. Loban's diachronic study of elementary schoolchildren in California over a period of years gives certain indications in the same direction (Loban, 1963). Restricted code speakers are usually of lower working-class background where there is not a high premium on the verbalization of experience, in contrast to middle-class speakers who have both restricted and elaborated codes. Restricted code speakers can communicate perfectly well in a restricted code situation but, to use Firth's image again, would find it very difficult to make contact by telephone with members of the community at large and would, one infers, find it difficult to understand the elaborated code (though no work seems to have been done on their reception as distinct from their production of language). In this sense they are isolated from the larger community; in this sense they are in prison.

One has been looking at cognitive matters in the preceding paragraph. Needless to say, attention to the spoken language also implies corresponding growth in the affective field. To develop oracy is to develop human personality more directly than is possible by other educational means. In a very real sense speech and personality are one.

III

Any training in oracy must involve both production and reception. The task of the teacher of English can be summed up by a variation of three words. He is to encourage the *verbalization of experience* and the *experience of verbalization*. His focus is on the language used.

With any normal spoken utterance there are always several factors determining the language used. Halliday (1965) classifies these under the heading of 'field', 'mode', and 'style'. A somewhat cruder description is offered here, as in the model below.

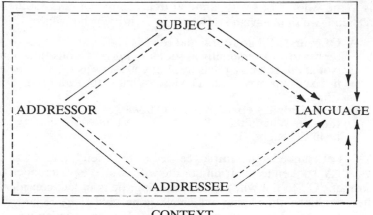

CONTEXT

The form of language is determined first and foremost by the speaker or Addressor, by his whole set. But he does not normally speak to nobody, and about nothing, so two more factors come in. His language will be shaped by the Addressee, and by the Subject talked about. But also he will be speaking at some particular time and place and occasion. And this may be the most important determinant of the language employed. In the model, all these factors are operating all the time, though they may have a major (thick line) or minor (dotted line) influence.

Language governed principally by subject could be characterized by the use of a special register:
He was caught in the leg trap off a googly.
ITA is claimed to have advantages over phonic and look-and-say.

Here the Addressees are taken into account as understanding the registers, but the situation is not mainly one raising the question of relationship. A non-expert Addressee will exercise influence on language in that it will have to be less technical, with more explanation implying an imaginative attempt on the part of the Addressor to see how the problem appears to him. A special register might still be employed but it will be glossed. Many situations in which the Addressor–Addressee relationship is paramount are non-technical, often social. In phatic communion for example, the subject is unimportant (the weather, the new hat, the traffic), the establishment of relationship all-important.

In the following three utterances the Addressor and the Subject are constant (the Addressor has been asked to see someone and agrees). The context, in so far as it is represented by a telephone conversation, is the same. Yet the language differs in each case. There are no modes of address, but if we are told that one utterance is to the Addressor's wife, another to his employer, and another to a friend, we shall have no difficulty in saying which is which.

A Of course. I'll go round and see Mr Harris straight away. I'll report to you personally as soon as I know. Good afternoon.
B Not at all. It'll be a pleasure. Let you know as soon as I've got it fixed up with the Davies. What's the address? O.K. Cheerio!
C Well, I could step in on the way home. Means I'd be a bit late though. What's the address? You're quite sure that's where he lives? Right. Bye for now.

'A' is of course to the employee, 'B' to the friend, and 'C' to the wife. 'A' spoken to the friend or the wife, would have sounded too formal. 'C', to the wife, is not grudging; he is in fact considering her, realizing the dinner will have gone cold if he is late, and asking whether she is prepared for this. He can question whether she's got the right address without seeming critical. But if he used the same words to the employer they would seem both grudging and critical. 'B', to the friend, is less formal in language than 'A', and contains the phrase 'It'll be a pleasure'. He would not use this to his employer as it would sound as if he were doing his job as a special favour: would not use it to his wife, as favours are out of place between husband and wife – their marriage is a joint enterprise in which, in one sense, they are always doing favours for each other, but neither think of their contributions in this way. 'A', to the employer, is much more formal and less personal than the other two. If the speaker has any doubts about the address of Mr Harris he keeps them to himself; he can always check with the secretary. A phrase like 'report to you' implies an employer/employee relationship.

The Context can also have a major influence on the language used. By Context here one understands the time, place, and occasion of an utterance. A degree-giving ceremony, or a school speech-day, compels a certain formality of language which the participants would not use to one another in the common-room. The five styles of discourse enumerated by Joos (1962) (from Frozen, Formal, Consultative, and Casual, to Intimate) are partly determined by context, partly by the Addressor/Addressee relationship. Again, the influence of the Context may be a matter of the presence or absence of objects spoken about; objects present might be indicated briefly or non-verbally, objects absent might have to be described.

All the factors in the model described above combine to produce a particular form of language, and the language itself, when produced, is a factor in the production of further language. They make up a speech situation. Together they create a tension in the Addressor which usually compels speech (tension which is too great, of course inhibits it). This tension may be produced by the sheer presence of another person, as in a railway carriage or lift: it might be heightened by a direct question ('How are you finding this party?'); it might arise from the need in the Addressor to explain, persuade, apologize, ingratiate himself. A certain form of language emerges.

IV

It is clear from the above that it is not helpful to think of 'correct' English as though there were one absolute standard. Rather, one is thinking of appropriate English, related to the whole situation. The educated adult reading this paper will have developed many appropriate ways of using language.

He has done this basically by being in situations where the

tension compels verbalization. But how does he in fact know which language to use? He must in some sense be aware of the appropriate one. The young child's speech is largely undifferentiated, yet a girl of four and a half was recorded talking to her doll as follows:

> Come on, drink up milkies. Oh, she's spilt it. Don't worry. Mummy will clean it up.

Obviously the model here was the child's own mother. During subsequent educational processes, children differentiate their language, not mainly by conscious training but by assimilation. Playground language is acquired from peers and elders. Classroom language, suitable for discussing ideas, from the teacher and the subject matter. A teacher's question, 'How far do you think William Pitt a satisfactory war leader?' is an invitation to a particular evaluative, unemotional use of language, and would largely preclude, by its style alone, answers couched in terms like 'smashing gaffer'.

This process of learning the rules of speech by being in the situation is obviously fundamental. It does not necessarily preclude some deliberate training however. There are some formulas which are very useful indeed – the modes of introduction, the language of procedure in committee, the devices of phatic communion. The Victorians faced up to this matter squarely and produced books of advice on good conversation and correct etiquette. We tend to be embarrassed by it, perhaps because it seems to imply unashamed social climbing. But there is nothing unworthy in knowing how to open up human relationships or ease them along. Formulas, whilst not creative uses of language in themselves, may provide the framework for such usages.

In fact the concept of register, of the form of English appropriate in a particular situation, causes us to look again at the function of conventional language. Words like 'jargon' and 'cliché' have been terms of abuse. Language follows certain conventions – of word order, for instance. Otherwise it would be incomprehensible. Structurally the possible orders are highly restricted, and the probability of certain words occurring together is high. This applies not only to groups like 'bacon and eggs', but to a phrase like 'difficult problem' (much more likely than 'easy problem'), 'main characteristics', 'social group'. In the phrase used above 'he was caught in the leg trap off a googly' the listener, knowing the subject, would have a fair chance of predicting what was to follow after the first three words. Such language is fairly predictable, yet it cannot be called an excuse for not thinking accurately, a charge levelled against the user of 'jargon' and 'cliché'. Lawyers' 'jargon' is in fact extremely accurate. Another factor to be taken into account is the context in which the conventional language is used. Because of the speed with which it goes over, many people would not object to 'black as thunder' in speech, whereas they would criticize it in writing. G. Hughlings Jackson (1932) made a useful distinction between two kinds of speech – 'old well-organized' and 'new now-organizing'. A good speaker will have both; ready made, well learned sequences and collocations on the one hand; and the ability to formulate new collocations and sequences on the other. As Frieda Goldman-Eisler shows (1961a) both are likely to occur in discussion and conversation; she demonstrates that both become more fluent, as measured by the speed of articulation, with practice under experimental conditions – the 'new now-organizing' becoming, in fact, 'old well-organized'. 'Fluency' for her is a fairly low level activity; it is opposed to the occurrence of unfilled 'pauses' which indicate cognitive activity and high level verbal planning is going on. Fluency is marked by high predictability, intolerance of silence, conventional language, indicating internal emotional activity. It should be said, however, that her experiments take place in situations which exclude as far as possible a real Context and Addressee; and thus no measure of effective communication, which is what speech is concerned with, can therefore be employed. (Goldman-Eisler, 1961, b and c).

V

If the model speech situation and the description of language learning going on within it are acceptable then the general implications for education in oracy can be drawn out. Basically one requires the construction of many different situations, for in these the student learns the rules and the language.

The Addressor brings certain predispositions. As Firth puts it 'What a man actually says in a given speech situation is at that moment a dominant process in the working of his "set" and perhaps also a dominant factor or term in the situation (1964, p. 90) and he defines "set" as including instincts, urges, sentiments, interests, abilities and the general patterns of his behaviour' (p. 79). Whatever else the Addressor has learnt, or done, will be relevant. Training in oracy is not something to be separated from other educational activities. The Addressor also brings a purpose, nearly always to affect the Addressee in some way – by instruction, persuasion, entertainment, disagreement, for instance. The Subject provides certain words and constructions, and – negatively – excludes others. The Context will have a considerable influence on amount and style of speaking.

The crucial relationship is that of Addressor and Addressee. The model snapshots this at a moment of time when the former speaks to the latter. But as a matter of fact theirs is usually a reciprocal relationship. The Addressee is sending back signals which may be non-verbal or pre-verbal: and he and the Addressor are constantly changing places. In a sense they create each other's utterances, for each utterance guides the choice of meaning and to some extent the language of the one following, if it is not inconsequential. Reciprocal speech is the normal mode in that people use it more than any other form. It implies productive roles on the part of both or all participants.

The conventional education situation imposes a receptive not a productive linguistic role on the pupil. It has given one-way communication, from the teacher to the taught. Many forces are combining to bring about changes here, particularly the psychologists' insistence on the essential activity of the learner, though the changes have gone further at primary level than the others. To give the pupil, as a pupil, a productive linguistic role implies a different relationship with the teacher, which many teachers find hard to accept. To give the pupil as potential citizen such a role is to encourage social change to produce freer citizens.

The new role of the teacher has several facets. First he will have certain attitudes towards language, informed by modern linguistic thinking. If for instance he accepts that 'appropriateness' rather than one absolute 'correctness' is a criterion for language he will be able to see in perspective the different codes that children use. The old attitude that the language of some homes is 'bad' and that of the school 'good' which has been one of the things which has caused 'working class' children to react against the 'middle class' school will be replaced by one which recognizes the home language as one which is very effective within its own situation, though, like any restricted code, it has not general use. The teacher will recognize it, further, as a badge of identity, which only changes slowly as identity changes. Again, if the teacher takes a scientific criterion for accent – that it is to be judged by how it helps or hinders communication, he will find himself up against hierarchical beliefs about it, which classify accents into first class (RP), second class (many regional accents) and third class (town accents). To challenge these beliefs is to challenge the social structure. It should be added that popular linguistic beliefs – that there is only one correct English, that there is one correct accent, that grammar is unknown to those who have not learned about it, that slang is *per se* 'bad' – are terribly disabling to ordinary speakers of English.

Second, the teacher, responsible for syllabus construction, will think with both oracy and literacy as basic terms, and with production (speaking, writing) and reception (reading and listening) as the aspects of these. The conventional English time-table assigned different aspects of the subject to different periods; Monday, third period – grammar: Tuesday, last period – composition, and so on. Now we think of the time-table in terms of a central continuing theme or experience out of which emerge opportunities for the various aspects of production and reception. We start, not with the 'skill' to be taught, but with the central experience upon which the 'skills' may operate. Within this framework many opportunities for speaking and listening occur naturally.

Third, the teacher will be thinking of himself rather less as pedagogue, more of organizer, co-ordinator, producer in the theatre sense, of situations. In the classroom the division of children into groups forms a useful basis for work in both literacy and oracy: they are not 'practising speech' but pursuing some common task requiring the use of oral skills. Children who are too diffident even to participate in small groups may be helped by division into pairs where the compulsion to contribute is greater. But the speech situations are not confined to the classroom. Projects in which the children seek information from various adults, social service in which visiting or shopping for old people involves communication in genuine situations, school functions at which the children are not merely passive spectators, but show visitors round and give them explanations, are some of the many types of possible activity.

Fourth, the teacher will be more conscious of the function of his interventions. In connection with Bernstein's work it was mentioned earlier that the pressure to verbalize experience in the restricted code home is low. Work is going forward under his direction to try to develop remedial programmes for young children. This verbalization is brought about partly by the nature of the prompts and questions the child is given; and in a good home, linguistically considered, these are offered constantly. The infant school attempts to reproduce this kind of pressure. It is seen in the question and answer techniques of the class teacher at all levels, and the pressure for exact definition from the sixth form teacher in discussion. But with large classes, and class teaching methods it is often possible for pupils to avoid such invitations. The result is not that the grammatical structures required for thought are absent in restricted code children (Lawson demonstrates this with 11- and 13-year-old boys) but that they are less easily employed than the middle-class children (Lawson, 1966).

VI

The foregoing has seemed to concentrate most on the Addressor; but of course the Addressor is also the Addressee in reciprocal situations. Oracy involves both speaking and listening. Research demonstrates that listening is not as efficient a function as it may be (for a summary of research see Wilkinson *et al.*, 1966), but this is not to say that we need 'listening programmes' specifically to train it, in isolation from other activities, like some of the American ones. There are, however, three reasons for considering it here. The first is that it is through listening that we acquire our own language, and the particular registers we need for all kinds of speech. Whether deliberately or accidentally, society is constantly provided speech models. In school we may do this deliberately; we may require the production on tape of a radio programme which requires the different registers and styles of news reader, commentator, interviewer, reader of poetry or short story, actor in a radio drama.

The second reason is that listening may be the basis for an exciting study of language in action, whose source materials can be obtained on tape from broadcasting and actuality. Corresponding to the literary classics one would look for radio plays, programmes, and speeches where the spoken mode is used creatively. One thinks, for instance, of Louis MacNeice's *Dark Tower,* or the *Big Hewer* and other radio ballads, produced by Charles Parker. But one would also concern oneself with questions about the language of young children, the language of the pop world, or advertising, the use of ambiguities by politicians, the differences between standard and non-standard speech, the accents of English and English speaking peoples, the functions of different registers, the breaking of register, the nature of cliché and jargon. A radio interview can be evaluated in terms of the completeness or otherwise of the questions asked, and whether they are answered or not. More difficult work would explore the nature of our understanding of the spoken language. One might for instance give part of a conversation – ask what came before, and what is likely to follow – and what clues there are which enable one to do this. It seems likely that the ability to make such predictions is an important part of understanding – the questions of what is good speech implied in this paper can be considered. How are pauses being used? How far is 'fluency' synonymous with oracy?

The third reason for mentioning listening here, however, is for what it implies about human relationships. One sometimes finds children (and adults too) whose monologues show no concern for the listener or his point of view. If there were no other reason for emphasizing it, listening would still be an essential component of oracy, for it implies respect for the other person as a person.

VII

Many aspects of the subject have been inevitably neglected. Oracy is not merely the concern of the English teacher, but of teachers in all subjects. It has implications for their class organization, and indeed for the organization of a school. A climate of oracy as well as literacy is desirable. It has implications for school architects also, and designers of school furniture, and canteen organizers. But none of these people are likely to be influenced until the English teacher himself recognizes its importance.

Nor has the examining of the subject been mentioned, partly because from one point of view it is a large and difficult matter, partly because from another point of view it is a trivial matter. An examination's main educational importance lies in the good or bad washback it has on the teaching, its ability to produce the desirable ends described above. There has been some interesting work (e.g. Hitchman, 1966; Southampton Institute, 1966; Manchester School of Education, 1966). At Birmingham it has been demonstrated that it is possible to produce a valid and reliable completely objective listening test for CSE candidates (Atkinson and Wilkinson, 1966); and work commissioned by the Schools Council is also going forward there into the construction of measures of both production and reception through the secondary range.

This paper was entitled *The Implications of Oracy*. But this was not intended to imply that all the implications can be fully perceived at the moment, let alone worked out. This is a matter for educational thought and the educational processes.

ACKNOWLEDGEMENT
Parts of this paper draw on discussions with Mr Leslie Stratta whose help I gratefully acknowledge.

Dialect in School

By J. Wight

Editor's Introduction

The word 'dialect' has frequently been used to mean one form of language which is different from the 'standard' in such features as grammar and vocabulary. The problem here is that the definition conveys a suggestion of something which is inferior to the standard, less systematic and incorrect. For this reason some people prefer the term 'variety' of language which suggests equality, for dialects (which may have social or geographical boundaries) are found to conform to rule-systems in the same way as standard forms, only these rule-systems are *different*.

We can perhaps accept the geographical boundaries more easily than the social. We discover, for example, that if we ask for *flan* in Spain we shall be served caramel custard; on the other hand we know that *burn, beck* and *brook* are really the same thing but have different names in different parts of the British Isles. Studies within particular regions have shown that certain features like double negatives (I ain't got none) and dropped 'h's' are significantly more common amongst lower classes than middle classes and these are features which have been more difficult to separate from notions of inferiority.

The classifications of pronunciation (long or short vowels in *garage*) or vocabulary (isoglosses for *mist* and *fret*) are arbitrary and many dialects or even quite different languages may exist together in the same community. The problem is complicated further by the fact that the functions and contexts of language affect which varieties are chosen. For example, the expression of group solidarity or social distance will affect the choice of grammar, pronunciation and vocabulary, and the context specific 'me Dad was scrapin' out' is appropriately less explicit than 'my father was scraping out the pigeon loft'.

So while the standard form is only one dialect among many that are *linguistically* equal, it is likely to be regarded as socially superior since it is the form most often chosen by those who have authority and power. Further, the notion of a 'standard' form does not mean that everyone can use it since there is a difference between what a person can understand in use and what he can put to use himself.

There are several implications for teaching here. First, the variety of language habitually used in the pupil's home and immediate environment should be valued for itself as a tool refined for particular needs and purposes. Then each person will need to extend his repertoire of varieties as he engages in different social relationships at school, and in wider society. Teachers can give a good deal of help and guidance here. In addition, teachers need to understand the problems of individuals and particular groups of pupils such as those referred to in *Education Survey* 13 (DES 1971):

> Some (pupils) may have a form of English so divergent from the standard form as to be almost unintelligible – a fact that they resent and find difficult to accept. (p. 10)

The teacher who is unaware, for example, that Jamaican Creole is not usually inflected may react badly to a sentence such as *I wake up early yeside,* and this lack of awareness may blind him to the great sensitivity a pupil often has as he develops his span of ability along a continuum from Creole through local forms to standard English.

Jim Wight discusses notions of dialect and in particular the way dialect can influence the performance of children in school. This is a matter which concerns all teachers, not only those responsible for reception classes, but those responsible for specialist teaching which uses sophisticated terms and abstract concepts in the standard variety.

B.W.

Terms of reference
Most of the observation, reading and discussion that has preceded this paper has been in the context of the particular educational needs of West Indian children in British schools. The home language of many West Indian children is an English based Creole. It is a question of debate whether Creole languages should be regarded as dialects or as languages in their own right. This is not the place to examine the arguments involved in that debate. In our work on the Project we have decided to regard these Creoles as dialects of English. This is because most of the children can with little conscious or systematic teaching modify their own language to the point where they achieve a classroom dialect that is relatively close to their teacher's standard. The point to remember is that most of the paper refers primarily to West Indian children and that many of

these find themselves in an extreme dialect speech situation. The paper first of all considers the inadequacy of definitions of dialect speech which are too rigid. It then discusses some of the ways in which dialect can influence the performance of children in school. It goes on to consider the notion that dialect is an indication of linguistic deficit, and concludes by summarizing the attitude of the Project towards dialect in the preparation of teaching materials.

1. The dialect continuum

WHEN describing a non-standard dialect the usual procedure is to compare it with the standard language and then to list the points of difference. It is then stressed that these contrastive features are not mistakes, but the product of different sets of rules which operate in the dialect. This method of description is excellent for most purposes. However, if one wishes to study the way in which dialect interferes with the linguistic performance of a child in school the description must be less static.

It is necessary to remember, for example, that in Britain the dialect speaking child is rarely restricted to a single dialect with a rigid set of phonological and grammatical rules. Rather he starts at school to operate along a dialect continuum. In most cases this is one dimensional, with the home dialect at one end and the school dialect at the other. In the case of a Creole speaking child the contrast between his home dialect and the immediate neighbourhood dialect introduces a second dimension which seems to increase the child's linguistic flexibility and sensitivity to varieties of lexis, phonology and syntax. It is difficult otherwise to account for the speed and skill with which many West Indian children acquire a more standard dialect for formal situations like school.

In addition to the differences in the child's speech brought about by different social contexts, a closer examination of quite short stretches of dialect speech shows that some of the 'rules' fluctuate in strength. Labov (1967) has shown that many of the distinctive features of Negro dialect are not invariable, that it is possible to measure their prevalence and to describe certain contextual conditions that influence the choices made (automatically) by the speaker. It is, for example, a feature of various Negro dialects (and of many West Indian Creoles) that certain final consonant clusters are reduced. Labov showed that the amount of final $/t/$, $/d/$ reduction (67%) is not much greater than is the case with the white speakers (57%), while the $/s/$, $/z/$ reduction is more distinctive of Negro dialect (50%: 14%).

To take another example, it is a 'rule' in Jamaican Creole not to mark the simple past tense by inflection. Consider, however, the following example of Jamaican Creole quoted by Cassidy (1967).

It is part of a story told by a cane-field labourer near Morant Bay in Jamaica:

> Nou, (Breda Anansi), pik up iz myuuzik man, wich iz tree kakruoch, dat i tuk intu a guodi, an wen ing riich about a aaf mailz, tu di King giet, im straik up di myuuzik man.

A standard translation would be:

> Now (Brother Anancy) picked up his music men, who were three cockroaches, that he took in a gourd, and when he reached about half a mile from the King's gate he struck up the music men.

In the original Jamaican Creole, four of the verbs (pick, is, reach and strike) are not inflected, though one verb (took) is inflected. This ratio of uninflected to inflected past verbs (4:1) is maintained throughout the story. In the children's school dialect the proportion of inflected past forms increases considerably. The following is a part of a discussion about the merits of air travel between a teacher and three twelve-year-olds recently arrived from Jamaica:

Glenville:	I never like the food, not all of it, only liked the spaghetti I did.
Pauline:	I never eat any spaghetti.
Sylvester:	I only drink the water.
Glenville:	I drink the orange and the tea.
Pauline:	We went to sleep on the plane and I first wake up and saw the telly was on.
Glenville:	I only went to sleep once I did.

2. Performance in school

It is not easy to summarize the position of the Creole speaking child at school, but certain generalizations can be made.

(1) He will soon speak at least two dialects.

(2) The formal school dialect will contain certain Creole features, but it will be intelligible to non-Creole speakers. (Spoken Creoles can be entirely unintelligible to outsiders.)

(3) In spite of this facility with the school dialect, Creole is the child's first language. At various points in his school career this Creole background places the child at a considerable disadvantage.

Attitudes vary about the role of dialect in school. Attitudes are also changing. Tolerance is on the increase. Correctness (i.e., conformity to standard rules) is less important in the hierarchy of English teaching objectives. There is a growing awareness that there are other criteria for judging 'good English', and that at certain stages in the child's education these criteria outweigh the value of insisting on standard spelling, standard grammar, etc.

However, the instinctive reaction of most teachers to such features as a double negative is still 'it's wrong', rather than 'it is not standard, but very common in various regional and social dialects'. It is difficult to know exactly what effect it has on young children to hear their own language, the language of their parents, described as wrong. In the case of a child for whom school represents a fair amount of failure in other respects this extra hurdle will certainly hinder his general school performance and may have much more serious psychological implications. A child's own language is a very personal possession.

(a) *Production – the written language*

The two most obvious areas of dialect interferences are seen in the children's writing. It will affect the spelling and the syntax. Any child learning to read and write comes face to face with the fact that the standard written language and his own spoken language do not match each other very well. At the age of six the Jamaican Creole equivalent of the notorious 'The cat sat on the mat' would be /dikyatsitpandimat/. It is written out without spaces between the words. This is because a five-year-old child cannot automatically and easily analyse and sequence the units of his spoken sentences in the manner required for writing. Mackay and Thompson (1968) report that the lexical items (words with high information content) are easily recognized and handled, but that there is some doubt in the child's mind about the status of the grammatical elements in the sentence. This is true for children whose spoken language corresponds fairly closely in syntax and lexis to standard English. For a five-year-old Creole speaker the intellectual problems of analysis and matching are much greater. In addition to analysing his spoken language into the appropriate sequence of units for writing, the dialect speaker has to fit the sounds of his spoken words to the written symbols. Teachers report that West Indian children who make reasonable progress learning to recognize whole words sometimes fail badly at phonic word building. This is hardly surprising when even the spelling rules which convert received pronunciation speech into writing would not win prizes for simplicity or logical consistency. But at least with that rule system the teacher can appreciate the ambiguities and make allowances for them.

To return to the Creole sentence above, the three words 'cat', 'sat' and 'mat' each have different central sounds, /ya/, /i/ and /a/, which must all be represented by the letter 'a' in the written sentence. It takes considerable time and sensitivity for a teacher without special training to make allowance for ambiguities of that sort even assuming that her analysis does not stop at a judgement of 'wrong pronunciation'.

(b) *Reception – the spoken language*

As mentioned above the dialect speaking child's approach to *written* English quickly reveals some of the more obvious problems. It is more difficult to assess the submerged difficulties that the children experience in their *oral* language transactions in the classroom. In the infant school the Creole speaking child is sometimes unintelligible. Differences of syntax and pronunciation will make a simple sentence hard for the teacher to understand. Unusual intonation and stress and a couple of unfamiliar lexical items will make the same sentence completely unintelligible. The most difficult question to answer, though, is how much the child understands the teacher.

Speaking to a group of children, a teacher can see if they are all listening. She cannot necessarily tell if they are all fully understanding. When a child fails to respond in the expected way to a question or an instruction, she can only guess at the reason. It might be the result of poor concentration, a short memory span, or limited experience. It might be a question of the child's confidence or intelligence. All these reasons are likely to suggest themselves before the possibility of dialect interference is considered. Yet if the teacher, a skilful listener with vocabulary and experience far greater than the child's sometimes fails to understand the child's dialect, the odds are that that child in an infant school frequently fails to understand the teacher.

Until some delicate testing procedure is available to measure the extent to which dialect interference is a factor in comprehension failure in young children, it is only possible to guess at the disadvantages of the Creole speaking child in the infant school. It should be mentioned, though, that Keislar and Stern (1968) investigated the hypothesis that Head Start children who receive instruction in a familiar dialect will learn more than a comparable group who receive the same instruction in Standard English. Their results gave no support at all to this hypothesis. In fact the groups instructed in Standard English achieved better results!

Whatever the actual situation is for the Jamaican Creole speaker in the infant class, it is certainly true that most suppositions made by linguists about the situation need testing before they can be confidently accepted. If however it is accepted that a Creole speaking background is likely to decrease the child's understanding in the infant school, there is some evidence that as the child grows older it becomes a less critical factor.

It is a truism that a child's ability to understand language exceeds his ability to produce it. This being so, the child's development of a more standard dialect for school use is likely to indicate an ability to understand dialects which are closer still to the standard.

The research (Wight and Norris, 1970) that preceded the Project's present development of teaching materials also suggested that where West Indian children do have difficulty in oral comprehension – Creole interference is not the principal cause. In this research phase a test was developed to examine the effect of Creole interference in situations where the teacher is talking to the whole class. The test was given to eight junior school classes in the 7–9 age range. It contained 50 items, 25 of which were designed to present special difficulty to Creole speakers. The other (control) items were designed to be of equal difficulty to both speakers of Creole and of Birmingham dialects. The special West Indian items focused on grammatical and phonological points of difference between Jamaican Creole and Standard English.

In Jamaican Creole, for example, the standard rules of subject verb agreement do not apply and there is a tendency not to mark noun plurals with the morpheme 's'. A sentence which begins 'When the horse comes back . . .' contains two grammatical clues for most English speakers that only one horse is likely to come back. It was assumed that for Jamaican Creole speakers these clues would be obscured. Therefore clauses like this were embedded in short stretches of narrative and the children asked to answer such questions as: 'How many horses were expected back?' The assumption was that West Indian children would find particular difficulty with items of this sort because of dialect interference. In fact the results obtained were far from those expected. By and large the West Indian children (both those born in England and those recently arrived from the Caribbean) scored significantly lower on *all* items. There was little evidence that the special West Indian items were creating relatively more difficulty than the control items. There was an exception to this. Children recently arrived from the Caribbean did have more difficulty with those items based on Creole pronunciation.

This test result suggested that Creole interference was not the principal cause of the children's comprehension failure. A small scale experiment carried out the year before also supported this view. In this experiment a number of 12-year-old West Indians who had been in England a relatively short while played a word association game. The teacher said a word and the children responded by writing down the first word that came into their minds. Many of the words were potentially ambiguous to the children because of differences in Creole pronunciation. By examining the children's responses it was possible to see which word the children had 'heard'. For example, a Creole speaker will pronounce the number 3 – /tree/. If the stimulus word therefore was 'tree', the associated response 'leaves' or 'wood', might be expected, but a response of 'four' or 'number', etc., would indicate

Creole interference. Only 6 per cent of the children's answers to potentially ambiguous stimulus words showed evidence of dialect interference. A number of the children who played this word association game spoke quite broad Creole themselves, yet they were able to adjust to the pronunciation of the English teacher so well that with impressive consistency they could interpret the teacher's words without the help of any context. This was a small scale experiment, but it suggests very sophisticated skills on the part of these children as they adjusted to a system of pronunciation quite different from their own.

The tentative conclusion to be drawn from all this is that although dialect will continue to have a marked influence on the child's language *production,* he will, provided he has reasonable exposure to the dialect of the teacher and the school, develop skills of language *reception* to cope with the contrasts between Creole and Standard English. This is not to say that there are not difficulties of comprehension for these older children, but it is likely that for them the principal sources of difficulty lie elsewhere. If there is dialect interference it operates like a filter on the communication channel when there are other non-dialect reasons which already make the communication difficult – such as the speed, or the intellectual complexity of the teacher's language, the novelty of the subject matter, etc.

3. Dialect difference and linguistic deficit

It is obvious that Jamaican Creole affects the child's ability to produce Standard English. There is though a much more fundamental consideration. Do the formal characteristics of a dialect – its lexis, phonology and especially its syntax have an effect on the child's ability to use language efficiently (as opposed to respectably)? Does a non-standard dialect automatically indicate linguistic deficit?

Now is not the time to examine the problems involved in defining or measuring linguistic deficit. It is assumed for the moment, that tests of verbal ability do measure important aspects of linguistic proficiency. On these tests middle-class children tend to score higher than working-class children. Also it does not need to be argued that middle-class speech is likely to be more standard than that of working-class children. Both these propositions may be true, but it needs to be demonstrated that there is a causal relationship between them.

There is moreover a very important point to remember. Some tests of language development examine the ability of children to produce Standard English. Berko's ingenious test examines, for example, the children's ability with the plural 's' morpheme. The Illinois test of psycholinguistic abilities also contains a section in which success depends on the mastery of Standard English grammatical rules. A verbally gifted Creole speaker might fail in sections of tests of this kind, but it would be a demonstration of linguistic difference not deficit.

In other words the conclusion that dialects are responsible for language deficit is sometimes the product of a circular argument which first defines linguistic competence in Standard English terms and then proves that dialect speakers are incompetent.

Baratz (1968) conducted an interesting experiment which makes this point perfectly. She constructed a sentence repetition test that contained 30 sentences – fifteen of these sentences were in Standard English.

> e.g. When the teacher asked if he had done his homework, Henry said, 'I didn't do it.'

The other fifteen sentences were in Negro non-standard:

> e.g. When the teacher asks Henry did he do his homework Henry say I ain did it.

The subjects of the experiment were drawn from a Washington Inner City Negro school and a suburban white school. The white subjects were significantly better than the Negro subjects at repeating the Standard English, but the Negro subjects were significantly better at repeating the Negro non-standard.

There is an expansion of the earlier simple question which deserves more serious examination. Is a non-standard dialect intrinsically a restricted type of language which therefore limits certain types of communication and retards the development of certain conceptual skills? A typical argument runs as follows:
(a) Jamaican Creole does not regularly indicate past tense.
(b) Jamaican Creole does not have the same number of tenses as English.
(c) Therefore, Jamaican Creole speakers have a restricted general concept of time.

This type of argument is difficult to answer conclusively. It implies that a Greek soldier doing his national service round the walls of Troy had a much more elaborated concept of time than we do simply because at first sight Homeric Greek has a much more complex tense system than standard English. Moreover there are areas where Jamaican Creole syntax makes more delicate distinctions than Standard English. Is it the case that in these areas a Standard English speaker has restricted concepts? For example, Bailey (1964) has shown that the sentence pattern *subject + verb 'to be' + complement* breaks down into three different sentence patterns in Jamaican Creole.

(a) When the predicate is an adjective there is no copula: di biebi ogli 'The baby is ugly'
(b) When the predicate is a noun the copula is *a* di biebi a gyal 'The baby is a girl'
(c) When the predicate is a locative phrase the copula is *de* di biebi de anda di tree. 'The baby is under the tree'.

Can one conclude from this that Standard English speakers have a restricted general concept of predication?

4. Familiarity and functional efficiency

Other evidence about the restrictive nature of dialect is sometimes drawn from the comparative studies of children's language. These studies take as a measure of linguistic skill the amount of complexity and variety in the children's language. A measure might be the proportion of subordinate clauses or adverbial phrases – the variety of vocabulary – even the proportion of sentences which lack a main verb.

In an interesting short study of this sort Mordecai (1966) divided West Indian children into three groups according to the length of their stay in England. In one of the sub-tests the children were asked to describe to the tester a series of pictures – the subjects of which were chosen carefully to avoid cultural bias against the most recent arrivals. The success of each child was measured by giving a score to the most complex sentence in each description. During the early stages of the Project a similar method of collecting children's language was employed. The tentativeness of the language and the lack of fluency was quite marked.

The most fluent descriptions were made by a very articulate self confident 12-year-old girl:

This is a child's lady . . . nurse. She's in the hospital dressing . . . cleaning out a little baby's hairs and he's got a wound on his forehead. And there is his shirt lift up and you can see his pure tummy. And her hands is betwixt the cot bars. This is a chinese lady. She's looking after the baby. She's a nurse and she has got on a watch and a nurse cap and a nurse dress. There is a saucepan there as well.

When the same children were asked to improvise a scene depicting the situation at home the morning after an imaginary robber, this girl slipped easily into the role of the bossy mother:

Look! There is footprints on the windowsill. It seems like we have got burglars here last night! Shall we look see if we lost our money? Look! There ain't any money in the drawer. Let's call the police!
Hallo is that BAR 999?
Yes, this is BAR 999, can I help you please?

O yes you can. It seems like we have got burglars here last night, because they have thief all of the money we have got in our drawer and then we have seen their footprints on the windowsill.

The contrast between these two stretches of language is obvious. There is a great deal more subordination and complexity in the second sequence. Although one hopes that robbers were not regular occurrences in her home – the language of the home and her mother's role were both familiar – and so fluent, complex, if not entirely standard language was the result. Describing a picture was on the other hand an unfamiliar task, even though she knew a fair amount about hospitals – from her mother who was a nurse. The result was a series of shorter less complex sentences.

Many studies which attempt to measure the development of children's language skills by examining factors like complexity run into this difficulty of creating a familiar context where the subjects can display a reasonable range of the resources available to them.

In observing children using the Project's pilot materials it appears that dialect itself very rarely effects the *functional* efficiency of their language production, *unless* part of the child's task is actually to produce Standard English. In a situation, for example, which calls for enquiry, the children rarely fail because of ignorance of the Standard auxiliary inversion rules or the appropriate intonation patterns. They do fail frequently because of difficulty in processing adequately the answers they receive – or because they are unaware of the power and relevance of certain lines of enquiry. This distinction between the form and the functional efficiency of children's language is discussed more fully elsewhere (Wight, 1971), but it is one of the reasons why only about a quarter of the Project's teaching materials focus on problems created for West Indian children by Creole.

5. Some conclusions

The Project's attitude towards West Indian children and their dialect can be summarized simply:

(1) The most important factor for a Creole speaking child is probably the attitude of the teacher and the school. Teachers need to be as informed as possible about Creole and able to approach the children's language learning problems from the child's point of view.

(2) Many West Indian children do have a range of severe language learning problems which have little to do with dialect *per se*. These are problems shared by many English children. The bulk of the Project's teaching materials focus on these non-dialect and general language development areas, and are not exclusively for West Indian children.

(3) One unit of the four which make up the materials does focus on dialect. Its aims are twofold. It is designed to help West Indian children write Standard English focusing on certain areas where there is persistent dialect interference. Its second, less publicized intention is to bring to the notice of the teacher many of the issues discussed in this paper.

Even with this fairly restricted aim we have been conscious of the danger of appearing to attack the child's own language. We hope to avoid this by presenting the Standard English structures which are to be taught, in the context of the conventions of the written language, emphasizing that nobody writes in exactly the same way as they speak.

The most effective way to guard against attacking the dialect is simply to place a positive value on it in class. Dialect differences can be considered objectively and older children can be encouraged sometimes to explore their own dialect and write in the style and manner of their culture. A teaching experiment (Muehl, 1970) with groups of Negro teenagers asked them to do a 'cooltalk' translation of the story of Faust. Quite apart from helping the students actually to enjoy a visit to Gounod's opera, the results are worth reading in their own right. The following is a version of Act I, the syntax of which has been standardized a bit, one suspects, by their teacher.

This old dried up cat named Fred was sittin down at the table one night, trying to dig on his philosophy. The folks outside were buggin his case, cause he was thinkin about goin sidewise. They kept on buggin his high. And then comes this cat, this cat from below the world, his main walk boy Satan. This cat put down the rap to him. 'I know all your git up and go has got up and went, but drink this juice man. Put glide in your stride, cut in your strut, and fill the hole in your soul! Make everything want to be mellow. Like look, Jack, drink this taste, and everything will be all right. We'll let you play the Sidney Poitier role.' So the dude turns around and what does he see but this babe standin there as cool as can be. So Fred agrees to turn in hisself to the happy huntin grounds, and give his soul to the man.

Language in a Social Perspective
By M. A. K. Halliday

Editor's Introduction

Whereas it is true that language in relation to context has always been a central concern of linguistics, not all linguists have demonstrated this concern. In some classrooms also there has been a tendency to examine bits of language independently of situations in which they are used or to view 'acquisition of vocabulary', for example, as a valid end in itself. However, as Halliday points out, learning is inevitably concerned with meanings. The paper which follows is important in the way that it directs attention to language as part of a system of alternatives open to a speaker concerning what can be meant in a given situation.

Halliday develops the theory underlying this position and distinguishes what he calls 'meaning potential' from notions of 'competence'. The implication for both teacher and researcher is that the focus for attention in sociolinguistic studies is language as used in its context. Halliday's paper lays the foundation for teacher and pupil to view language as an infinitely variable tool and to consider appropriateness of its usage as a more useful concept than correctness. This view is a wide one. For example, it enables the teacher to see that appropriate language use in speech differs from writing; that entirely appropriate accents and dialects may influence spelling and syntax as pupils learn to widen their repertoire; that specialist subject areas may introduce difficulty by their use of language (familiar or unfamiliar) in a specific context; that any study of language must be related to who speaks to whom and on what occasion. The reader will discover other insights and pointers for informed practice. Halliday's explorations of relationship between context and language provide a fertile field of theory which contributes substantially to a rationale for language study and language use.

B.W.

THE studies which are described in the series of monographs entitled *Primary Socialization, Language and Education,* edited by Basil Bernstein, show how in a coherent social theory a central place is occupied by language, as the primary means of cultural transmission.

What is the nature of language, when seen from this point of view? There are two sides to this question. The first is, what aspects of language are highlighted – what do we *make* language look like, so to speak – in order to understand its function in the socialization of the child, and in the processes of education? The second is the same question in reverse: what do we learn about language – what *does* it look like, in fact – when it is approached in this way?

1. Language as social behaviour an acknowledged concern of modern linguistics, and not limited to the study of instances

It has been suggested that one of the main preoccupations of the 1970s will be a concern with social man. This implies not simply man in relation to some abstract entity such as 'society as a whole' but man in relation to other men; it is a particular facet of man in relation to his environment, only it shifts the emphasis from the physical on to the human environment – on to man in the environment of men. The individual is seen as the focus of a complex of human relationships which collectively define the content of his social behaviour.

This provides a perspective on language. A significant fact about the behaviour of human beings in relation to their social environment is that a large part of it is linguistic behaviour. The study of social man presupposes the study of language and social man.

A concern with language and social man has for a long time been one of the perspectives of modern linguistics. In 1935 J. R. Firth, introducing the term 'sociological linguistics', discussed the study of language in a social perspective and outlined a programme of 'describing and classifying typical contexts of situation within the context of culture . . . [and] types of linguistic function in such contexts of situation' (p. 27). We tend nowadays to refer to socio-linguistics as if this was something very different from the study of language as practised in linguistics *tout court*; but in a way new 'sociolinguistics' is but old 'linguistics' writ large, and the linguist's interests have always extended to language as social behaviour.

It was Malinowski from whom Firth derived his notions of 'context of culture' and 'context of situation' (Malinowski, 1923);

This paper was first prepared for the Second International Congress of Applied Linguistics, Cambridge, September, 1969. A revised version of it was presented to the Oxford University Linguistic Society on 21 October 1969.

and Malinowski's ideas about what we might call cultural and situational semantics provide an interesting starting point for the study of language and social man, since they encourage us to look at language as a form of behaviour potential. In this definition, both the 'behaviour' and the 'potential' need to be emphasized. Language, from this point of view, is a range of possibilities, an open-ended set of options in behaviour that are available to the individual in his existence as social man. The context of culture is the environment for the total set of these options, while the context of situation is the environment of any particular selection that is made from within them.

Malinowski's two types of context thus embody the distinction between the potential and the actual. The context of culture defines the potential, the range of possibilities that are open. The actual choice among these possibilities takes place within a given context of situation.

Firth, with his interest in the actual, in the text and its relation to its surroundings, developed the notion of 'context of situation' into a valuable tool for linguistic enquiry. Firth's interest, however, was not in the accidental but in the typical: not in this or that piece of discourse that happened to get recorded in the fieldworker's notebook, but in repetitive patterns which could be interpreted as significant and systematizable patterns of social behaviour. Thus, what is actual is not synonymous with what is unique, or the chance product of random observations. But the significance of what is typical – in fact the concept 'typical' itself – depends on factors which lie outside language, in the social structure. It is not the typicalness of the words and structures which concerns us, but the typicalness of the context of situation, and of the function of the words and structures within it.

Malinowski (1935) tells an interesting story of an occasion when he asked his Trobriand Island informant some questions about the Trobrianders' gardening practices. He noted down the answers, and was surprised a few days later to hear the same informant repeating what he had said word for word in conversation with his young daughter. In talking to Malinowski, the informant has as it were borrowed the text from a typical context of situation. The second occasion, the discussion with the little girl, was then an instance of this context of situation, in which the socialization of the child into the most significant aspect of the material culture – the gardening practices – was a familiar process, with familiar patterns of language behaviour associated with it.

There is not, of course, any conflict between an emphasis on the repetitive character of language behaviour and an insistence on the creativity of the language system. Considered as behaviour potential, the language system itself is open-ended, since the question whether two instances are the same or not is not determined by the system; it is determined by the underlying social theory. But in any case, as Ruqaiya Hasan (1971) has pointed out, creativeness does not consist in producing new sentences. The newness of a sentence is a quite unimportant – and unascertainable – property, and 'creativity' in language lies in the speaker's ability to create new meanings: to realize the potentiality of language for the indefinite extension of its resources to new contexts of situation. It is only in this light that we can understand the otherwise unintelligible observation made by Katz and Fodor (1963), that 'almost every sentence uttered is uttered for the first time' (p. 171). Our most 'creative' acts may be precisely among those that are realized through highly repetitive forms of behaviour.

Firth did not concern himself with Malinowski's 'context of culture', since he preferred to study generalized patterns of actual behaviour, rather than attempting to characterize the potential as such. This was simply the result of his insistence on the need for accurate observations – a much-needed emphasis in the context of earlier linguistic studies – and in no way implied that the study of language could be reduced to the study of instances, which in fact he explicitly denied (1968). More to the point, Firth built his linguistic theory around the original and fundamental concept of the 'system', as used by him in a technical sense; and this is precisely a means of describing the potential, and of relating the actual to it.

A 'system', as the concept was developed by Firth, can be interpreted as the set of options that is specified for a given environment. The meaning of it is 'under the conditions stated, there are the following possibilities'. By making use of this notion, we can describe language in the form of a behaviour potential. In this way the analysis of language comes within the range of a social theory, provided the underlying concepts of such a theory are such that they can be shown to be realized in social context and patterns of behaviour.

The interest in language and social man is thus no new theme in linguistics. It is also predominant in the important work of Pike (1967, first published 1954–60). Its scope is not limited to the description of individual acts of speech; more significant has been the attempt to relate grammatical and lexical features, and combinations of such features, to types of social interaction and, where possible, to generalized social concepts. From a sociological point of view it would be of no interest otherwise; a social theory could not operate with raw speech fragments as the only linguistic exponents of its fundamental ideas.

2. Language in a social perspective interpreted through the concept of 'meaning potential'

If we regard language as social behaviour, therefore, this means that we are treating it as a form of behaviour *potential*. It is what the speaker can do.

But 'can do' by itself is not a linguistic notion; it encompasses types of behaviour other than language behaviour. If we are to relate the notion of 'can do' to the sentences and words and phrases that the speaker is able to construct in his language – to what he can say, in other words – then we need an intermediate step, where the behaviour potential is as it were converted into linguistic potential. This is the concept of what the speaker 'can mean'.

The potential of language is a meaning potential. This meaning potential is the linguistic realization of the behaviour potential; 'can mean' is 'can do' when translated into language. The meaning potential is in turn realized in the language system as lexico-grammatical potential, which is what the speaker 'can say'.

Each stage can be expressed in the form of options. The options in the construction of linguistic forms – sentences, and the like – serve to realize options in meaning, which in turn realize options in behaviour that are interpretable in terms of a social theory.

We can illustrate this point by reference to Basil Bernstein's work in the area of language and social structure (Bernstein, 1967, 1970). On the basis of a theory of social learning. Bernstein identifies a number of social contexts which are crucial to the socialization of the child, for example contexts in which the mother is regulating the child's behaviour or in which she is helping him in learning to carry out some kind of task. These are 'typical contexts of situation', in Firth's sense, but given significance by the theory underlying them.

For any one of these contexts Bernstein is able to specify a range of alternatives that is open to the mother in her interaction with the child. For example, in regulating the child's behaviour she may adopt one (or more) of a number of strategies, which we might characterize in general terms as reasoning, pleading, threatening, and the like, but which the theory would suggest represent systematic options in the meanings that are available to her. Bernstein in fact makes use of the term 'meanings' to refer to significant options in the social context; and he regards those as being 'realized' in the behaviour patterns. But this is realization in exactly the linguistic sense, and the behaviour patterns are, at least partly, patterns of meaning in the linguistic sense – the mother's behaviour is largely language behaviour. So the chain of realizations extends from the social theory into the language system.

Hence the behaviour potential associated with the contexts that

Bernstein identifies may be expressed linguistically as a meaning potential. Some such step is needed if we are to relate the fundamental concepts of the social theory to recognizable forms and patterns of language behaviour.

A word or two should be said here about the relation of the concept of meaning potential to the Chomskyan notion of competence, even if only very briefly. The two are somewhat different. Meaning potential is defined not in terms of the mind but in terms of the culture; not as what the speaker knows, but as what he can do – in the special sense of what he can do linguistically (what he 'can mean', as we have expressed it). The distinction is important because 'can do' is of the same order of abstraction as 'does'; the two are related simply as potential to actualized potential, and can be used to illuminate each other. But 'knows' is distinct and clearly insulated from 'does'; the relation between the two is complex and oblique, and leads to the quest for a 'theory of performance' to explain the 'does'.

This is related to the question of idealization in linguistics. How does one decide what is systematic and what is irrelevant in language – or, to put the question another way, how does one decide what are different sentences, different phrases, and so on, and what are different instances of the same sentence, the same phrase? The issue is a familiar one to readers of the *Educational Review*, from the article by Peter Geach in the volume *The Place of Language* (Wilkinson, 1969). Geach's argument is, that in order to understand the logical structure of sentences we have to 'iron - out' a lot of the differences that occur in living speech: '. . . idealization which approximates slightly less well to what is actually said, will, by the standards of logical insight into the structures of sentences, pay off better than some analyses that try to come closer to what is actually said' (p. 23).

The philosopher's approach to language is always marked by a very high degree of idealization. In its extreme form, this approach idealizes out *all* natural language as irrelevant and unsystematic and treats only constructed logical languages; a less extreme version is one which accepts sentences of natural language but reduces them all to a 'deep structure' in terms of certain fundamental logical relations. Competence, as defined by Chomsky, involves (as Geach objects) a lower degree of idealization than this. But it is still very high from other points of view, particularly that of anyone interested in language as behaviour. Many behaviourally significant variations in language are simply ironed out, and reduced to the same level as stutterings, false starts, clearings of the throat and the like.

It might be claimed at this point that linguistics is anyway an autonomous science and does not need to look outside itself for criteria of idealization. But this is not a very satisfactory argument. There is a sense in which it is autonomous, and has to be if it is to be relevant to other fields of study: the particulars of language are explained by reference to a general account of language, not by being related piecemeal to social or other non-linguistic phenomena. But this 'autonomy' is conditional and temporary; in the last analysis, we cannot insulate the subject within its own boundaries, and when we come to decide what features in language are to be ignored as unsystematic we are bound to invoke considerations from outside language itself. The problem is met by Chomsky, who regards linguistics as a branch of theoretical psychology. But one may agree with the need for a point of departure from outside language without insisting that this must be sought in one direction and no other – only in psychology, or only in logic. It may just as well be sought in a field such as sociology whose relationship with linguistics has been no less close.

Sociological theory, if it is concerned with the transmission of knowledge or with any linguistically coded type of social act, provides its own criteria for the degree and kind of idealization involved in statements about language; and Bernstein's work is a case in point. In one sense, this is what it is all about. There is always some idealization, where linguistic generalizations are made; but in a sociological context this has to be, on the whole, at a much lower level. We have, in fact, to 'come close to what is actually said'; partly because the solution to problems may depend on studying what is actually said, but also because even when this is not the case the features that are behaviourally relevant may be just those that the idealizing process most readily irons out. An example of the latter would be features of assertion and doubt, such as *of course, I think,* and question tags like *don't they?*, which turn out to be highly significant – not the expressions themselves, but the variations in meaning which they represent, in this case variation in the degree of certainty which the speaker may attach to what he is saying (Turner and Pickvance, 1969).

In order to give an account of language that satisfies the needs of a social theory, we have to be able to accommodate the degree and kind of idealization that is appropriate in that context. This is what the notion of meaning potential attempts to make possible. The meaning potential is the range of *significant* variation that is at the disposal of the speaker. The notion is not unlike Dell Hymes' (1970) 'communicative competence', except that Hymes defines this in terms of 'competence' in the Chomskyan sense of what the speaker knows, whereas we are talking of a potential – what he can do, in the special linguistic sense of what he can mean – and avoiding the additional complication of a distinction between doing and knowing. This potential can then be represented as systematic options in meaning which may be varied in the degree of their specificity – in what has been called 'delicacy'. That is to say, the range of variation that is being treated as *significant* will itself be variable, with either grosser or finer distinctions being drawn according to the type of problem that is being investigated.

3. Language as options

Considering language in its social context, then, we can describe it in broad terms as a behaviour potential; and more specifically as a meaning potential, where meaning is a form of behaving (and the verb *to mean* is a verb of the 'doing' class). This leads to the notion of representing language in the form of options: sets of alternative meanings which collectively account for the total meaning potential.

Each option is available in a stated environment, and this is where Firth's category of system comes in. A system is an abstract representation of a paradigm; and this, as we have noted, can be interpreted as a set of options with an entry condition – a number of possibilities out of which a choice has to be made if the stated conditions of entry to the choice are satisfied. It has the form: if *a*, then either *x* or *y* (or . . .). The key to its importance in the present context is Firth's 'polysystemic principle', whereby (again following this interpretation) the conditions of entry are required to be stated for each set of possibilities. That is to say, for every choice it is to be specified where, under what conditions, that choice is made. The 'where', in Firth's use of the concept of a system, was 'at what point in the structure'; but we interpret it here as 'where in the total network of options'. Each choice takes place in the environment of other choices. This is what makes it possible to vary the 'delicacy' of the description: we can stop wherever the choices are no longer significant for what we are interested in.

The options in a natural language are at various levels: phonological, grammatical (including lexical, which is simply the most specific part within the grammatical) and semantic. Here, where we are concerned with the meaning potential, the options are in the first instance semantic options. These are interpreted as the coding of options in behaviour, so that the semantics is in this sense a behavioural semantics.

The semantic options are in turn coded as options in grammar. Now there are no grammatical categories corresponding exactly to such concepts as those of reasoning, pleading or threatening referred to above. But there may be a prediction, deriving from a social theory, that these will be among the significant behavioural categories represented in the meaning potential. In that case it should be possible to identify certain options in the grammar as being systematic realizations of these categories, since presumably they are to be found somewhere in the language system. We will not expect there to be a complete one-to-one correspondence between the grammatical options and the semantic ones; but this is merely allowing for the normal phenomena of neutralization and diversification that are associated with all stages in the realization chain.

There is nothing new in the notion of associating grammatical categories with higher level categories of a 'socio-' semantic kind. This is quite natural in the case of grammatical forms concerned with the expression of social roles; particularly those systems which reflect the inherent social structure of the speech situation, which cannot be explained in any other way. The principal component of these is the system of mood. If we represent the basic options in the mood system of English in the following way:

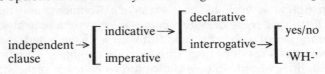

(to be read 'an independent clause is either indicative or imperative; if indicative, then either declarative or interrogative', and so on), we are systematizing the set of choices whereby the speaker is enabled to assume one of a number of possible communication roles – social roles which exist only in and through language, as functions of the speech situation. The choice of interrogative, for example, means, typically, 'I am acting as questioner (seeker of information), and you are to act as listener and then as answerer (supplier of information)'. By means of this system the speaker takes on himself a role in the speech situation and allocates the complementary role – actually, rather, a particular choice of complementary ones – to the hearer, both while he is speaking and after he has finished.

These 'communication roles' belong to what we were referring to as 'socio-semantics'. They are a special case in that they are a property of the speech situation as such, and do not depend on any kind of a social theory. But the relationship between, say, 'question' in semantics and 'interrogative' in grammar is not really different from that between a behavioural-semantic category such as 'threat' and the categories by which it is realized grammatically. In neither instance is the relationship one to one; and while the latter may be rather more complex, a more intensive study of language as social behaviour also suggests a somewhat more complex treatment of traditional notions like those of statement and question. Part of the grammar with which we are familiar is thus a sociological grammar already, although this has usually been confined to a small area where the meanings expressed are 'social' in a rather special sense, that of the social roles created by language itself.

However, the example of the mood system serves to show that, even if we are operating only with the rather oversimplified notions of statement, question, command and the like, categories like these occupy an intermediate level of 'meaning potential' which links behavioural categories to grammatical ones. We do not usually find a significant option in behaviour represented straightforwardly in the grammatical system; it is only in odd instances that what the speaker 'can do' is coded immediately as what he 'can say'. There is a level of what he 'can mean' between the two.

The relation between the levels of meaning and saying, which is one of realization, involves as we have said departures from a regular pattern of one-to-one correspondence. In any particular sociolinguistic investigation, only some of the total possible behavioural options will be under focus of attention; hence we shall be faced especially with instances of 'one-to-many', where one meaning is expressed in different forms. But in such instances we can often invoke the 'good reason' principle, by which one of the possibilities is the 'unmarked' one, that which is chosen to express the meaning in question unless there is good reason to choose otherwise. For example, a question is typically realized in the grammar as an interrogative, and there has to be a 'good reason' for it to be expressed in some other form, such as a declarative. And secondly, the implica'ion of 'one meaning realized by many forms', namely that there is free variation among the possibilities concerned, is unlikely ᴗ be the whole truth; it nearly always signifies that there is a more subtle choice in meaning that we have not yet cottoned on to, or that is irrelevant in this particular context.

So a category like that of 'threat', assuming that such a category is identified within the meaning potential, on the basis perhaps of a theory of socialization, will be realized in the language system through a number of different grammatical options. These might include, for example, declarative clauses of a certain type, perhaps first person singular future tense with a verb from a certain lexical set (often identifiable in Roget's *Thesaurus*!), and with attached *if* clause, e.g. *if you do that again I'll smack you*; but also certain other forms, negative imperative with *or* (*don't do that again or* . . .), conditioned future attributive clauses with *you* (*you'll be sorry if* . . .), and so on. These may appear at first sight to be merely alternative ways of expressing a threat, in free variation with each other. But it is very likely that on closer inspection they will be found to represent more delicate (though perhaps still significant) options in the meaning potential. At the same time it might be the case that one of them, possibly the first one mentioned above, could be shown on some grounds to be the typical form of threat (perhaps just in this context), the others all being 'marked' variants; we are then committed to stating the conditions under which it is *not* selected but are not required to give any further explanation when it is.

4. An example

Let us consider a hypothetical example of the behaviour potential associated with a particular social context. We will keep within the general framework of Bernstein's theory of socialization, and take up the type of context already mentioned, that of parental control; within this area, we will construct a particular instance that will yield a reasonably simplified illustration. It should be said very clearly that both the pattern of options and the illustrative sentences have been invented for this purpose; they are *not* actual instances from Bernstein's work. But they are modelled closely on Bernstein's work, and draw on many of his underlying concepts. In particular I have drawn on Geoffrey Turner's studies, in which he has made use of the linguistic notion of systems representing options in meaning for the purpose of investigating the role of language in control situations (Turner, 1973).

Let us imagine that the small boy has been playing with the neighbourhood children on a building site. His mother disapproves both of the locale and of the company he has been keeping, and views with particular horror the empty tin or other object he has acquired as a trophy. She wants both to express her disapproval and to prevent the same thing happening again. She might say something like 'that sort of place is not for playing in', or 'I don't like you taking other people's things', or 'they don't want children running about there', or 'just look at the state of your clothes', or 'I'm frightened you'll hurt yourself', or many other things besides.

Various means are open to the mother here for making her intentions explicit. Now, in terms of the actual sentences she might utter, the range of possibilities is pretty well unlimited. But a particular theory about the function of the regulatory context in the socialization of the child would suggest that she is actually operating within a systematic framework of very general options, any one of which (or any one combination) might be expressed through the medium of a wide range of different lexico-grammatical forms. These options represent the meaning potential lying behind the particular instances.

We will assume that the mother is using some form of appeal, as distinct from a direct injunction or a threat. She may simply enunciate a rule, based on her authority as a parent; or she may appeal to reason, and give an explanation of what she wants. Let us call this 'authority or reason'. Secondly, and at the same time, she may formulate her appeal in general or in particular terms, either relating this event to a wider class of situations or treating it on its own; we will say that the appeal may be 'general' or 'particular'. And she may slant her appeal away from the persons involved towards the material environment and the objects in it ('object-oriented'); or she may concentrate on the people ('person-oriented') – in which case the focus of attention may either be on the parent (the mother herself, and perhaps the father as well) or on the child. Finally, if the orientation is towards people, there is another option available, since the appeal may be either 'personal' or 'positional': that is, relating to the child or herself either as individuals, or in their status in the family, the age group and so on. Thus *you* may mean 'you, Timmy'; or it may mean 'you as my offspring', 'you as a young child' or in some other defined social status.

We may now represent these possibilities in the following way as a network of alternatives:

This represents the meaning potential that is open to the mother in the situation, as far as we have taken it in the present discussion.

The categories in this semantic network are not immediately recognizable as linguistic categories. There is no category of 'object-oriented' or 'positional' in the grammar of English, no grammatical system of 'authority/reason'. But if this network of options is a valid account of a part of the range of alternatives that are open to the mother as regards what she 'can mean' in the situation, then the implication is that these options will be found to be realized somewhere in the linguistic system, in the things that she can say.

Any one selection from within this range of options could be realized through a wide range of different grammatical categories and lexical items. Take for example the combination 'authority, general, object-oriented'. The mother might say *that sort of place is not for playing in,* or she might say *we don't go into places like that,* or *other people's things aren't for playing with,* or *we don't take other people's property;* all of these would be instances of the particular combination of options just mentioned. Here we have alternative forms of expression for what are, within the limits of the few distinctions recognized in our illustration, the same selections in meaning. As far as their grammar and vocabulary is concerned, there are certain things common to two or more of these examples which can be related to their common element in their meanings: for example the form . . . *(is/are not for . . . ing (in/with)*, the form *we don't . . . ,* the reference to *place,* and so on. But in other respects they are very different, and involve categories that might not otherwise be brought together from their different places in the description of the grammar, such as *we don't X with/in Y* and *Y is not for X-ing with/in* as forms of disapproval, or the different categories represented by the words *place* and *thing* (including *property,* which can be interpreted as either). Note that *place* and *thing* are grouped together under the option 'object-oriented'; no doubt if the analysis was carried through to a more delicate stage they would then be distinguished, since although both represent non-personalized forms of appeal there is a difference between the notion of territory and the notion of ownership that might be significant. Meanwhile they serve to illustrate a further point, that the analysis seeks to specify as far as possible the contribution made by each particular option to the form of the sentences used. Here, for example, the feature of 'authority' is reflected in the negative and in the modal forms; that of 'general' in the tense and the noun modifiers *that sort of . . ., . . . like that;* that of 'object-oriented' in the words *place, thing* and *(other people's) property,* coupled with the absence of individualized personal pronouns.

Even though the forms used to express any one meaning selection are very varied, they are nevertheless distinct from those realizing other selections: we must in principle be able to tell what the mother means from what she says, since we are crediting the child with the ability to do so. Here to complete the illustration is a set of possible utterances by the mother representing different selections in the meaning potential. These are not intended to cover the whole of the mother's verbal intervention; some of them would need to be (and all of them could be) accompanied by an explicit injunction such as *you're not to do that again.* They exemplify only options in the type of appeal she is using; as such, each one could occur either alone or in combination with an appeal of one of the other types. The figures following each example indicate, by reference to the network, the options it is assumed to express.

other people's things aren't for playing with (135)
you know you don't play with those sort of boys (1368)
they don't want children running about there (1369)
Daddy doesn't like you to play rough games (1378)
that tin belongs to somebody else (145)
you can go there when you're bigger (1469)
I was worried, I didn't know where you'd got to (1478)
you'll ruin your clothes playing in a place like that (235)
it's not good for you to get too excited (2368)
boys who are well brought up play nice games in the park (2369)
we don't want people to think we don't look after you, do we? (2379)
that glass they keep there might get broken (245)
you might have hurt yourself on all that glass (2468)
I'd like you to stay and help me at home (2478)

Not all the possible combinations of options have been exemplified, and some of them are unlikely in this particular instance, although probably all could occur. Let us stress again here that both the examples and the network of options, although inspired by Bernstein's work, have been invented for the present discussion, in order to keep the illustration down to a manageable size.

A system network of this kind is open-ended. It may represent only certain very gross distinctions: in the simplest case, just a choice between two possibilities, so that all the meaning potential associated with a particular social context is reduced to 'either this or that'. But it is always capable of accommodating further distinctions – of being made more and more 'delicate' – when these are brought into the picture. Each new distinction that is introduced has implications both 'upwards' and 'downwards': that is, it is significant as an option in behaviour, and it is systematically (however indirectly) expressed in the language. Only in very restricted types of situation can anywhere near all the linguistic features of an utterance be derived from behaviourally significant options; but then there is no such thing as 'all the linguistic features of an utterance' considered apart from some external criteria of significance. The point is that, as further specification is added to the semantic systems, so more of the linguistic features come to be accounted for. This can be seen in Turner's work, already referred to, in which he is investigating the meaning potential associated with certain contexts of the general kind we have been illustrating.

5. Interpretation of linguistic forms determined by reference to concepts of social theory

In understanding the nature of 'social man', and in particular the processes – and they are largely linguistic processes – whereby the child becomes social man, we are likely to be deeply concerned with those aspects of his experience which centre around social contexts and settings of the kind just exemplified.

We shall not of course expect to assign anything like the whole of an individual's language behaviour to situations of this kind, which can be investigated and interpreted in the light of some significant social theory. The meaning of a poem, or a technical discussion, cannot be expressed in terms of behavioural options. (It can, on the other hand, be related to a set of generalized functions of language which define the total meaning potential of the adult language system; cf. the discussion in the next section.) At the same time, the social contexts and settings for which we can recognize a meaning potential in behavioural terms are not at all marginal or outlandish; and they are contexts which play a significant part in the socialization of the child. The importance of such contexts is given by the social theory from which they are derived.

Not all the distinctions in meaning that may be associated with a context of this kind can be explained by reference to behavioural options which are universally significant in that context. Within the actual words and sentences used there is bound to be much that is particular to the local situation or the shared experience of the individuals concerned. In the illustration given in the last section, the reference to breaking glass or getting hurt by it is obviously specific to a small class of instances of a control situation; and it is likely to be significant only in relation to that setting. It is possible, however, that a highly particular feature of this kind could be the local realization of an option having a general significance: there might be some symbolic value attached to broken glass in the family, having its origin in a particular incident, and we could not know this simply from inspecting the language. And there are general shifted meanings too, extended metaphors whereby, especially in the interaction of adult and child, behavioural options are encoded in highly complex, more or less ritualized linguistic forms; for example the bedtime story, where the princes and the giants and the whole narrative structure collectively express patterns of socialization and interpersonal meanings. Here we are led into the realms of literary interpretation, of levels of meaning in the imaginative mode, of the significance of poetic forms and the like.

Looking to the other end of the scale, we can find settings, for example games where the language plays an essential part, like pontoon or contract bridge, for which a system of meaning potential will account for a very high proportion of the words and sentences used by the participants (Mohan, 1969). These restricted settings are interesting from the point of view of sociolinguistic method, since they illustrate very well the principle of language as behaviour potential. But they may have little or no significance in themselves as social contexts, relative to any general theory of social behaviour.

What we are referring to as a 'social context' is a generalized type of situation that is itself significant in terms of the categories and concepts of some social theory. The theory may focus attention on different facets of the social structure: not only on forms of socialization and cultural transmission, but also on role relationships, on the power structure and patterns of social control, on symbolic systems, systems of values, of public knowledge and the like. Our example was drawn from the socialization of the child, because that is where most work has been done; but systematic options in language behaviour are not limited to situations of this type. Any situation in which the behavioural options open to the participants are, at least in part, realizations of some general theoretical categories is relevant as a 'social context' in this sense. Hence a particular linguistic feature may have a number of different meanings according to the type of context in which it occurs: for example, *they don't want children in there* might not be any kind of appeal – it might occur in a context that had nothing to do with socialization, not being addressed to a child at all. We could not simply take the linguistic forms for granted, as having just one behavioural interpretation.

More important, perhaps, or at least less obvious, is the fact that even within the same context a linguistic form may have different meanings, since there may be sub-cultural variants in the meaning potential (different 'codes', in Bernstein's sense; cf. Hasan, 1973) typically associated with that context. In other words, assuming that the sentence above was in fact being used in a regulatory context such as the one invented for the illustration, it might still have more than one meaning, given two distinct social groups one of which typically exploited one area of meaning potential (say, 'elaborated code') and the other another ('restricted code'). Within a 'code' in which the typical appeal was positional and non-discretionary, this example would be interpreted as an imperative, whereas in one tending towards more personal and more challengeable appeals it could be taken as a partially explicit rule. The meaning of selecting any one particular feature would be potentially different in the two 'codes', since it would be selected from within a different range of probable alternatives.

We have suggested that this use of a social context corresponds to what Firth meant by the 'typical context of situation', and that it makes the link between the two Malinowskian notions of 'context of situation' and 'context of culture' referred to at the beginning of this paper. It is the social context that defines the limits of the options available; the behavioural alternatives are to this extent context-specific. But the total range of meanings that is embodied in and realized through the language system is determined by the context of culture – in other words by the social structure.

The study of language as social behaviour is in the last resort an account of semantic options deriving from the social structure. Like other hyphenated fields of language study, socio-linguistics reaches beyond the phonological and morphological indices into the more abstract areas of linguistic organization. The concept of socio-linguistics ultimately implies a 'socio-semantics' which is a genuine meeting ground of two ideologies, the social and the linguistic. And this faces both ways. The options in meaning are significant linguistically because selections in grammar and vocabulary can be explained as a realization of them. They are significant sociologically because they provide insight into patterns of behaviour that are in turn explainable as realizations of the pragmatic and symbolic acts that are the expressions of the social structure.

In principle we may expect to find some features of the social structure reflected directly in the forms of the language, even in its lower reaches, the morphology and the phonology. The pheno-menon of 'accent' is a direct reflection of social structure in the phonetic output. Such low level manifestations may be of little interest, although Labov's (1968) work on the New York dialects showed the potential significance of phonological variables in the social structure of an urban speech community. There is an analogy within the language system itself, where sometimes we find instances of the direct expression of meanings in sounds: voice qualities showing anger, and the like. But in general the forms of expression involve a number of levels of realization – a 'stratal' system (Lamb, 1966) – even within language itself; and this is the more clear when linguistic features are seen as the expression of meanings derived from behaviour patterns outside language: we will not expect to find a direct link between social content and linguistic expression, except in odd cases. The socio-semantics is the pivotal level; it is the interface between the two. Any set of strategies can be represented as a network of options; the point is that by representing it in this way we provide a link in the chain of realizations that relates language to social structure.

6. Importance of socio-linguistic studies for understanding of the nature of language

The investigation of language as social behaviour is not only relevant to the understanding of social structure; it is also relevant to the understanding of language. A network of socio-semantic options – the representation of what we have been calling the 'meaning potential' – has implications in both directions; on the one hand as the realization of patterns of behaviour and, on the other hand, as realized by the patterns of grammar. The concept of meaning potential thus provides a perspective on the nature of language. Language is as it is because of its function in the social structure, and the organization of behavioural meanings should give some insight into its social foundations.

This is the significance of functional theories of language. The essential feature of a functional theory is not that it enables us to enumerate and classify the functions of speech acts, but that it provides a basis for explaining the nature of the language system, since the system itself reflects the functions that it has evolved to serve. The organization of options in the grammar of natural languages seems to rest very clearly on a functional basis, as has emerged from the work of those linguists, particularly of the Prague school, who have been aware that the notion 'functions of language' is not to be equated merely with a theory of language use but expresses the principle behind the organization of the linguistic system.

The options in the grammar of a language derive from and are relatable to three very generalized functions of language which we have referred to elsewhere as the ideational, the interpersonal and the textual (Halliday, 1970). The specific options in meaning that are characteristic of particular social contexts and settings are expressed through the medium of grammatical and lexical selections that trace back to one or other of these three sources. The status of these terms is that they constitute a hypothesis for explaining what seems to be a fundamental fact about the grammar of languages, namely that it is possible to discern three distinct principles of organization in the structure of grammatical units, as described by Daneš (1964) and others, and that these in turn can be shown to be the structural expression of three fairly distinct and independent sets of underlying options.

Those of the first set, the ideational, are concerned with the content of language, its function as a means of the expression of our experience, both of the external world and of the inner world of our own consciousness – together with what is perhaps a separate sub-component expressing certain basic logical relations. The second, the interpersonal, is language as the mediator of role, including all that may be understood by the expression of our own personalities and personal feelings on the one hand, and forms of interaction and social interplay with other participants in the communication situation on the other hand. The third component, the textual, has an enabling function, that of creating text, which is language in operation as distinct from strings of words or isolated sentences and clauses. It is this component that enables the speaker to organize what he is saying in such a way that it makes sense in the context and fulfils its function as a message.

These three functions are the basis of the grammatical system of the adult language. The child begins by acquiring a meaning potential, a small number of distinct meanings that he can express, in two or three functional contexts: he learns to use language for satisfying his material desires ('I want an apple'), for getting others to behave as he wishes ('sing me a song'), and so on. In a paper in a previous volume of this journal I suggested a list of such contexts for an early stage in his language development (1969; cf. Wilkinson, 1971). At this stage each utterance tends to have one function only; but as time goes on the typical utterance becomes functionally complex – we learn to combine various uses of language into a single speech act. It is at this point that we need a grammar: a level of organization intermediate between content and expression, which can take the various functionally distinct meaning selections and combine them into integrated structures. The components of the grammatical system are thus themselves functional; but they represent the functions of language in their most generalized form, as these underlie all the more specific contexts of language use.

The meaning potential in any one context is open-ended, in the sense that there is no limit to the distinctions in meaning that we can apprehend. When we talk of what the speaker can do, in this special sense of what he 'can mean', we imply that we can recognize significant differentiations within what he can mean, up to some point or other which will be determined by the requirements of our theory. The importance of a hypothesis about what the speaker can do in a social context is that this makes sense of what he does. If we insist on drawing a boundary between what he does and what he knows, we cannot explain what he does; what he does will appear merely as a random selection from within what he knows. But in the study of language in a social perspective we need both to pay attention to what is said and at the same time to relate it systematically to what might have been said but was not. Hence we do not make a dichotomy between knowing and doing; instead we place 'does' in the environment of 'can do', and treat language as speech potential.

The image of language as having a 'pure' form *(langue)* that becomes contaminated in the process of being translated into speech *(parole)* is of little value in a sociological context. We do not want a boundary between language and speech at all, or between pairs such as langue and parole, or competence and performance – unless these are reduced to mere synonyms of 'can do' and 'does'. A more useful concept is that of a range of behaviour potential determined by the social structure (the context of culture), which is made accessible to study through its association with significant social contexts (generalized contexts of situation), and is actualized by the participants in particular instances of these contexts or situation types.

There is no need to wait until some speaker is observed to produce a particular utterance, before one can take account of the relevant features embodied in it. Socio-linguistic studies are not bounded by the accidental frontiers of the data collected, although they do take such data rather seriously. As Bernstein's work has shown, there are many ways of investigating the language behaviour associated with a social context, ranging from hypothetico-deductive reasoning through various forms of elicitation to hopeful observation. All these are valid parts of the investigator's equipment.

The study of language in a social context tends to involve a rather lower degree of idealization than is customary in a psycho-philosophical orientation, as we have noted already. But there is always some idealization, in any systematic enquiry. It may be at a different place; the type of variation which is least significant for behavioural studies may be just that which is most faithfully preserved in another approach – variation in the ideational meaning, in the 'content' as this is usually understood. We might for example be able to ignore distinctions such as that between singular and plural, or between *cat* and *dog* – if we were using the notion of competence and performance, then these distinctions would be relegated to performance – while insisting on the difference in meaning between *don't do that, you mustn't do that, you're not to do that,* and other variants which differ simply in intonation, in pausing and the like.

This overstates the position, no doubt. But it serves to underline the point made earlier: that the object of attention in linguistic studies is not, and never can be, some sort of unprocessed language event. When language is studied in a social perspective, the object of attention is what is usually referred to as 'text', that is, language in a context; and the text, whether in origin it was invented, elicited or recorded, is an idealized construction. But all this means is that a linguistic item – a sentence, or whatever – is well-formed if it is well-formed; there must be criteria from somewhere by which to judge. It is not easy to find these criteria within language; in 'autonomous' linguistics it is in practice usually the orthography that is used to decide what the limits of relevant differentiation are, since the orthography is itself a codified form of idealization (rather as the 'text' of a piece of music is the score). Criteria are found more readily at the interfaces between language and non-language, by reference to something outside language; in a social context, the degree and kind of idealization is determined at the socio-semantic interface. In principle, what is well-formed is whatever can be shown to be interpretable as a possible selection within a set of options based on some motivated hypothesis about language behaviour, and 'motivated' here means extrinsically motivated by reference ultimately to (a theory about) some feature of the social structure.

The perspective is one in which there are two different but related depths of focus. The more immediate aim, from the point of view of linguistics, is the intrinsic one of explaining the nature of language. This implies an 'autonomous' view of linguistics. There is also a further, extrinsic aim, that of explaining features of the social structure, and using language to do so. This implies an 'instrumental' approach. But ultimately the nature of language is explained in terms of its function in the social structure; so the pursuit of the first aim entails the pursuit of the second. To understand language, we examine the way in which the social structure is realized through language: how values are transmitted, roles defined, and behaviour patterns made manifest.

The role of language in the educational process is a special aspect of the relation between language and social structure. Bernstein's theories concerning the linguistic basis of educational failure are part of a wider theory of language and society, which encompasses much more than the explanation of the linguistic problems imposed by the educational system on the child whose socialization has taken certain forms. Bernstein's concern is with the fundamental problem of persistence and change in the social structure. Language is the principal means of cultural transmission; but if we seek to understand how it functions in this role, it is not enough just to point up odd instances of the reflection of general sociological categories in this or that invented or recorded utterance. An approach to this question presupposes not only a theory of social structure but also a theory of linguistic structure – and hence may lead to further insights into the nature of language, by virtue of the perspective which it imposes. The perspective is a 'socio-semantic' one, where the emphasis is on function rather than on structure, where no distinction is made between language and language behaviour; and where the central notion is something like that of 'meaning potential' – what the speaker 'can mean', with what he 'can say' seen as a realization of it.

Preoccupations of a sociological kind, which as was pointed out at the beginning have for a long time held a place in linguistic studies, assume a greater significance in the light of work such as Bernstein's: not only because Bernstein's social theory is based on a concern with language as the essential factor in cultural transmission, but also because it has far-reaching implications for the nature of language itself. And these, in turn, are very relevant to the educational problems from which Bernstein started. Bernstein has shown the structural relationship between language, the socialization process, and education; it is to be expected, therefore, that there will be consequences, for educational theory and practice, deriving from the perspective on language that his work provides. Some concept of the social functioning of language must in any case always underlie the approach of the school towards its responsibility for the pupil's success in his mother tongue.

What's the Use?
A Schematic Account of Language Functions
By James Britton

Editor's Introduction

It is perhaps surprising in view of the vast output of writing demanded by some school systems that theories about developing written competence have frequently had limiting effects and have inhibited students rather than extended their abilities.

It is fortunately rare nowadays that a pupil is given a model passage to imitate in constructing 'A conversation between the willow tree and a scarecrow'. Chomsky's work has shown that language is not acquired piecemeal passively by imitation. However, even more recent theories of stimulating creative writing by direct experience have omitted the important fact that writing can equally proceed from *reflections* about experience or constructions of imaginary experiences. Where pupils have never been encouraged to reflect, their progress has been limited and remaining at the level of spontaneous recording of observations can be stultifying. Other views have stressed the primacy of 'technique' or the study of language through exercises and where these notions have prevailed, development may have been constrained. Postman and Weingartner (1966) reflect on the detrimental effects of such a partial view of language on the pupil:

> The most common result of the teaching of English and composition is not the creation of good writers and speakers, but the creation, in most of the public, of a lifelong fear of grammatical errors. . . . To be sure, we help some of our students to speak and write better. But the majority of fair-to-middling students leave the English class feeling that 'correct English', like moral perfection, is something that they cannot hope to attain.

Complementing their views, a fifteen-year-old student when recently asked why he had written only a few sentences replied: 'Well, the more you write the more trouble you gets into.'

In the paper which follows, 'What's the Use?', James Britton attempts to build a model of language functions which is more complete and which allows consideration of writing as both an end in itself and as a means to accomplish some end. The classification scheme focuses upon the intention of the writer and the use to which he puts language rather than upon technique and example practice. It allows Britton to develop the hypothesis that the POETIC and TRANSACTIONAL functions, which are particular forms of discourse in writing, develop by 'dissociation' from beginnings in written-down speech. Further, they allow writing to be considered in relation to the writer's intention and the kinds of constraints that are imposed upon writing by the context provided for it in school. The ideas in this paper have been used to underpin two major research projects, the results of which can be read in Britton (1975) and Martin (1975) and some criticisms may be found in Williams (1977). Britton offers an important aid to any teacher who wishes to study writing systematically.

B.W.

---

1. A preliminary note

WE shall be concerned in this article with the functions of extended discourse – a text or a piece of extended speech (not excluding dialogue). Thus, the notion of an overall function, a function that dominates in a hierarchy of functions, must be kept in mind.

We shall be concerned with 'typical function': necessarily so if we are to face up to the distressing facts that a speaker may have hidden and devious intentions in making himself heard; that he may fail to do what he intended; that the effect of an utterance may differ for each member of an audience; and that an utterance may set up a chain of consequences with no determinable cut-off point.

Our salvation lies in the notion of 'context' as Lyons has interpreted it:

> I consider that the idea of context as 'universe of discourse' (in Urban's sense) should be incorporated in any linguistic theory of meaning. Under this head I include the conventions and pre-suppositions maintained by 'the mutual acknowledgement of communicating subjects' in the particular type of linguistic behaviour (telling a story, philosophizing, buying and selling, praying, writing a novel, etc.). . . . (Lyons, 1963, pp. 83–84).

Thus 'the conventions and presuppositions maintained by the mutual acknowledgement of communicating subjects' provide a mature speaker or writer with a repertoire of known choices of function within our culture, and enable a mature listener or reader to recognize which choice has been made.

The rules of the game operate within 'the mutual acknowledgement of communicating subjects' and are therefore open to change. If advertisers, for example, insist on writing what seem to be fragments of autobiography for the purpose of selling tours, additional rules come to be written in.

2. The process of representation

Some of the things we say suggest that we may use words to support more general ways of classifying or representing experience: more general and perhaps more elementary ways. Thus (as has often been noticed) we speak of 'sinking into despair' and 'rising to the height of our ambitions'; we 'fall into disfavour' and 'rise to an occasion', and we call education 'a ladder'. It seems likely that some general spatial sense of height and depth constitutes a non-verbal mode of classifying, and that this underlies the habits of speech by which the things we aspire to or strive for are located 'up above', while the things we shun or are at the mercy of are located 'down below'. (When we speak of 'the height of folly' or 'the height of the ridiculous', we are probably mocking some instance by giving it, so to speak, a prize – a booby prize.)

Certainly language, as a way of representing the world, is inextricably interwoven with other forms of representation. My example was trivial, but the statement is crucial, and takes us on to an even more important hypothesis, that what distinguishes man from the other animals is not language *per se*, but the whole process of representation.

It is the process of representation that makes a man's view of the world (if we interpret behaviour aright) so vastly different from that of the other animals who live in it with him. Indeed, to speak of an animal's 'view of the world' at all is probably misleading; whereas man's every response to the environment is likely to be mediated by his total view of the world as he knows it. By symbolizing, by representing to himself the world as he experiences it, man creates, if Cassirer is right, a retrospect which by projection gives him also a prospect. (Cassirer, 1946, p. 38). In the human world, the here-and-now is set in a rich context, a world constructed of experiences derived from elsewhere and other times. In such a world, what goes away may be expected to come back, 'out of sight' does not mean 'out of mind', change need not be kaleidoscopic, and very little that happens to us will be wholly unforeseen.

I have laboured the point because I want to suggest that it is typically human to be insistently preoccupied with this world representation, this retrospect and prospect a man constructs for himself. It is of immense importance to him, I believe. It is his true theatre of operations since all he does is done in the light of it; his hopes for the future depend upon its efficacy; and above all his sense of who he is and what it is worth for him to be alive in the world derive from it. We might even say that he is more pre-occupied with it than he is with the moment by moment interaction with environment that constitutes his immediate experience. A man's consciousness, in fact, is like the little dog with the brass band: it is for ever running ahead, or dropping back, or trotting alongside, while the procession of actual events moves steadily on.

Our world representation may owe its vividness to sense images and the symbols (however we think of them) that mark emotional categories: for its *organization* it relies very largely upon language. As we talk about events – present, past or imagined – we shape them in the light of, and incorporate them into, the body of our experience, the total. We may of course fail in our attempt to adjust the corpus and digest the new event: life does sometimes make irreconcilable demands upon all of us. To preserve the order, harmony, unity of our represented world we may ignore the recalcitrant event (or aspect of events); or we may, over a period of time, continue the effort to come to terms with it. Those who too readily ignore disturbing aspects of experience are destined to operate in the actual world by means of a represented world that grows less and less like it: and so the fool has his paradise.

3. The expressive function
If human consciousness is like the little dog with the brass band we may expect to find its volatile nature revealed in a man's expressive speech. Being more or less intimate, unrehearsed, such speech is free to follow the shifting focus of attention, clothing a speaker's preoccupations the more faithfully because it is committed to no other task, meets no demands but his own, takes for granted a listener's readiness to be interested both in the speaker and his message.

Expressive speech is language close to the speaker: what engages his attention is freely verbalized, and as he presents his view of things, his loaded commentary upon the world, so he also presents himself. Thus, it is above all in expressive speech that we get to know one another, each offering his unique identity and (at our best) offering and accepting both what is common and what differentiates us.

Secondly, it is in expressive speech that we are likely to rehearse the growing points of our formulation and analysis of experience. Thus we may suppose that all the important products and projects that have affected human society are likely to have been given their first draft in talk between the originator and someone who was sufficiently 'in the picture' to hear and consider utterances not yet ready for a wider hearing. Such a listener would ideally concern himself first with the speaker and his thinking, those mental processes that lie behind the utterance; though, having 'understood', he might take account also of the forms of the utterance itself and assist in its modification to suit a wider audience.

But of course our use of expressive speech is not limited to the original and far-reaching. It is our principal means of exchanging opinions, attitudes, beliefs in face-to-face situations. As such, I would judge it to be a far more important instrument for influencing each other and affecting public opinion and social action than any sermon, political speech, pamphlet, manifesto or other public utterance.

'Expressive' is one of the three principal language functions in the scheme I want to outline. It is a scheme that was worked out in the course of classifying some two thousand pieces of written work, in all school subjects, produced by boys and girls of eleven to eighteen, though its application is not confined to the written language. In order to explain the remaining terms, I need to refer back to the general theory with which I began.

4. The roles of participant and spectator

Once we suppose that man operates in the actual world by means of his representation of it, we can see for him an alternative mode of behaviour: he may operate *upon the representation itself* without seeking any direct effect in the actual world. We may in fact see in this formulation a way of describing a great deal of his spontaneous image-making. (Susanne Langer calls man 'a proliferator of images' and postulates a new need not recognized in the other animals, a 'need of symbolization'.) (Langer, 1960, p. 41). These two kinds of behaviour seem to me essentially and interestingly different. (For a fuller discussion see Chapter II in my *Language and Learning*.) 'Operating in the actual world' I want to call 'being in the role of participant': 'operating directly upon the represented world' (improvising upon past experience, for example, or supplying gaps in our picture by drawing upon other people's experiences – but both taken up out of concern for our world picture and not as a means to some end in the actual here-and-now) — this I want to call 'being in the role of spectator'. Contrast Othello telling the story of his life to Desdemona and her father (where all three are in the role of spectator) with a beggar telling a hardluck story to enhance his appeal, or a historian reading a novel, or any other narrative, in order to check on a point of historical fact (each of them, in pursuing his own current ends through the agency of the narrative being in the role of participant).

To be in the role of spectator is to be concerned with events not now taking place (past events or imagined events), and to be concerned with them *per se* (as an interruption to or a holiday from the march of actual events) and *not as a means to some ongoing transaction with the actual.*

Suppose I recount an interesting experience to a friend – for his entertainment and my own pleasure in doing so. I shall continue to breathe, stand up, sit down, drink maybe, or eat, attend occasionally to what is going on around me – offer him another drink, move nearer the fire if I am cold, answer a child's question, and so on. But mentally I am 'living in the past' – these other things are seen as unattended background to, or interruptions of, what I am principally concerned to do; which is to rehearse in mind an experience that is not now going on, but has been experienced in the past.

What I feel as background or interruption to my spectator role activity is likely to be similarly felt by my listener. In other words, in sharing this past experience with him I induce him also to take up the spectator role. But it is an experience I had, he did not. It follows that I may similarly take up the role of spectator of experiences *I* have never had – and that, I suggest, is what I do when I read a novel or watch a film, or when I enter into possible future experiences in my day-dreaming.

When we use language to get something done, we are in the role of participants – participants in a very general sense in the world's affairs: and, as we have suggested, this must be taken to include the use of language to recount or recreate real or imagined experience in order to inform, or teach, or make plans, or solicit help, or achieve any other practical outcome.

We must note finally that taking up the spectator role does not indicate any lack of involvement in the experiences being recounted: we do indeed 'participate' in the story or the fiction or the dream, but since the events that involve us are distinct from ongoing events, and not subordinated to ongoing events as means to end, this participation does not put us in the role of participant.

5. The three main categories

The two roles of participant and spectator are thus seen to represent two different relationships between what is being *said* (or written or thought) and what is being *done,* and to cover between them all uses of language. We see our three main function categories, Transactional, Expressive and Poetic, related to the two roles as follows:

Participant		Spectator
role		role
TRANSACTIONAL ———	EXPRESSIVE ———	POETIC

When the demands made of a participant (in the world's affairs) are at a maximum, we have called the function 'transactional', a term that will need no explaining. Where the use of language in spectator role achieves its fullest satisfactions, we have called the function 'poetic', a term meant to include any example of the verbal arts. The expressive function straddles the participant/spectator distinction, but the dividing line at this mid-point is a shadowy one, and expressive language, as we have seen, is loosely structured, free to fluctuate. Thus, to modify an earlier example, if I recount the story of my recent holiday for your entertainment (and to enjoy it myself in retrospect), the talk is likely to be expressive, in the spectator role. If as you listen you become interested in the place I am describing as a possible holiday trip for yourself, you may ask for information about it – switching to participant role, but probably staying in the expressive. If, however, you pursue this line of enquiry and begin seriously to plan your holiday, your questions, directing my answers, may have the effect of shifting us both into transactional speech. A less likely alternative: if you were to become so interested in my account *as narrative*, and if under your encouragement I warmed to my task of constructing a story (and had the talent to do so), my language might move from the expressive to the poetic function. Finally (lest it appear that the expressive function operates only as a stage *en route* to something else) if as you listen to my talk we warm *to each other*, we may begin to exchange experiences, opinions, evaluations, and – now in spectator role, now in participant – intensify the reciprocal processes of exploring the other and revealing the self that constitute the expressive function of conversational utterance.

6. The poetic function

D. W. Harding long ago laid the foundations of the theory that associates literature with the role of spectator (Harding, 1937). He saw gossip and the novel as two instances of 'imaginary spectatorship in a social setting', and suggested that in each a *detached evaluative response* to the possibilities of experience was being offered by the speaker (writer) and invited of the listener (reader). 'The result,' he said, 'is a vast extension of the range of possible human experience that can be offered socially for contemplation and assessment.' Though as participants we evaluate a situation in order to operate within it, as spectators we are able to relate events more amply to a broader spectrum of values. 'Detached and distanced evaluation is sometimes sharper for avoiding the blurrings and bufferings that participant action brings, and the spectator often sees the event in a broader context than the participant can tolerate. To obliterate the effects on a man of the occasions on which he was only an onlooker would be profoundly to change his outlook and values.' (Harding, 1962, p. 136).

To put this point very simply: freed of a participant's need to *act* (to interact socially, to keep his end up, to turn events to his own advantage, etc.), a spectator is able to attend more fully and more exclusively to the evaluative processes. I want now to add a new point within the same framework: freed of the necessity for action, a spectator is able to attend more fully to the utterance *as utterance* – that is to say, to its forms of language and to formal features of whatever the language portrays: the pattern of events in a narrative; the configuration of an idea or a theory; and, above all, the pattern of feelings evoked – the rise and fall of emotional tension, the succession of love, hate, anger, fear, relief, pity that may attend his response to the experiences portrayed. I say 'above all' because I believe Harding's view of the detached evaluative response may be enhanced by recognizing that the effect of feeling upon a participant has this marked difference from its effect upon a spectator. As we participate in events, feeling seems to operate primarily as a spur to action: we might even say that it discharges itself in action. As spectators, we hold it to savour it; and as we read on (or listen, or speak, or write), to savour not simply an emotion but the formal design created by a complex of emotions dynamically related.

If gossip and the novel are linked as exemplars of language in the spectator role, they are differentiated in the degree to which they realize the opportunities for formal organization. In our terms, most gossip will be expressive in function (as will be also the loosely autobiographical written narratives of the English lesson): the novel, the play, the poem, on the other hand, take on the poetic function in so far as they achieve the necessary degree of formal organization, formal unity. (What is the necessary degree will be an arbitrary decision related to the purpose of making an analysis.)

For the poetic utterance is a construct or artifact, a verbal object. To exaggerate the matter, as many poets and critics have done, its function is not *to say*, but *to be*: or – more commodiously – where other utterances have *meaning*, a poetic utterance has *import*. This is a matter we shall return to in a moment.

7. The transactional function

Transactional language has two main sub-divisions which we have labelled, familiarly enough, *informative* and *conative*. The informative covers both the giving and the seeking of information; the full range of what is meant by 'information' takes us into considerable complications in the way of sub-categories. The conative is quite straightforward in theory since we have chosen to define it narrowly, but applying the distinctions in practice presents difficulties. For language to qualify as conative in function, the speaker's intention to change his listener's behaviour, opinions or attitudes must be deliberate and recognizable – recognizable, that is, to an observer even where it is so disguised as to deceive a victim to whom it is addressed.

8. Transactional and poetic contrasted

Before describing further sub-categories of the transactional, let us attempt to clarify some of the major issues, first by briefly contrasting the two poles of the system, transactional and poetic language.

TRANSACTIONAL (Participant role)	POETIC (Spectator role)
The utterance is an immediate means to an end outside itself.	The utterance is an immediate end in itself, and not a means, i.e. it is a verbal artifact, a construct.
The form it takes, the way it is organized, is dictated primarily by the desire to achieve that end efficiently.	The arrangement *is* the construct i.e. the way items are formally disposed is an inseparable part of the meaning of the utterance.
Attention to the forms of the language is incidental to understanding, and will often be minimal.	Attention to the forms of the language is an essential part of a listener's (reader's) response.
The speaker (writer) is concerned in his utterance to enmesh with his listener's relevant knowledge, experience, interests: and the listener is at liberty to contextualize what he finds relevant, selectively. This 'piecemeal contextualization' we take to be a part of the conventions governing transactional language.	The speaker (writer) is concerned to create relations internal to the utterance, and achieve a unity, a construct that is discrete from actuality. Thus he resists piecemeal contextualization; i.e. the conventions holding between speaker and listener in poetic language call for 'global contextualization'.

9. Contextualization of the poetic

The difference in mode of contextualization (the manner in which we relate what is in the utterance to what we know, think, feel already) is a crucial one. As we read a poetic text we must of course draw at all points upon our own experience in order to interpret what is on the page: but, if we are responding according to the conventions governing poetic language, our principle of selection and organization of this material will be one of subordination to every clue the text can offer us. This process, then, might be thought of as the converse of 'piecemeal contextualization'

– in fact the converse of contextualization itself. When we have completed the structuring of the raw material of our own experience in obedience to the demands of the text – having as it were recreated the construct as a unity – we may then go on to relate its total import to our own experience as a whole, our general views and beliefs on the issues involved.

It is in this way that the artist with a message gets his message across. A work that invites piecemeal contextualization must forgo the formal coherence and unity of the poetic construct: its message may be forceful, but it is not poetically conveyed: we should classify it as 'transactional'. On the other hand, the first thing to record about the poetic work is to classify it as 'poetic': however, we may then go on and allot it to a second category in accordance with the function that seems appropriate to its 'global contextualization'. We might for example call *1984* or *Catch 22* 'Poetic (Conative)'; C. P. Snow's *The New Men* or Patrick White's *The Tree of Man*, 'Poetic (Informative)'; and perhaps Lowry's *Under the Volcano* and Joyce's *Ulysses*, 'Poetic (Expressive)'. That the scheme should make room for such judgments is more important than that we should agree in making them – mercifully. And for the vast majority of works of literature all we shall need to say, or want to say, will probably be said in classifying them as 'Poetic'.

As far as satire is concerned, our claim that the poetic function should rank as primary is perhaps somewhat encouraged by the consideration that most of the satires that continue to be read concern themselves with causes which, if not lost, are at least won.

10. Sub-categories of the informative

Of the many possible ways of subdividing informative uses of language, we have chosen one based on James Moffett's analysis of the relation between a speaker and his topic: between the 'I' and the 'it', where 'I', 'you' and 'it' represent the three components of a communication situation. (Moffett, 1968). He calls his analysis 'an abstractive scale', and sees it as operating in close interconnexion with a 'rhetorical scale' representing the range of relations between the 'I' and the 'you'. He marks off four positions on his abstractive scale, moving from the least to the most abstract, from the 'codification of our world that most nearly reflects the structure of that world to codification that more and more resembles the structure of the mind'. (Moffett, 1968, p. 9). Here, more or less in the form that he gives them, are his four categories:

1. Recording: the drama of what is happening.
    Chronologic of perceptual selectivity.
    (e.g. an on the spot recording of what is happening before the guillotine.)

2. Reporting: the narrative of what happened.
   Chronologic of memory selectivity.
   (e.g. an eye-witness account of what happened one day during the French Revolution.)
3. Generalizing: the exposition of what happens.
   (e.g. a historical generalization about the Reign of Terror.)
4. Theorizing: the argumentation of what will, may, happen.
   Tautologic of transformation.
   (e.g. a political scientist's theory about revolutions.)

(Moffett, 1968, pp. 34, 35 and 47.)

Having acknowledged a substantial debt (which will become obvious), I shall leave Moffett's account in bare outline and go into greater detail in explaining the modified form of scale we have used to subdivide our informative category.

But first to make a more general point: Moffett in fact applies his scale to all forms of discourse: we have used it where it seemed focal, where it systematized observed differences between utterances that seemed important. The relation between a speaker and his topic is likely to be crucial in the informative category, which is after all the category Jakobson called 'the referential function' and which he defined as 'focus upon the topic'. (See Sebeok, 1960, p. 357). The scale might be applied to expressive discourse, but would not add a great deal of information, or to conative discourse, but somewhat irrelevantly. To apply it to poetic discourse would, I suspect, be to introduce an alien concept (and our notion of global contextualization will suggest reasons).

Basing our requirements on the data to be classified – the two thousand scripts collected from secondary schools – we finally introduced three transitional categories, making seven out of Moffett's four.

(i) *Record.* The speaker records what is going on *here and now*, and/or describes what is to be observed here and now. (Compare what is often called 'running commentary'.) The principle of organization is chronological or 'spatial' (qualitative, descriptive).

We have made the assumption that the prerequisite classifying processes are no more demanding if one says, 'The policeman's coat is blue with silver buttons' than if one says, 'The policeman is shouting and waving his baton': i.e. that *describing* is not *per se* a generalizing activity and thus related to the analogic in a way *narrating* is not.

(ii) *Report.* The speaker reports what went on or what was to be observed on a particular occasion at a particular place. The principle of organization is, again, chronological/spatial. Note that the speaker, since he takes up a retrospective stance, has a basis of selection not available to the speaker of *record*.

Some historical statements are in this category since they deal with directly observable events: e.g. 'In May 1836 an exploring expedition led by the surveyor-general attacked a party of aborigines killing seven and wounding four.' But more commonly, historical statements are generalizations based upon scattered observations and observations over a period of time: e.g. 'The record of relations between the settlers and the natives was an unhappy one.' Such statements, in themselves, are *analogic* (Category (v)). However, isolated sentences of either type are likely to be embedded in a text that contains both types: classification will in any case be in accordance with what seems to be dominant, and in this particular case a balance of analogic statements with related statements of report is likely to be characteristic of the best analogic discourse.

(iii) *Generalized narrative or descriptive information.* The speaker reports what goes on (or used to go on) habitually, or what might be, or have been, habitually observed over a series of occasions in a series of places. E.g. What we do on Sundays; what coffee-houses were like; how we get our water supply. Classes of events or of 'appearances' are organized on a chronological/spatial principle. This category thus marks the first step towards generalization, away from the particularity of report.

We include in this sub-category a great deal of everyday informational discourse, discourse in which the speaker generalizes from a number of observable events or procedures or concrete situations (e.g. recipes, practical hints, descriptions of simple processes or procedures).

(iv) *Analogic, low level of generalization.* An arrangement of loosely related and low-level general statements: a concatenation or agglomeration of such statements, for example about the industries of Scotland or the effects of the Thirty Years War. The principle of organization is, however, classificatory rather than chronological/spatial.

(v) *Analogic.* This, rather than (iii) or (iv), is Moffett's 'generalizing' category. Here generalizations are made and are related hierarchically or logically: i.e. the principle of organization is again classificatory, but more rigorously so than in (iv).

A great deal of scientific and historical discourse will come into this category, but it will include any attempt to relate statements on the basis of their respective levels of generality, from whatever areas of experience they may be drawn. E.g. 'The differences are large and variable. Taking an objective view of my parents as the adults I know best, an obvious difference is that I am at school learning, whereas they have left school and work. This means that they bring home the money and I do not. I am dependent on them and responsible to them.'

(vi) *Speculative (Analogic/tautologic)*. This is another transitional category that seemed to be required since a great deal of open-ended speculation arises when a speaker makes, as it were, horizontal moves in his thinking – framing general hypotheses on the basis of general propositions – and yet does not reach conclusions which would provide a genuinely theoretical analysis.

(vii) *Tautologic (Moffett's 'theorizing')*. Here the systematic combining of abstract propositions leads to new conclusions, which form a further extension of the system or theory. The basis of organization is, in a strict sense, *theoretical*.

Though its claim to belong to this category can hardly be sustained on the evidence of one sentence, we judged the school-boy's piece from which this was taken to qualify for inclusion: 'The social life of man is characterized not by virtue of his being a tool-using animal but by virtue of his being a language-generating animal.'

At this point I imagine a reader might be tempted by common-sense to ask with me a low-level question: What then becomes of these high-level abstractions? Do they reverberate for ever in a perpetual tautology? And I suppose our answer should be along these lines: that we give them intellectual assent in so far as (1) we accept as valid the steps in thinking by which they were arrived at and (2) they support or strengthen important ideas or beliefs we already hold; and perhaps (3) they modify some lesser beliefs or replace them with ones that fit better into the total edifice: then presumably at some points in the whole network there will be tests applied which show whether the system works in practice, whether it provides reliable guidelines to choice at the level of behaviour.

What is important is to realize, as Moffett points out, that the more abstract processes derive from *and remain dependent on* those at lower levels. Thus, the series of categories from (i) to (vii) has clear developmental implications: to say this, however, is to broach an important aspect of our study which this article cannot attempt to deal with.

11. Sub-categories of the conative

We distinguish two sub-categories of the conative, *regulative* and *persuasive*. The regulative represents a direct exercise of influence, and it aims more often at affecting action or behaviour than at changing attitudes, opinions or beliefs. It covers on the one hand simple requests such as 'Pass the mustard', and on the other, rules and instructions issued to those obliged to obey them, and recommendations that carry the weight of authority or the force of a speaker's wishes.

It should be noted that recipe books, and a great many other varieties of technological discourse, may use a conative form, but

since their function is informative they are classified in the informative categories.

In ordinary polite society a request to pass the mustard is not
expected to be refused: the regulative utterance is enough. In
authority situations those giving the instructions speak in the
expectation that they will be obeyed. Persuasive language, the
second sub-division of the conative, is employed where no such
expectation of compliance operates: usually because it is
inappropriate, but sometimes in cases where the expectation has
met disappointment, or the speaker has chosen not to invoke it
although he might have done. Here the speaker's will is, as it were,
diverted into an effort to *work upon* the listener in support of the
course of action he recommends, or (more typically perhaps) the
opinion, attitude, belief he is putting forward. Thus it is one
strategy of persuasive language to foresee and counter possible
objections, bringing the weight of logical argument to bear; it is
another strategy to work upon a listener's feelings, employing
perhaps the wiles of classical rhetoric, whether recognized as such
or not.

12. What's the use?
So there it is – the outline of a scheme in progress (an appendix
gives the category numbering). If it seems to us rather tenuous at
times we take heart from the thought that we shall understand it
much better when we have completed a study of the two thousand
scripts, and have applied it also to a four-year follow-up study of
the school-work of about a hundred eleven-year-olds and a
hundred fourteen-year-olds.

We believe it may offer one approach to the consideration of
'language across the curriculum' – an undertaking that must call
into question some very general matters concerning teachers'
objectives, as well as some very particular ones regarding the
diverse linguistic demands made on children as they move from
one lesson to another in the day's programme.

Of the general matters, it is the interrelationships of the main
categories that interest us most – as well as the *interrelatedness* of
the various linguistic demands and achievements. We would hope,
for instance, that expressive language may be increasingly seen to
play a key role in all learning (even the most subject-oriented) as
well as in learning to use language; and that the educational value
of spectator role activities may come to be better understood and
more convincingly argued. We see such activities indeed as
reflecting a concern for 'the compleat man': for it is the corpus of
an individual's experience that makes him the person he is; that
generates the pluses and minuses of his fluctuating verdict on the
world, his fluctuating acceptance of the human condition, his

fluctuating faith in himself. And spectator role activities, across the whole range from expressive to poetic utterance, represent a concern for this corpus.

Appendix

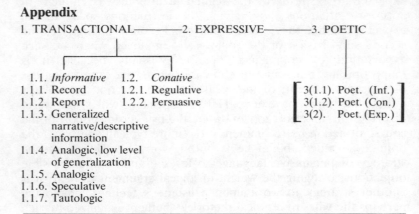

1. TRANSACTIONAL————2. EXPRESSIVE————3. POETIC

1.1. *Informative*   1.2.   *Conative*
1.1.1. Record   1.2.1. Regulative   3(1.1). Poet. (Inf.)
1.1.2. Report   1.2.2. Persuasive   3(1.2). Poet. (Con.)
1.1.3. Generalized   3(2).   Poet. (Exp.)
       narrative/descriptive
       information
1.1.4. Analogic, low level
       of generalization
1.1.5. Analogic
1.1.6. Speculative
1.1.7. Tautologic

ACKNOWLEDGEMENTS
Acknowledgements are due to my colleagues in the Schools Council Writing Research Project: Miss Nancy Martin, Dr Harold Rosen, Messrs Tony Burgess, Dennis Griffiths, Alex McLeod and Bernard Newsome.

Language and Meaning
A Study of Adolescents and Young Adults
By E. A. Peel

Editor's Introduction

Whereas meaning has not always been a major concern for linguists, it has been a central issue for teachers and for those who study learning in school. Therefore it is important to discuss meaning in relation to language. Even in school subjects such as foreign languages, where language itself is learned rather than being the medium of instruction, early emphasis on grammatical accuracy has been replaced by valuing all-round competence in communication (Littlewood, 1974).

Although the importance of meanings has been recognized in school learning, the different kinds of meaning and the particular types which lead to optimum learning at different ages are matters which require investigation. Edwin Peel uses empirical methods to investigate the differences between semantic, syntactic, and conceptual meanings. He suggests that, while young children learn referential meanings and words similar in sound to those already known, older children can cope with syntactic (knowing, for example, that a word changes meaning when used as a different part of speech) and conceptual (knowing, for example, that the prefix 'tele' retains the consistent meaning 'at a distance' in several words) meanings. His work has strong implications for the teaching of reading in secondary schools. He reports from a study which suggests that only in mid-adolescence and beyond is there evidence that pupils make use of 'the whole logical structure of the textual material available'. The developmental conclusion is possible: that pupils are not intellectually mature enough to make deductive conceptualizations. It is also possible that the teaching of reading over-emphasizes decoding at the sentence level and that, if pupils are not taught advanced reading skills in the secondary school, they will only slowly and haphazardly acquire the crucial ability to obtain meaning from context.

B.W.

I DO not need to elaborate upon the theme of the importance of language in the production of ideas and meanings during secondary and higher education. But I may remind readers that although many of the basic language-thought mechanisms which emerge during childhood have been extensively discussed and investigated, relatively little has been done with older age groups. There is much of interest to be extracted from a study of such older pupils and students. The topics of meaning, concept formation, understanding and judgement, evaluation and creative use of English may all be fruitfully explored.

In this paper I propose to survey and discuss briefly ideas and studies in the psycho-linguistics of meaning. Different meanings emerge both from the *practice* of language and from *thinking* associated with it which reveal differences and possibly developments during and after adolescence.

First, a word about the main principle underlying both the theorizing and the research technique which forms the basis of our discussion. It has been to think about and produce a verbal situation involving nonsense syllables, words, sentences or paragraphs, open in that it provides the subject with fairly unrestricted opportunity to reveal his meanings, to construct his ideas and make his judgements, evaluations and creations. This sometimes means that qualitative differences or responses have to be recognized, graded, and agreed upon by judges, but the gain in more revealing replies is most valuable for it takes account of the structural quality of the language-thought processes. The somewhat open test paragraph, sentence, or word list with accompanying verbal preparation is itself a structure, comprehension of which reveals the deeper, wider structure in the cognitive life of the person tested.

Readers acquainted with the interest among contemporary linguists, anthropologists and sociologists, in structural and holistic modes of theorizing and investigation (Piaget, 1970; Lane, 1970), will realize that much of what follows fits well into this topical scene. The recognition of structure has been a part of psychological theory and practice for a long time, first by the Gestalt psychologists and later more fully and penetratively by Piaget.

The Geneva use of the concept of structure in explaining thought (Inhelder and Piaget, 1959) includes the basic notions of holism, transformation, and homeostasis. But Piaget does not fall into the trap of assuming that ready-made structures appear *ab initio*. They emerge with experience and even in adolescence there is still plenty of scope for further structural development in cognition. Meaning is essentially a structural phenomenon, for it may be constructed out of many parts and relations in the language-thought whole.

Discussion of meaning in relation to language tends to get shelved by educationalists and others writing about cognitive processes in the school setting. This appears strange since the experience of meaning by the pupil is something the teacher tries to promote and utilize. The apparent lack of interest may have several causes.

First the word is unpopular because it has longstanding connections with the 'idea' of an object – as something existing *a priori* and outside the learner's mental life. But the dualism between word and idea disappears if we hold the view that learning is construction and that the only difference between learning and thinking is in the degree of control exercised by the speaker over his own utterances.

Secondly, meaning in language is too often assumed to be merely that of reference of a word to an object or other words as in lexicography and translation. This interpretation is patently so incomplete in foreign language learning that the whole concept tends to be rejected.

Thirdly, the concept of meaning as a primary feature of mental life, irreducible to other simpler psychological phenomena such as association (Humphrey, 1951), conditioned connections between stimuli or mediation by pure stimulus acts (Hull, 1952) has been rejected on psychological grounds. The educationalist may also be tempted, therefore, to exclude it from his own discussions. This will not do, for educationally the problem is both real and complex.

There are several kinds of meaning and the explanation of each is equally varied. The confusion is increased by the interest of different disciplines in the problem which includes that of philosophy, general linguistics, psychology, sociology, and education.

Prominent among English specialists are Ogden and Richards who wrote in the vein of association psychology and were concerned with referent-meaning, and Firth (1958) the most positive advocate of the idea of poetic meaning and also vigorous in insisting upon the inclusion of the study of meaning in language research. Among psychologists we may note the unique theoretical and experimental contribution of Osgood, Suci and Tannenbaum (1957) in their analysis of general meaning into the three dimensions of: value, potency, and movement.

Educational studies of meaning in English are not numerous. My own inquiries (Peel, 1962) on word learning, to be mentioned later, started from a psychological standpoint, but were developed to include the learning of foreign language vocabulary (Luckman, 1964). This work was restricted to word learning (and nonsense syllables) which, however, was related to the learner's language and thought structures. The aim was to promote certain structures and then to see how far they affected verbal learning.

Before I consider obvious interpretations of the word 'meaning' I can demonstrate to the reader how the semantic element, shown in the attitudes held and meanings constructed by the thinker, is reflected in sentence test material, designed primarily to educe syntactic idiosyncrasies.

The purpose was to investigate grammatical peculiarities, not necessarily inaccuracies, which might be used by people having English as a second language. They were given a set of incomplete sentences which they had to fill in. The missing parts were so chosen that the blank spaces allowed some degree of freedom in the insertion of the completing material. One of the tests was as follows:

> Task: Complete the following sentence by inserting two words in the place provided:
> At the end of the visit, because the children were hungry and tired we .... make them wash their hands before eating.

Although it was intended to test syntactical oddities, the first thing we noted was that there are two broad classes of reply, which show that the subjects started off from two opposing *attitudes* about hunger and cleanliness. The sentence reflected these meanings. There were people who put hunger before cleanliness and those who put cleanliness before hunger. Those people who put hunger before cleanliness provided a preponderance of 'did not' answers (mainly among native English speakers) and those who put cleanliness before hunger gave a preponderance of 'had to' answers (mainly among people with English as a second language). This is a psychological or semantic element which has to be cleared away before we can look at the answers structurally. We see that any attempt to make a syntactical analysis of connected English will require also some combination with semantic analysis.

Psychologically, meanings can be said to begin when the thinker has any mental structure at all into which the new experience can be assimilated and which structure itself in the process may become accommodated to the new experience. Meanings, then, are instances of what Piaget calls equilibration. This suggests that we must widen the concept of meaning far beyond that of ideational reference. Thus it can include clang or phonetic likeness, orthographical similarity, unusual, linguistic, metaphorical shapes and structural or syntactic patterns. Even when we see meanings as having mainly a referent significance, we may usefully distinguish between a simple sign-significate connection, and a richer conceptual meaning which takes account of the fact that a single sign and a single significate may each be a part of a wider matrix of related signs or significates.

Thus our account of meanings has to provide for clang (homophonic) and orthographic similarity, unusual juxtaposition of words and ideas, metaphor, *Times* crossword clues, sign-significate reference, conceptual meaning, syntactic patterns and contextual meaning.

(a) *Poetic Meaning*

Let us first analyse the meanings which words acquire by their phonetic and phonological qualities and which phrases acquire by virtue of the imaginative juxtapositioning of words, as in the metaphor. We may call this poetic meaning. Firth (op. cit.) gave the best single account where on page 192 he set forth his overall view as follows:

> To make statements of meaning in terms of linguistics, we may accept the language event as a whole and then deal with it at various levels, sometimes in a descending order, beginning with social context and proceeding through syntax and vocabulary to phonology, and even phonetics, and at other times in the opposite order, which will be adopted here since the main purpose is the exposition of linguistics as a discipline and technique for the statement of meanings without reference to such dualisms and dichotomes as word and idea, overt expression and overt concepts, language and thought, subject and object.

First docs not deny the concept of mind but he is not concerned with referent meaning nor with contextual meaning but with the meanings associated at the lowest levels with sounds. To quote him (op. cit. p. 193)

> Whenever a man speaks, he speaks in some sense as poet. Poets have often emphasized that a great deal of the beauty and meaning of the language is in the sound of it.

and further (op. cit. p. 194)

> Alliteration, assonance and the chiming of what are usually called consonants are common prosodic features of speech, and from the phonological point of view can be considered as markers or signals of word-structure or of the word process in the sentence.

This he called the prosodic mode of meaning and is a feature of good dialogue in contemporary drama and other forms of prose. Such might be the use of the consonant digrams.

  CR in *cr*ash, *cr*ack, *cr*umble
  SL in *sl*iding, *sl*ithery, *sl*ippery, *sl*ush

This interest by linguists in the semantic power of sounds is matched at a more behaviouristic level by psychologists' attempts to discover whether a clang (homophonic) preparation is more or less effective than a meaningful preparation (by synonyms) for the subsequent learning of lists of words and nonsense syllables. The idea for such experiments followed from the behaviourist concept of primary (homophonic) and secondary (mediated) stimulus generalization. Thus Cofer and Foley (1945) tested five matched groups of 25 learners respectively with a list of ten words, after each group had been presented with four readings of a list of homophones, a second list of homophones, a list of synonyms, a second list of synonyms of the first synonyms and a control list of 10 independent words. The 10 words lists included the two following words:

PREPARATIONS

Test Words	Homonyms I	Homonyms II	Synonyms	Synonyms of Synonyms	Control List
pear	pare	pair	fruit	result	palm
right	write	rite	just	barely	very

The results were as follows and appear to suggest that homophonic was more effective than ideational preparation.

RESULTS

	Mean recall of words in test list
1st Homophone Group (best homophones)	6.72
2nd Homophone Group	5.64
Synonyms Group	5.88
Synonyms of Synonyms Group	5.24
Control Group	4.80

Other results showed the opposite tendency, so the state of knowledge was far from clear. These earlier attempts could be faulted as experiments. But for me they neglected the important variable of age. It is common educational experience to find that children and younger adolescents learn new words in the mother tongue and in foreign languages more easily by clang rhyming than by semantic connections. Older people on the other hand may find semantic associations more helpful. I am using semantic here in its referent connotation.

It is possible to test how far a referent or semantic connection as opposed to homophonic association aids the learning of new material. In one experiment (Peel, 1962) a list of ten nonsense syllables, once presented, formed the learning task. Before the list was run through, each nonsense syllable was linked with other nonsense syllables and words. The groups of children and students so prepared were chosen at random. Each received four presentations of the list to be learned (the subjects did not know that this was to be the learning list), with the particular nonsense syllables or words paired with the list.

Thus NAR and GOM were two of the ten nonsense syllables to be learned and their preparation were as follows:

			Nature of preparation
Group 1.	VOK-NAR	LEK-GOM	control
Group 2.	VAR-NAR	LOM-GOM	clang N.S.
Group 3.	dress-NAR	church-GOM	word, semantic or referent
Group 4.	car-NAR	Tom—GOM	clang word

The four different preparations of connections were tried with 300 training college students in randomly selected groups of 75 each, and 200 secondary modern school pupils in groups of 50 with the following results:

	Group 1	*Group 2*	*Group 3*	*Group 4*	
	Mean number of correct responses				*n each*
	Control	*Word*	*Clang NS*	*Clang word*	*group*
Training College Students	6.0	6.4	5.5	5.8	75
School Pupils	3.9	3.9	4.3	3.9	50

The differences which are statistically significant show that semantic connections help the maturer learner whilst the clang connections appear to inhibit him. On the other hand the school pupils appear to be helped by clang association; meaning appears to exercise little if any influence.

Returning to poetic meaning, Firth drew attention at a higher level to the effect of putting together of words not usually associated with each other. This is meaning by collocation and, we are told, is not to be confused with contextual meaning. It is indeed a creative metaphorical and not a generic extension of the meaning of the terms put together: *spent night, joyful morn.*

Firth also cites Swinburne's lines:

> Welling water's winsome word,
> Wind in warm weather,

to demonstrate the power of the initial *w* as promoting these senses of meaning. It also illustrates his point that phonological meaning is not capable of translation into another language. His extension of the idea of collocative meaning to include the association of synonyms, antonyms, contraries, and complementary couples in one collocation, takes the concept into the realms of ideas and values. This is very evident in Pope's poetry.

> Most strength the moving principle requires;
> Active its task, it prompts, impels, inspires.
> Sedate and quiet the comparing lies,
> Formed but to check, deliberate, and advise.

One can sense here the phonological meaning in the propelling p . . . p . . . p . . . of the second line followed by the halt sign *sedate* and rounding off in the slower tempo of the *d*s of the last line, all being integrated by the pentameter rhythm.

The highest level of collocative meaning is revealed in the situation where there is speaker (or writer) and audience (or reader) each of whom, to use a behaviourist term, reinforces the actions of the other by persuading and convincing verbal forms. This collocative language comes into being as a result of the frequent occurrence of hitherto unused combinations of words and their consequent acceptance in the language. This collocation may be of several origins, as for example, idiomatic, or metaphorical.

> *it makes no matter*
> *there is nothing in it*
> *as well as its clear-cut issues . . . .*
> *London proposes, Paris coy*

These are meanings which stem from the effective use of language in itself as it were, and without reference to the meaning of words in the ordinary semantic sense. This use of language can be made at different levels, phonetic, phonological, prosodic and collocative – in poetry and in the social situations where a speaker is trying to influence his audience within the setting of their common society.

In broad terms the type of meaning discussed so far justifies the name of poetic meaning. Its experience has an essential aesthetic quality and making a pupil sensitive to it is an important aim in teaching literature, drama and poetry.

Where should we put the peculiar phonological fragmentations and lexical collocations which make up *Times* crossword clues such as:

Clue	Solution
Lucy Aston and Catharine Glover, we hear, for instance.	Scotswomen
Meaning power of attorney.	Significant
Spanish royal is east, understand.	Realise (Real is E)
Hug me back and get two!	Embrace (Me reversed brace)

These nearly resemble collocative grouping, and call for a play with words whose first rule is that the solver should not take any sequence of words or sounds in their normal structured or contextual setting. The solver must look for other groupings and meanings. Such meanings are not strictly poetic and metaphorical but they arise in collocations which are not the usual ones making up accepted English phrases and sentences.

(b) *Referent versus Syntactic Meaning*
In its wider educational setting meaning has the qualities suggested in the theory of signs, which suggests (Morris, 1956, p. 217) that a sign functions semantically, pragmatically and syntactically. Semantic meaning is the usual referent meaning of sign to significate. The latter may be an object, word, class, relation, operation, etc., as for example, word APPLE – fruit apple, russian *louk* – English *onion*, n = number of beans, ÷ is dividing. Such hooking up of signs forms a large part of early learning in any language.

Pragmatic meaning is more closely linked with the motivation of learning. It links the sign with the purposes and consequences of its significate for its users and experience. Thus the sign *arithmetic* or *school* has a different pragmatic meaning for successful and unsuccessful school pupils. Many politically toned words operate in this way, as for example: *apartheid, tory* and *reactionary*.

Syntactic meaning is the relation between a word or symbol and other words or symbols located with it in a sentence or equation. The word *on* takes on different meanings according to the sentences:

On you go! The electricity is on. Put the book on the table.

On departing he thanked his host. Go *on*! You're having me on.

In learning a foreign language syntactic meanings are often much more important than simple semantic meanings. Thus in French we have *in = dans,* but, *in the hand = à la main.*

The suggestion that words, besides carrying a simple referent meaning, also have a syntactic meaning is capable of experimental testing. The ten nonsense syllables referred to above, NAR, GOM, etc., were also each put into a different sentence as under:

I am fat NAR my wife is lean

In the Summer the woods are GOM.

These sentences were presented four times in random order with the same instructions as given for the other preparations described on p. 130, and then the learning list NAR, GOM . . . . was run through once in the same way as in the first experiment.

Two kinds of preparation were compared.

(1) Semantic or referent as, e.g. in dress-NAR, church; GOM.

(2) Syntactic as exemplified in

I am fat NAR my wife is lean.

The comparison was carried out with two groups of subjects; secondary modern school pupils in their first and fourth years, mean ages 11½ and 14½ years respectively.

In the first experiment the pupils within each age group were divided on the basis of equal scores on a buffer test for the two kinds of preparation: semantic and syntactic.

1st year	*Score on a prelim. buffer list of 8 words* (STEM)	*Score on the NAR-list of 10 NSs*	n
Semantic preparation Dress-NAR	4.2	3.5	51
Syntactic preparation I am fat NAR my wife is lean	4.2	3.2	45
4th year			
Dress-NAR	5.0	5.1	40
I am fat NAR my wife is lean	5.0	5.3	40

There is a slight but not statistically significant trend towards a greater effect of syntactic preparation with older pupils. More might be done along these lines.

(c) *Conceptual Meaning*

The four kinds of meaning so far discussed: poetic, semantic or referent, pragmatic and syntactic, do not, however, account for all that we observe in the effectiveness of meaning in school learning. For instance, the following extract from a Latin vocabulary revision session reveals something more than the influence merely of referent meaning.

Teacher: What does existimo mean?

Pupil: I exist.

Teacher: Wrong, I judge, value or appraise from *ex* and *aestimo* – I estimate.

Here an incorrect meaning is constructed from a false generalization, existimo-exist. Also the correct meaning is substituted and supported by a valid generalization aestimo + ex, estimate, etc.

It is quite easy to demonstrate the difference between this learning in which the response forms a member of an extended class and that in which it is merely a single referent. Under certain conditions foreign words like stein, kirche, louk (Russian onion), each of which fits into the learners' existing repertoires of responses,

Stein – stone, stane, rock, quarry . . . . .

Kirche, kirk, church, chapel, cathedral . . . . .

Louk – leek, onion, shallot, are more easily recorded and retained than those which have no obvious classes to join. Such may be sad (garden) – we assume the learner is naïve enough not to connect sad with the English sed – words of Latin, sedere – connection. A garden in Russian is where one puts down (seats) seeds – or Chleb (bread) from Russian.

A simple experiment with adult learners demonstrates the power of conceptual meaning and also the importance of the direction of the learning. Forty made-up words were put in a list with their English equivalent. Half of the forty pairs of words were chosen so that a meaningful association was suggested, as, for example, in the pairs:

wall . . . . steyn

violin . . . . skreepon

whereas as far as could be ascertained the other twenty items were composed of pairs of words not so obviously associated, such as

picture . . . . kuplo

knowledge . . . . vardin

Similarly in the test of twenty items, ten items consisted of closely connected pairs and ten of less obviously connected pairs. These associations are called strong and weak respectively.

TABLE OF MEAN CORRECT SCORES
(Maximum 10)

		Group A: Recall Learning Translating English to New Language allowing up to 3 spelling errors if the right word had been chosen		Group B: Recognition Learning Translating the New Language to English	
Testing	Period	Strong Ass.	Weak	Strong	Weak
1st	immediate	5.3 (4.0)*	1.4 (0.9)	6.3	2.5
2nd	after 15 mins.	6.7 (5.4)	3.1 (2.2)	7.8	4.4
3rd	,, 1 week	5.2 (4.1)	1.5 (1.0)	7.7	3.3
4th	,, 1 month	5.5 (4.0)	2.1 (1.3)	7.4	3.0
5th	,, 3 months	5.3 (4.0)	1.3 (0.9)	2.7	6.9

* These are the mean scores from answers spelled completely correctly.
Note: The figures in the brackets refer to mean score when correct spelling was insisted upon.

In order to test the effect of direction, the same test was presented in two forms, one requiring a translation from English to the 'new language' and the other requiring the reverse order of translation. An adjustment has to be made to allow for spelling mistakes in the new words. Spelling mistakes would be made only very rarely in giving English words, but might occur quite frequently in giving words in the 'new language'.

The results were calculated as mean scores for each of the two groups of people tested.

If the pairs of columns marked strong and weak are compared, it is clear that the strong connections are more readily learned, in the 1st and 2nd tests, and retained, in the 3rd, 4th and 5th tests.

In all, this evidence supports the view that 'meaning' contributes to more efficient learning of paired associates, but modern language learning entails of course far more than the acquisition of vocabulary, essential as this is. When a pupil first learns a new word in a foreign language, say PUT in Russian meaning WAY, ROAD or ORBIT he will best do no more than tie PUT to his picture or experience of WAY at the barest level of a contact word (Skinner's tact). Next PUT will become an indication word *PUT is a way*. At this stage PUT has referent or semantic meaning. When, however, the pupil begins to learn that puteshestbye means journey, S*put*nik means fellow-traveller, or Satellite, that Ras*put*in was allegedly so named because he deviated from the straight and narrow way, that is because he was dissolute, then PUT takes on a richer meaning for the learner. The essence of this meaning is that of a *relationship between the sign* PUT and the *signs* puteshestbye, sputnik, Rasputin . . . . . . *of similar significates*. For this reason we could well call it *conceptual meaning*. We may note here that it is not the same thing as *syntactic* meaning.

We can use this idea of conceptual meaning to help distinguish between pairs of words which may be confused.

(a) stationary – adjective ending – ary
    stationery – stationer – gro*cer*   winery (USA) – grocery, etc.

(b) fewest – few many *number*
    least – little less *size*

(c) kirche – kyriake (of the Lord), kirk, church (no s)
    kirsche – kera*s*os, cera*s*us, ceri*s*e – cherry
    (*s* dropped in error, compare pea from pois, from the erroneous belief that the 's' was a plural marker).

When we do this it suggests that the distinguishing generalizations or classes are orthogonal to the confusing ones

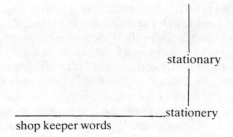

stationary

_____stationery
shop keeper words

Since they direct the learning we may call them *vectors*. If we admit orthogonal vectors why not others at various angles. A word is now seen to be a crossing point of various vectors, its meaning being carried in each vector. Thus the word *mean* is at the crossing point of at least four concept-vectors.

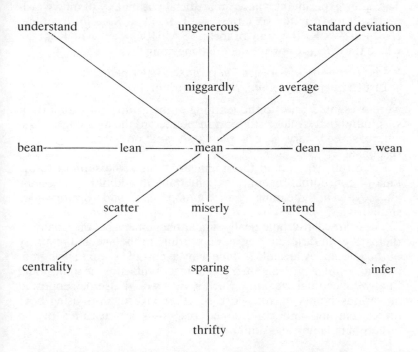

So far our progress from conceptual meaning to an extended vector theory of meaning has been speculative. How does it stand up to objective experiment? We may attempt such an experiment by first presenting lists of words bearing on some of the words to be finally learned, the former being studied and even learned prior to the giving of the second list of test words. We could use both primary or homophonic lists and secondary or meaningful lists.

For example, a test list consisted of the words *ton, rib, den, cup, bag, pin, rod, gun, pad, met,* of which the word *cup* is regarded as the key word. Two groups of preparatory thinking lists were given, one consisting of the words, *rub, hug, mud, but, pun* being the instances of primary generalizations and the other list consisting of the words, *beaker, saucer, glass, tumbler, tankard.* The control group of subjects had the preparatory list *god, dun, set, pod, kin.* After giving the preparatory list we then give the test list and count the frequencies of a correct cup response. With College students the *beaker* preparation list was more effective than both the homophone list and the control list. The homophone list showed no improvement on the control list. This would seem to suggest that with the mature students, a meaningful preparation involving the concept of liquid container does aid the memorizing of verbal material.

A later experiment where an artificial vocabulary of nine words was built up from the six letters, A, I, K, P, R, S, as for example, Hospital – SIKPRA and branch – SAPIRK was carried out, in which the effects of two conceptual meaning lists:

List A: *poorly, doctor, sickness, nurse, sick* (medical)
List B: *tree, leaf, sapling, twig, sap* (arboreal)

were presented prior to the learning of the artificial vocabulary. It was found that College students responded to the meaningful lists, whereas secondary school pupils showed no evidence of such response.

From this experiment there appears to be some support to the idea of conceptual meaning as something in addition to *semantic* and *syntactic* meaning and *homophonic* and *orthographic* similarity.

These are all psychologically similar phenomena but they manifest themselves in different degrees according to the age and maturity of the learner. A feasible sequence by age would seem to be homophonic similarity, semantic meaning, syntactic meaning, and finally conceptual meaning. Such a view would also be supported at various points by the work of other investigators using both direct learning and conditioned responses as measures of the effects of meaning and similarity.

(d) *Meaning from Context*
Lastly we turn to the comprehension of meaning from context. Often a new term, strange in its appearance, is introduced in a piece of text. The meaning of the new term has to be constructed from the context in which it is embedded. Linguistic and logical cues help in this mental act, and all the types of meaning so far outlined could enter into the process. Recently De Silva (1969)

made an interesting attempt to discover what psychological and logical elements in the whole test situation contributed to the construction of the meaning of a single term in context. He was more concerned with thoughts and their development processes but the technique could well be applied also with linguistic structures in mind.

De Silva used material from secondary school history texts and coded in the test word, whose meaning was to be constructed, by an unknown word. The pupils came from five years in a comprehensive school. He chose ten history concept words in context, of which *monopoly*, coded by KOHILAK was one:

KOHILAK (Monopoly)
The East India Company was the first and the greatest of the companies which was to play a leading part in the development of the British Empire. Financed chiefly by the City merchants, it held a virtual *kohilak* of trade with India, and was frequently accused of having too restrictive an outlook. Yet for many years it was the only source of capital for English enterprises in India, owned or chartered ships which carried goods to and fro, and made arrangements to market them at their own destination.

The subjects were asked 'What is KOHILAK? Why do you think so?' He was able to categorize the answers into the following four classes beginning with the least and ending with the most mature.

1. *Logically restricted* – 'These immature responses are not oriented to reality but are tautological, inconsistent, directly contradictory, irrelevant or otherwise irrational and display a gross lack of comprehension of the passage.'
2. *Circumstantial Conceptualization* – 'This form of signification is characterized by attempted analysis in terms of one aspect of the presented data and failure to grasp the essential features of the problem.'
3. *Logical Possibilities* – 'In this category of response subjects engage in realistic appraisal showing capacity to combine two or more pieces of evidence and ability to relate cause and effect.'
4. *Deductive Conceptualization* – 'In responses falling within this category the subject generally explores the content of the passage in almost its entirety in a deductive way and draws integrated, reasoned, penetrating and imagined inference.'

The preparation of answers made in the different categories set against the ages of the subjects was as follows:

| | *Percentages of Frequency* | | | | |
Age	12	13	14	15	16
No Response	4.0	3.5	6.5	9.5	5.5
Limited Response	71.0	68.8	63.0	47.0	40.0
Circumstantial Conceptualization	10.0	9.3	10.5	15.5	16.5
Logical Possibility	4.5	6.0	4.3	8.8	3.5
Deductive Conceptualization	10.5	12.5	15.8	19.0	34.5

From the above table it is apparent that only in mid-adolescence and beyond does one get marked evidence of the use of the whole logical structure of the textual material available. An interesting investigation would be where one could use the same broad mode of attack combined with an analysis of the answers in terms of the linguistic terms characteristic of the passages. This would, of course, necessitate the choice probably of differently structured passage material.

I have set out some half dozen different sources of the meaning of any word or phrase; phonological, collocative, referent, pragmatic, syntactic and conceptual. These different conceptions of meaning are not mutually exclusive and in some degree all may contribute to the meaning of any particular word or phrase. However, some may be more dominant at different levels of intellectual and linguistic maturity than others. In general conceptual meaning is a feature of later adolescence. Phonological meaning may have greater significance for the young learner of language. The one important value of the concept of collocative meaning is that it shows that any novel lexical combination brings about a new meaning. In a way referent meaning is a special case of collocation and since often it is not two words which are collocated, but word and object, such meaning comes to have a sort of objectivity which obscures the original arbitrary pairing. Hence we tend to get a separation of word and thought and a failure to recall that all meaning originates in language usage.

Criteria of Language Development
By Andrew M. Wilkinson

Editor's Introduction

The term 'language development' is often used very loosely at present. It can mean a school subject or part of the curriculum, like 'physical activities', and then its meaning depends on a school's or particular teacher's view of language. If, for example, 'vocabulary' is deemed important, pupils might be 'developed' by exercises such as including words like 'obelisk' and 'salamander' in original sentences; on the other hand if 'grammar' is considered crucial, exercises on the feminine forms of *bullock* and *duke* might feature strongly. At its worst this kind of teaching can be sterile and divorced from the pupil's experience of what language is and does; at its best it is limited by what, as teachers, we each know about language, by our linguistic prejudices.

For most people, development will also include some notion of growth and change, and the concept will be dynamic. Our increasing knowledge of how children acquire language and use it in various modes for various purposes and audiences is of help in constructing a rationale for progress in language. There is a need also for the criteria by which we judge progress to be carefully specified, but this rarely occurs.

Clearly it is as unhelpful to have no criteria as it is to have restricted ones such as 'use of subordinate clauses' or 'length of sentences' which could not alone give valid assessments of a child's development. Andrew Wilkinson's paper is an attempt to provide a model for considering the development of language despite the difficulties. His focus here is on the details of linguistic, stylistic, and content measures of language and he presents an affective model which he applies to four passages of writing by middle school pupils. Clearly there are many other possible and useful applications, including those to spoken forms of the language: a recent review (Wade, 1978) suggests that, even in formal assessment, criteria are sometimes confused or contradictory. It is valuable to have criteria for differentiating between children's abilities to master and organize experiences and feelings, to reveal self awareness and sincerity. Other parts of the model draw attention to features such as appropriateness and effectiveness of language and the writer's intention as well as to various aspects of cognitive judgements of content. As well as providing insights into assessment and development this paper could usefully form the basis for constructing a school's language policy.

B.W.

Abstract
'Language Development' has been insufficiently considered as a whole. The article surveys linguistic measures of which there are many; stylish measures which have not on the whole been seen developmentally; cognitive measures of which there are few; and affective measures particularly in relation to 'maturity' of which there are scarcely any. As pilot an affective model is offered and applied to samples of children's written work on the theme of 'the happiest day of my life'. Only tentative conclusions are suggested as the article is intended to open up the field.

What is 'Development'?

IT was easy for the old textbook writers. They assumed that English developed in 'stages'. So they chose their series title ('The Path to Glory' or whatever) and called the volumes Stage One, Stage Two, and so on. However, English is not a linear subject, and a person's language abilities are complex, so that progress cannot be described by a set of crude markers. And yet there are clearly differences between, say, the language of a one-year-old, a five-year-old, a ten-year-old. Development obviously takes place, but does not take place obviously. 'Language development' is a popular phrase, but its meaning has been insufficiently pursued.

The Making of Judgements
As a way of doing so let us first of all consider the traditional methods of arriving at a judgement on an English essay. It was advocated that one should assign marks under headings of the type Language, Style, Content, and Mechanical Accuracy (principally spelling and punctuation). A fair amount of investigation into the reliability of examiners using such 'code marking' went on (Hartog and Rhodes, 1936, being the classic) until Wiseman's work (1949) showed that 'impression marking' was just as reliable, faster and probably more valid. The impression markers were doubtless using internalized criteria derived from their experience; probably many of the code makers were doing the same and finding in the

code system a simplified rationale for these. What such criteria are, however, has not been pursued. Let us therefore take Language, Style and Content as heads for discussion, since we need to establish some criteria for judging one piece of language before we can compare another with it. Content we shall consider in two aspects – cognitive on the one hand and affective on the other.

Linguistic Judgements
For a period of over fifty years research workers particularly with a psychological background, have attempted to measure the language development of children objectively – by classifying and counting certain language features. These include quantity (the number of words, the mean sentence length). They include variety (the number of *different* words, the variety of parts of speech – adjectives and adverbs appearing to indicate greater maturity than nouns and verbs). These last two measures are of course calculated in relation to the total words used. Obviously there is much more likelihood of variety in ten sentences than in two. Thus what is called the type-token ratio is calculated – the number of words under study (e.g. adjectives) being expressed as a ratio of the total number of words. Again the use of unusual words has been regarded as significant (for instance words not occurring in basic vocabulary lists such as Thorndike's (1944)), as has also the variety of sentences used (question, statement, exclamation, etc.). Often the occurrence of basic sentence patterns, or 't units', sometimes modified by considering them as 'phonological' or 'communi-cation' units, has been employed. The degree of sentence complexity, counting subordinate phrases and clauses, has been widely employed as a measure. Thus Loban (1963) used a 'weighed index of subordination' giving one point for each dependent clause, and a similar type of weighing for other subordinate features. There have also been analyses using transformational and systemic grammar. Coherence and completeness have also been included.

A recent study by Harpin *et al.* (1973) will serve as an example of the types of analysis which might be used. This study, concerned with writing development in the junior school, used the following measures: sentence length, clause length, subordination index, Loban subordination scale, use of simple sentences, use of complex sentences, use of 'uncommon' subordinate clauses (all except adverbial clauses of time and noun clause objects), the incidence of non-finite constructions in the main clause, general index of personal pronoun use, the proportion of first person and of third person uses, the proportion of personal pronoun uses other than as subject.

If we may generalize from the results of numerous studies (for summaries of the research see, e.g. McCarthy, 1954; Carroll, 1968) it seems that in *pre-school children* language maturity is marked by greater number of words, greater mean sentence length, greater variety of words and parts of speech, greater use of usual words, use of varied sentence types, greater complexity of structure, and superior coherence. However, we have to be cautious in considering these findings. Early researchers do not seem to have been sufficiently aware of the importance for its linguistic content of the situation in which the language was produced. Harpin *et al.* (1973) with junior school children find that their results agree with those of other research workers (p. 132) on the importance only of sentence length, clause length, and to a less extent on index of subordination. They point out that the most important source of variability in all measures is the *kind* of writing required.

The growth of linguistics from c. 1960 onwards, together with the advent of the tape recorder, gave impetus to the examination of the language of pre-school children, under the stimulus of Chomsky's work *Aspects of the Theory of Syntax*, 1965, particularly. McNeil produced a notable description in *The Acquisition of Language* (1970). The child was seen to move from holophrases to phrase structures (with an apparently pivot-open class grammar unlike adult systems) to the transformational rules and rules of accidence. Meaning was not considered except incidentally. After 1970, however, with the writings of such workers as Brown, Bruner, and Wells, the behaviour of the child and its meaning has been seen as prior to the language. Thus the apparent simplicity of the pivot-open class, for example, covers up a variety of different meanings. Even so in the language of pre-school children workers do not hesitate to talk about 'stages'.

After the age of four-and-a-half years Crystal discerns what, in his nomenclature, is a seventh stage which he characterizes thus: 'In short what the child has to learn after the age of five is that there are layers in the interpretation of a sentence that are not immediately apparent from the perceived form of the sentence. Sentences do not always mean what they seem to mean' (1976, p. 49). The work of Carol Chomsky (1969) demonstrates this. For five-year-olds Bill does the shovelling in 'John promised Bill to shovel the driveway' on analogy with 'John told Bill to shovel the driveway'. It is only by the age of ten years that nearly all of them understand the two constructions.

Study of the acquisition of further syntax seems to be rare. Yerrill (1976) examines a number of parenthetical, appositional and related items in various adult spoken and written texts to establish categories which he applies to the spoken and written language of 9–18-year-olds. Constructions such as non-embedded, participal, and relative clauses, and appositions, as well as parentheses proper, are included. He concludes that syntactic development, as evidenced by such items, continues into the later secondary stage, and it is the written rather than the spoken word that plays the important part in this development. But a good deal more work would have to be done in a variety of situations to see if this thesis could be sustained. The parentheses in spoken language (asides, *sotto voce* explanations, reciprocal devices) are not necessarily of the same kind as in the written language. But that such syntactic development does take place in the written language seems sufficiently demonstrated.

Stylistic Judgements
It is clear that teachers make judgements of children's writing on 'stylistic' grounds, as well as on others.

There is a difficulty of definition. Crystal and Davy (1969, pp. 9–10) distinguish four commonly occurring senses of 'style' – the language habits of a person, or of a group of people, the effectiveness of a mode of expression, and the idea of style as 'good' writing. The first two may be described largely objectively; the second two are partly evaluative. For our purposes we may perhaps equate the first two with the use of the appropriate register – the employment of a certain variety of language for a particular purpose in a particular situation. This is a feature which linguistics has sharpened up for us. The second two are derived from literary criticism, and assume a standard of 'good' or 'fine', or on the other hand of 'effective' writing – these are the ones which most often occur in teachers' judgements.

Perhaps many teachers nowadays would relate style to effectiveness, asking how successfully has the writer carried out his intention. This is of course pure Pope, 'In every work regard the writer's end' (*Essay in Criticism*, line 255). They would probably take his advice also to 'survey the WHOLE' (line 235) and, like him, be very cautious of 'fine writing'.

> Words are like leaves; and where they most abound
> Much fruit of sense beneath is rarely found
> (lines 309–10)

Nevertheless teachers' judgements, as we shall see below, still reward 'fine writing', and there is indeed sometimes a stage when young people grow intoxicated with words, which it is felt ought not to be discouraged.

Examples of judgements commonly employed is provided by Knight (1977, p. 25) who studies 'O'-Level examiners' reports:

> A few examples from the recurring phrases of commendation and reproof will indicate the consensus; 'ability in vocabulary';

'good correct style'; 'everyday slipshod speech patterns'; 'good standard of written English'; 'cogent, succinct and accurate writing'; 'graces of fancy and style'; 'distinction in content or style'; 'proper and exact use of the English language'; 'neat conclusion'.

Some of these judgements are, of course, question begging, but one is not concerned to criticize them or the assumptions behind them, merely to demonstrate that 'stylistic' judgements of a kind are in common use.

To arrange a hierarchy for style similar to that for young children's language would be a difficult and perhaps not very rewarding task. For style defined as appropriateness there could clearly be some progression – one would take it as axiomatic that the ability to employ a greater number of styles or functions is a mark of development. For style as effectiveness the criterion for success lies within the intention and communication – and there is no reason why a ten-year-old in these terms shall not be as successful as a fifteen-year-old. Style as decoration or 'fine writing' ('the graces of fancy and style') presumably indicates a certain facility with words which tends to come in adolescence rather than earlier, but it would scarcely be possible to map the stages leading to it.

Judgements of Content
There are, of course, models of human development, expressed in affective rather than cognitive terms. Perhaps the locus classicus, at least in psycho-analytical literature, is Erikson's 'Eight Ages of Man' (1965, p. 264). Each stage from birth to death is seen in terms of a polarity, from 'basic trust v. mistrust' at the 'oral sensory stage', to 'ego integrity v. despair' at 'maturity', which is the last stage of life. Obviously such a model is too comprehensive for our purposes. The two polarities relevant to the ages of schooling are 'industry v. inferiority' and 'identity v. role confusion'. In the first the child has to adjust to 'the inorganic laws of the tool world' (p. 251) – he must be able to cope, organize, to do, not merely to be done to. In the second he must have the 'accrued confidence' of one's 'inner sameness' and 'continuity of one's meaning for others' (p. 253).

The definition of 'maturity', i.e. later life, given here is clearly not one which is intended in the judgement on a 'mature style' quoted above, or on so many similar judgements in literary criticism. It is equally clearly not implied in the title of such a well-known book as Holbrook's *English for Maturity* (1961), though what *is* actually implied is uncertain, for one ransacks the book in vain for any attempt at definition. The problem is related to that of meaning of 'development' already mentioned in so far as it refers to development through language or to the meaning of the equally popular term 'growth' as in Dixon's title *Growth through English*.

Affective development is sometimes called the 'education of the emotions'. Yarlott surveys the literature and finds confusion on every side:

> In the presence of so many widely differing aims and criteria the ordinary teacher is apt to be perplexed about the purposes of emotional education. Is the basic aim to control emotions, to nourish them, to refine them, or to provide therapeutic release for inhibited feelings? Or should it be to help children to achieve depth and sincerity of emotion, to develop self awareness, and to make them more considerate for the feelings of others.
> (Yarlott, 1972, p. 3)

However, since Yarlott wrote there have been two interesting attempts to face up to the meaning of 'personal development'. Witkin (1974, p. 49) defines it in terms of 'the child's progressive mastery of new and more complex levels of sensate experience' and he is concerned to discover what this means in the practices of arts (English, drama, music, and art) teachers. Harrison's (1974) work is more closely related to the argument of this paper, in that he takes the written work of adolescents and classifies them in five stages. It would be unfair to distort his categories by a summary, but they perhaps represent one of the most significant attempts yet made to classify 'development' in the context of English teaching.

Cognitive development has received more attention than affective development. Piaget's stages – sensorimotor, preoperational, and operational (concrete and formal) – are seminal in the field. Bruner suggests a movement from the enactive, via the iconic to the symbolic. All models offered agree on a movement from an undifferentiated world to a world organized by the mind, from a world full of instances to a world related by generalities and abstractions. The hierarchy of Bloom's cognitive domain (1956) from knowledge of specifics to synthesis and evaluation follows this progress in some detail.

Even so there have been few attempts to evaluate the cognitive aspects of writing, though Peel *et al.* have assessed the cognitive judgements made by pupils of writing. Moffett's (1968) comes nearer to the line we are pursuing when he classifies discourse into four categories:

what is happening – drama – recording
what happened – narrative – reporting
what happens – exposition – generalizing
what may happen – logical argumentation – theorizing

(p. 35)

He sees this in some relationship to Bernstein's codes:

> The code differences run along the same line as the develop-
> mental shifts we have discussed; implicit to explicit; ethnocentric
> to individualistic, increasing choice, increasing consciousness
> of abstracting (speech being an object of special perceptual
> activity), increasing elaboration (p. 58).

Drawing on and developing Moffett's categories, Britton (1971) in
turn erects a hierarchy of 'transactional' categories from recording
at the bottom (writing 'what is going on *here* and *now*') to the
tautologic at the top ('the systematic combining of abstract
propositions leads to new conclusions').

It will be noted that these studies are concerned with the written
language. Attempts to judge the spoken language have mainly
been in connection with external examinations such as CSE, and
to a lesser extent 'O'-Level. Here a variety of criteria have been
employed (voice, content, fluency, reciprocity, interpretation)
though there is inevitably a strong element of impression about the
marking (Wilkinson, 1965, chapter iv). It is only in recent work on
function categories such as that of Tough with younger children
that the spoken language has been looked at for its cognitive
qualities. Thus one conversation is examined for 'strategies' such
as 'recognizing causal and dependent relationships', and 'reflecting
on events and drawing conclusions' (Tough, 1976, p. 130).

A Developmental Model for Middle School Writing

The attempt to construct a model of language development is
fraught with difficulties. To simplify matters we shall concern
ourselves only with the written, not with the spoken language,
though the work reported forms part of a larger investigation.

The difficulties lie in the variables in the communication
situation – particularly writer, audience, task, referent. The same
writer will perform inconsistently from day to day; the assumed
audience will influence the writing, one type of writing will exhibit
very different features from another (a running commentary is all
present tenses, a piece of history all past); one subject will highly
motivate one writer, bore another. Is it in fact really possible
under the circumstances to say that students *in general* at one stage
will display certain characteristics, and that at another stage
certain other characteristics? The attempt would seem worth
making, and indeed in certain areas has been made, as we have
seen. Here the discussion will concern all four areas of judgement
– linguistic, stylistic, affective, and cognitive – but, with cursory
attention to the linguistic since so much work has been devoted to
it.

The Sample
Four children, two in the first year of an 8–12 years middle school, and two in the final year, were asked to write on 'The happiest day of my life'. The pieces are as follows:

Peter:
I got up from bed and in front off me was lods of parcels I opending them, And there was a England football kit. A ball a pair of football boots I was ever so happy. Then I went down stairs and thier was a huge dinner on the table then I rember it was my bithday I had a nother supise as well my anty came round for tea and she gave me three pounds and we had a tea party. I was ever so good that night so my mum let me stay up and watch match of the day then I went to bed that was the happest day of my life.

Pauline:
I had just moved into a new house. I had no friends my sister was only about 4 years old I looked for some friends but I couldn't find any. Then I heard a noise someone was bouncing on a matrue then I looked over the wall and there I found somebody I said who are you? what is your name? she said the same to me it was my old friend I knew in play school (she is in this school now) she is called nicola Thorn. We played skipping until it was time for me to go in. I had my tea and I watched television and I went to bed I said to myself I think that was the happiest day in my life. Nicola has been one of my Greasest friends right from that day. And she sometimes breaks but with me but she soon comes running to me when she is my friend again.

Jack:
The best day of my life was when I got my bike. It was in the morning, I had just got up feeling very happy. I put my clothes on and went down stairs, I told my mum and dad that I was going up David Tregit's house. When I got there he was just having his breakfast. When he had finished we went outside and opened the shed. He had cleaned it up and had put some new things on it. he was selling it because he was getting a moped. The next day I went up again, to collect it, we went down to my house to show my dad. My dad had a very long look at it, and said 'How much will you sell it for'. '25 pounds' 'ok'. And for the rest of the day I was riding my bike feeling very happy.

Jill:
The best day of my life was at Barry island. We were all staying at butilands holiday camp. It was the last day, we woke up to the sounds of the sea crashing against the rocks. My sister and me got up early and got dressed went into the kitchen and took some money and went out. We left a note for mum and dad to say gone to get the paper and to go along the sea front. We did not wake my brother up. When we got out it was a lovely day

with the sun shinning and a cool breeze. We went out of the camp site and down on to the sand. We took our sandles of and went in to the sea it was cold but refreshing. Then we played hit but it was not very good with just two of us. Then we wrote names in the sand. Then got the paper and came back when we got back everyone was up we had breakfast then dad said Debras the greatest is she. He had seen what my sister wrote in the sand. Then we all went out and saw a realy funny fight no one got hurt then we went and bought some presents and things and went on to the beach. Had our lunch in a restruant. Went back and packed our bags. Then went to the station. we did not want to go, we walked through the fair to the station. Got on the train which was crowed it was very hot. when we got back home we had tea unpacked wtached t.v. then we went to bed. When we got in bed my sister and me talked about the day.

Analysis of Sample

Linguistic
On such a small quantity of text very little can be deduced from an analysis in terms such as we described earlier in this paper. It is perhaps worth recording, however, that the results are in general within expectation. On measures of total length the younger children write marginally less (c. 100 and 140 words) than the older (c. 150 and 260 words). The mean sentence length with the younger girl is 8 words, with the older children 9.9 and 10. The younger boy has a figure of 11 caused by the disproportionate weighing of a single sentence in a short composition. On complexity the younger children record a single subordinate clause, the older girl three, the older boy six, as well as infinitive phrases.

Stylistic
We have above defined style as appropriateness, effectiveness, and decoration.

Examples of all three types occur in the judgements of experienced teachers on the passages. Judgements on appropriateness concentrated largely on the spoken/written dimension 'has mastered the written idiom', 'sense of essay', 'a well rounded narrative', 'spoken idioms (lots of, ever so)', 'absence of preplanning (information suddenly inserted) typical of spoken language'. Jill's change into notes towards the end was taken as characteristic of the written mode.

Amongst judgements on effectiveness were: 'effective opening', 'neat conclusion', 'remembers what was said', 'gives direct words', 'economical in presentation', 'feeling for words', 'brings the incident to life', 'insight into character' (had a very long look at it –

Jack), 'sets the scene for the reader's benefit', 'variety of synonyms for "happy"'.

Judgements on decorative style were confined to the piece by Jill where the scene setting was commented on, particularly phrases such as the 'sea crashing against the rocks' and 'a lovely day with the sun shinning and a cool breeze'. Several judges saw these phrases as defects, as clichés (though not necessarily to the writer) and considered the piece to improve after this point where it was recording genuine observations rather than fulfilling expectations of an 'essay'.

It should be said that the majority of the experienced teachers judging these pieces had no difficulty in deciding which belonged to the younger and which the older children, though other criteria of judgement besides the stylistic doubtless weighed with them also.

Content – Affective

In terms of existing cognitive categories as reviewed above, these pieces do not reveal much – they are simply autobiographical reports. As such they are rooted in the concrete so that a concrete-abstract dimension is of little use in measuring them. Even so the teachers' judgements do discern differences which may be classified as cognitive – the sequencing or otherwise of events, a sense of relevance, the absence of preplanning in the younger children's work, the superior understanding of the situations described by the older children, extending to comment and explanation as appropriate.

However in terms of affective content these pieces are, as one would expect, much more revealing. Teachers' judgements (apart from question begging words like 'mature') reveal an ego/socio-centric dimension is being used ('self-involved', 'includes other people as independent entities', 'sense of audience'). There is a self/environment dimension ('she appreciates the seashore', 'he tells us where he was'). There is an implicit/explicit dimension – 'too much is assumed on the part of the reader'. There is also hinted at a simple-complex dimension ('gives the bare facts', 'awareness of what's going on', 'conscious of other people's viewpoints', 'much more relevant information', 'a sense of irony').

Using such judgements in part as a basis, an attempt was made to draw up a series of categories set down on the self/other person/other thing dimension, with the simple/complex dimension often implied under the separate headings.

The Affective Model

The self/other dimensions can be briefly characterized as follows:

A.1 *Self*

The individual's expression of his emotion and his awareness of the nature of his own feelings

A.1.1 emotion expressed (some written work very mechanical), its uniqueness, how far are these the writer's own feelings

A.1.2 emotion expressed and evaluated (e.g. 'I felt as though I was going to burst')

A.1.3 self image, awareness of how one appears or might appear (e.g. 'I looked very silly')

A.1.4 awareness of the springs and complexities of emotion (e.g. 'I suppose I must have been jealous to behave like that').

A.2 *Others*

The awareness of others both in relation to himself and as distinct identities

A.2.1 Existence of – the mere recording of other people as having been present. This is the single dimension. The following are ways in which the distinct identity of the person may be realized

A.2.2 What do they say? To record the exact words of others may be an elementary skill. Children who are not distinguishing between spoken and written registers may do so. But in any case it indicates their separateness

A.2.3 What do they think? To record the real or imagined thoughts of others

A.2.4 What do they feel? To record the real or imagined feelings of others

A.2.5 Attitudes to – from a simple expression of feeling 'I hate you' to a complex 'I didn't like her much but I'd no one else to play with'.

A.3 *Environment*

An awareness of the physical or social surroundings. On the one hand a 'restricted code' may not offer necessary context. On the other hand the environment may be a source of special stimulus

A.3.1 assumed environment

A.3.2 described or explained environment

A.3.3 environment responded to as significant or stimulating.

A.4 *Addressee*

It is often argued that writing to an unknown or not-envisaged addressee will be poorer in quality since it lacks focus. Certainly the imaginative leap into the mind of another so that one grasps what terms have meaning for him must characterize effective communication

A.4.1 addressee unknown

A.4.2 addressee defined – a person or type of person in mind

A.4.3 addressee specifically catered for, e.g. by an aside or explanation.

A.5 *Reality*
Basically this is concerned with how far a distinction is recognized between the world of phenomena, and the world of imagination, between magical and logical thinking; with how far the student's own preferences or beliefs can come to an accommodation with external reality, particularly if it is unpleasant; with how far the literal-metaphorical aspects of experience can be perceived in complexity
A.5.1 the world of fantasy/the world of reality and recognition of the two
A.5.2 the acceptance or otherwise of the world of reality
A.5.3 the recognition of the literal-metaphorical nature of reality – experiencing at more than one level.

The Model Applied

Peter
Peter is a delightful example of complete self-involvement. All the emotion is felt but in no sense evaluated. Other people are recorded as being present (A.2.1) but only just – they are entirely in a servicing role to him as bringers of gifts and bestowers of just rewards. They have no words, thoughts, feelings (A.2.2–4). Environment is assumed (A.3.1). The Addressee is unknown (A.4.1). Hold of Reality is shaky (A.5.1) – the incident has something manufactured about it – he doesn't remember until halfway through that it is his birthday. We may describe Peter then in terms of the earlier items in each category.

Pauline
Pauline, so characteristically in girls of that age, needs a 'best friend' and finds one in Nicola. She expresses her own needs (A.1.1) and meeting the other girl answers her cry from the heart – there is no self-analysis. Her awareness of the Other comes in so far as she quotes her verbatim (A.2.2), but her comment that breaking friends is inevitable but temporary shows quite a complex attitude (A.2.5). Basic details of the Environment are given (A.3.2). An especial attempt to interest the reader by the bracketed explanation (A.4.3) is to be noted. Her Reality is literal with exact details ('watched tv and went to bed') (A.5.1). Although some of Pauline's responses fit into earlier items in the categories, others indicate a greater 'maturity'.

Jack
With Jack there is direct expression of emotion (A.1.1), but much of it emerges indirectly in the tension of having to wait. In particular is he aware of the presence (A.2.1) of others, but also of their distinct identities; how the older boy keeps him waiting, and how he has cleaned up the bicycle for selling; and in particular how his Dad thinks and feels (A.2.3/4) and what he says (A.2.2). One can feel his sense of the complexity of his own feelings – his impatience, anxiety, joy (A.2.5). Environment is largely assumed (A.3.1). No Addressee is detectable, though he seems to expect an interested one. The piece is very much Reality-based (A.5.2) – 'Dad's very long look' speaks volumes. As far as the categories are concerned, Jack has more of the later items.

Jill
Jill does not on the whole express emotion directly. She is very much aware Others have to be taken into account – baby brother, and particularly mum and dad so they will not be anxious (A.2.1). Particularly insightful is her quotation of dad's remark ('Debras the greatest is she?') which shows a real perception of his wit and character (A.2.2–A.2.4) – indeed the appreciation of the two levels of meaning in the irony indicates more than this (A.2.5). Jill is the girl who responds positively to the Environment (A.3.3) and by implication keeps the needs of the Addressee well in mind (A.4.2) with details and explanations (in effect so that mum and dad would not be worried). This piece is a literal description of Reality; perhaps stylistically there are too many details: but the two levels of meaning in her father's irony indicate her appreciation that all things are not what they seem. For largely the same reasons as Jack's, Jill's writing is a much more mature piece than those of Peter and Pauline.

Discussion
The affective model is clearly very imperfect, but in these four cases it does at least succeed in differentiating the writing of the students on these grounds alone, if it is accepted that the polarities offered are legitimate ones.

It may of course be argued that the model is open to many objections. For example an objective or transactional piece of writing may be largely free of features to which it applies. But this is only to say that the 'maturity' of transactional writing need not be, judged by the same criteria – one would need in part at least a cognitive model. The work discussed here is part of ongoing research which is attempting to draw up criteria of development in cognitive and affective, as well as stylistic and literary terms, for both the spoken and written language. For the description of a representative sample of the work of any one student, criteria from all four areas would apply at one point or another. For reasons of manageability it has only been possible to outline the application of one set of criteria (the affective) to one language mode (the written), and to one style of writing (the autobiographical), but perhaps this has given some indication of the potentialities of the line of enquiry.

Transmission and Interpretation
By Douglas Barnes and Denis Shemilt

Editor's Introduction

It is well known that words have both a denotative and a connotative meaning. The word 'father', for example, designates a class of persons and a particular relationship; it also raises associations and emotions which may vary considerably from person to person. Even the referential meanings of a word depend upon agreed definitions, but connotations are freer floating partly idiosyncratic and partly shaped by culture ('red' having associations of 'golden' or 'value' in Russia rather than 'anger', 'embarrassment', 'violence' or 'radical').

So when we come to examine teachers' attitudes to aspects of the curriculum there are two main difficulties. First, an attitude is a convenient construct not a commodity or behaviour and so can be measured or observed only by what people say they will do or by what actions they take. A famous study by La Prière (1934) showed that intentions may be radically different from actual behaviour. The second problem is that words mean different things to different people. For example, 'finding out for oneself' may be interpreted as 'obtaining ready made information from books' or 'using one's own language to make sense of and to order experience'. But these different interpretations are likely to lead to very different views about the curriculum, about the business of teaching and learning and about the learners themselves.

Barnes and Shemilt in the paper which follows investigate teachers' attitudes to writing in schools. Their results show a pattern of attitudes into categories which they label *Transmission* and *Interpretation*. They suggest that the 'Transmission' teacher sees writing as an exercise in memorizing information and checking what a pupil has learned. Such teachers therefore assess and correct but tend not to make constructive comments or utilize pupil's writing as a means of communication or further learning. If, as the authors suggest, 'a substantial body' of teachers view writing in this way then certain consequences follow for their pupils. First, they may not get the chance to use writing to make sense of their world and to explore new experiences. Second, they may not receive the advice, help and encouragement they require as learners.

Barnes and Shemilt therefore touch on crucial areas which may not be easy to research but which have considerable implications for learning and teaching. Implicit beliefs held by teachers about communication in their classrooms affect the ways in which learners are able to use language.

B.W.

Abstract
Secondary school teachers' responses to questions about the setting of written tasks to pupils were categorized and shown to fall upon a dimension called Transmission-Interpretation. Half of the variance accounted for by this dimension was related to the subject taught. It is then suggested that the Transmission-Interpretation dimension could be used to relate the teacher's view of what constitutes knowledge with his expectations about the learner's and the teacher's classroom roles.

1. Introduction

EDUCATION is a kind of communication. Although this communication constitutes a large part of every teacher's professional activity, we cannot expect teachers to be highly aware of its nature. Like everyone else, they are more aware of the people they communicate with, and of their own purposes, than of the act of communicating. Nevertheless teachers do hold views about classroom communication and its functions, though these views tend to be intuitive and inexplicit. This study was designed to find how teachers differed in their tacit assumptions about classroom communication.

Teachers' attitudes to speech may have great influence on learning, yet these are likely to be less well articulated than their attitudes to writing, partly because our educational tradition has put much greater weight on writing than on speech. It was hoped that by asking secondary teachers about the written work which they set, it would be possible to throw light upon teachers' implicit beliefs about communication and learning as a whole.

2. Teachers' Responses
The teachers in eleven secondary schools were asked to complete a questionnaire. The schools were chosen to sample comprehensive, secondary modern and secondary grammar schools, and to sample boys', girls', and mixed schools.

	Boys	*Girls*	*Mixed*
Comprehensive	0	0	2
Secondary Modern	1	2	2
Secondary Grammar	1	2	1

Teachers were asked to have a third year group (13-year-olds) in mind in answering the questions. An attempt was made through the head teachers to persuade all who taught a third-year class to complete a questionnaire, even though some would be nil returns. Of the 246 questionnaires returned by teachers, only 125 have been used. Nil returns from teachers of subjects not involving writing were omitted. It was decided to omit returns from mathematicians, since it proved impossible to distinguish those for whom 'writing' meant using mathematical symbols. A number of teachers had failed to complete one or other of the four main questions, and these too had to be omitted for reasons which will become apparent.

The main section of the questionnaire contained these four items:

1. This question relates to why you set written work, and what value you believe it to have for your pupils. Please fill in one or more of the following, according to the number of different answers which are true for you.
   When I set written work I do so primarily because...................
2. This question relates to what you think is most important to bear in mind when you set written work. Please fill in as many of the following as necessary.
   When I set written work I usually make sure that ....
3. This question relates to what you do with pupils' work when they have handed it in. Please fill in one or more of:
   When I mark written work I usually take care to ....
4. If, after taking in and 'marking' work you usually hand it back to pupils with just a few informal comments please put a tick here ☐
   If, under certain circumstances you make further use of pupils' written work please indicate this by filling in one or more of these sentences:
   I often ....

Spaces were provided so that, as they chose, teachers could give one to four answers to each of the questions. All answers were to be treated as of equal importance, and their order ignored.

The questions were deliberately vague, since in attributing a meaning to them the respondent would be compelled to utilize his own covert assumptions about written work. This meant however that the respondents' replies had to be interpreted and categorized, and this proved to be the most delicate part of the study. We began with hypotheses about what patterns the responses would fall into, and these hypotheses gave us the first set of categories for analyzing responses. When all the responses had been allocated to one or other of these categories, the results were factor-analyzed to find whether they were random or fell into a pattern. On the first factor analysis there were signs of pattern but these were not very clear-cut so the categories were rearranged, and a second set arrived at by subdividing or combining the categories of Set One. This was done twice, and the third set of categories showed a very clear pattern in the responses. Thus the factor analysis was used as a device for clarifying a pattern already hypothesized.

Fig. 1. *Categories used in Interpreting Responses*

Question 1

Reasons for Setting Written Work	Percentage Teachers		Loading on FPC
Recording	36%	Group Two	(−.43)
Acquisition of Information	44%	Group Two	(−.42)
*Feedback	54%		(−.12)
*Acquisition of Skills	39%		(.04)
Cognitive Development	30%	Group One	(.60)
Personal Development	24%	Group One	(.82)

Question 2

What Teachers Keep in Mind When Setting Written Work			
Product	26%	Group Two	(−.44)
Task	54%	Group Two	(−.35)
*Oral	30%		(.01)
*Objectives	18%		(.06)
*Abilities	26%		(.19)
Context	22%	Group One	(.78)

Question 3

How Teachers Receive Written Work (i.e. 'marking')			
Assessment	41%	Group Two	(−.47)
*Errors	76%		(−.16)
Replies and Comments	21%	Group One	(.61)
Concern for Pupil's Attitude	30%	Group One	(.63)

Question 4

The Use Made of Written Work			
No or Minimal Follow-up	69%	Group Two	(−.32)
Corrections	37%	Group Two	(−.45)
*Supplementary Teaching	36%		(.12)
Future Teaching	22%	Group One	(.70)
Publish	25%	Group One	(.64)

Fig. 1 lists the third set of categories and indicates the percentage of teachers making a response in each category. Those categories marked with an asterisk were randomly distributed, that is they were equally likely to be given by any teacher. For example, 54 per cent of teachers valued written work as a source of *Feedback* about pupils' understanding of the work they were doing, and 76 per cent mentioned the indicating of *Errors* as being part of the function of marking. No particular pattern was found in the distribution of these two categories of response, nor of the other five marked with an asterisk.

All of the other responses were very clearly patterned however. The factor analysis showed that they loaded either positively or negatively on the First Principal Component (F.P.C.): no other significant factor emerged. That is, the 125 teachers of our sample fell into a clear-cut pattern along one dimension, which will be called the Transmission-Interpretation dimension. (The nature of the dimension will become clear once the categories have been explained.)

TRANSMISSION   INTERPRETATION

<————————————————————————————>

Group Two categories	Group One categories
(Negative loadings on	(Positive loadings on
F.P.C.)	F.P.C.)

This means that any teacher who makes a response which falls into one of the categories which have been called Group Two (in Fig. 1) will tend to make other responses in Group Two, and will tend not to make responses in Group One. Similarly a teacher who makes one response in Group One is likely to make others, and to avoid responses in Group Two. A high loading such as 0.82 for Personal Development means that a teacher whose response falls in that category is highly likely to choose only other Group One responses, and that it is extremely unlikely to be chosen by a teacher with mainly Group Two responses. A lower loading such as -0.32 for No or Minimal Follow-Up shows that although it is mainly associated with other Group Two responses, there are cases where it is used by a teacher who mainly gives Group One responses.

Thus we are able to say that teachers' responses to the four questions are on the whole systematic, and that they fall somewhere along a dimension which runs from purely Group Two responses to purely Group One responses. We shall say that teachers who give mainly Group Two responses have a Trans-mission view of classroom communication, and that those who give mainly Group One responses have an Interpretation view of it. To understand the nature of this dimension from Transmission to Interpretation it will be necessary to look closely at the categories into which teachers' responses were sorted.

3. Group One Categories (Interpretation)
Cognitive Development. Responses in this category indicated that teachers saw writing as a means of persuading pupils to think for themselves, including learning to think deductively, and learning

to correlate and interpret information. They related to the development of cognitive powers, in contrast to the learning of particular content or skills. Examples are, 'They need to discipline themselves to think and write coherently'; 'It is necessary for a thorough understanding, to correlate information on paper'; 'This increases their powers of deduction and perception'.

Personal Development. Responses in this group centred upon the idea that writing was a means by which pupils developed awareness of themselves and the world they live in. Typical of these responses is: 'Through writing, using one's imagination and describing real experiences, can often come a deeper awareness of the world around one and one's place in it.' Other related responses in this category included concern with pupils' motives in writing, respect for the pupils as a person, and the wish to learn about pupils' own views and responses to experience. Examples of these latter include, 'It may be an opportunity for the child to do something on his own without friends or teachers present'; 'I desire to stimulate new interests among the class'; 'I wish to discover their personal response to the work it has arisen from'.

Context. Into this category were placed responses which showed awareness that pupils do not write in a social vacuum, but are influenced by aspects of the context in which they write. This context includes the audience which the writer is addressing, the purpose which he envisages, the preliminary experiences and discussions in which audience, purpose and topic have been defined, the range of choices open, and the physical and social conditions under which they write. This category included responses such as: 'There is no shortage of either ideas discussed in class or source material (filmstrips, books, etc.)'; 'The stimulus has been such that every child in a mixed ability group feels able to write on a given subject.'

Replies and Comments. Responses which indicated that teachers tried to give a reply to what their pupils had written fell into this category. It did not include comments on the standard of the work or comments correcting errors, which were categorized as Assessment and Errors respectively. Reference to individual discussion with pupils were included here. Examples include: 'Write a personal advice to the pupil'; 'Make additions to half-developed ideas.'

Concern for Pupil's Attitude. Responses in this category show teachers who are concerned about the pupil's attitude to the task he is attempting, and see this as affecting how he will write, e.g. 'Provide a comment which is constructive and as encouraging as possible.'

Future Teaching. This category contrasts with 'Corrections' and 'Supplementary Teaching' and refers to using what pupils had contributed in their writing as a springboard for a new piece of work, as in 'Use individual studies to stimulate further group or class projects.' (When teachers wrote of giving lessons over to the further study of the subject matter these responses were categorized as 'Supplementary Teaching'.)

Publish. Teachers whose responses fell into this category showed interest in having their pupils write for a wider audience, and mentioned ways of publishing pupils' writing: 'Have a few differently treated pieces of work read out to the class'; 'Occasionally put good work on display in the History room'.

4. Group Two Categories (Transmission)

Recording. Responses were placed in this category when the teacher indicated that he saw writing as a means of storing knowledge. One example of this was: 'They will need the notes for revision purposes at a later date'.

Acquisition of Information. The responses in this category were those which connected writing with accumulating or memorizing information. Some implied memorizing, such as 'To learn facts' and 'To facilitate later recall' but others saw writing as a means for making information gathering the pupil's responsibility: 'I want to accustom the children to extracting information from books, documents, etc.'.

Product. Some teachers, when asked what they kept in mind when they set written work, showed by their replies that their attention was primarily directed towards the characteristics of the writing that they wanted their pupils to produce – the content, presentation and accuracy of the work – as against any awareness of writing as communication in a social context. Examples of responses in this category are: 'Factual details are correct' and 'The spellings of Geographical names and terms are copied from the board'.

Task. This category of response implies that the teacher is viewing writing more as the carrying out of a predetermined exercise than as communication between people. It includes responses that refer to the need to ensure that the task is suitable, that pupils are clear about its nature, and that it will be carried out in the manner required. Examples are: (When I set written work I usually make sure that) 'They know exactly what the question is'; 'They work to a definite plan'; 'They do it'. Responses in this category imply that the kind of writing done is highly controlled by the teacher.

Assessment. Included in this category were those responses in which 'marking' meant either numerical grading or the enforcing of predetermined standards. Two examples illustrating these are: 'Record the marks before handing back the books', and 'Point out to careless pupils that written work must be well presented and in good English'.

No or Minimal Follow-Up. Most of the responses in this category came from teachers who indicated that they seldom or never made any further use of pupils' writings after marking them. We added to these a small group of responses from teachers who mentioned using pupils' writings to demonstrate to the class the importance of high standards: this latter group of responses seems to indicate that no use is made of the writing as a message, but only as a model of good or bad practice. (E.g. 'Sometimes use books – without warning their owners – to show exactly what I expect of a diagram or homework.')

Corrections. Responses in this category indicated that the teacher used lesson time for pointing out errors of content and expression in the writing which his pupils had done. 'Take a mistake that has been made by many children and spend time explaining its correct use.' (This category was carefully distinguished from Supplementary Teaching which implied a more general re-examination of the topic written about, and Future Teaching which implied using what pupils had written as a springboard for new work.)

5. Contrasting Stereotypes

In order to interpret the results we now intend to present them in terms of two imaginary teachers, an Interpretation teacher and a Transmission teacher. These two contrasting stereotypes may make clearer the significance of these results, provided the reader keeps in mind that these two teachers are artificial constructions. It will be necessary to extrapolate from teachers' attitudes to writing in order to reconstruct their attitudes to knowledge and to the act of learning. That is, this part of the report should be read as having a more hypothetical status than the earlier parts have.

The Interpretation teacher sees writing as a means by which the writer can take an active part in his own learning: as pupils write they can – under certain circumstances – reshape their view of the world, and extend their ability to think rationally about it. He believes that the social context in which the writing takes place will partly determine whether it performs this function. He tries to ensure that his pupils see the written work as relevant to their own purposes, and sees writing as contributing to a dialogue in which he plays a crucial part. He therefore writes replies as well as comments, gives his pupils' writings the added status of wider publication, and allows it to influence the direction of lessons, thus encouraging pupils to play an active part in the shaping of knowledge.

The Transmission teacher on the other hand, is primarily aware of writing as a means of measuring the pupil's performance against his own expectations and criteria. When he sets written work his attention is focused upon the kind of writing he wants, so that he is careful to ensure that his pupils understand what he wants of them. He assumes that it is his business to define the task for his pupils, and to provide them with information about their success in measuring up to his standards. He values writing as a record to which his pupils can later look back, but assumes that they will address it to a general disembodied reader rather than to themselves or to him. He believes his main responsibility in receiving pupils' writing to be the awarding of a grade. Usually he continues with the lessons which he has already planned, and does not refer back to pupils' previous work, which he regards as completed when he hands back his assessment to pupils. On the occasions when he does mention pupils' work in class he uses it either as a means of correcting errors in content or manner, or as an opportunity to emphasize to the class the need to preserve high standards in written work. On the whole he regards writing as a record for future reference rather than as a means of learning; when he does think of writing as contributing to the learning of his subject it tends to be in terms of the memorizing of factual information.

Interpretation teachers tend to view writing as a productive dialogue between pupil and teacher, in which the pupil uses language to reshape knowledge for himself. Transmission teachers tend to view writing as an opportunity for pupils to memorize what has been taught to them, and as a means of finding out whether they have done so. It is clear that these different attitudes to the functioning of writing are related to other sets of assumptions about the nature of classroom learning, curriculum content, standards, and so on. Our enquiry into writing has, in fact, allowed us to observe one aspect of the processes by which teachers sustain their own definition of situation with respect to what goes on in their classrooms.

One unexpected result deserves comment here. Nearly half of the responses categorized as Acquisition of Information referred to the use of writing as a means of persuading pupils to find out information for themselves. Such an emphasis on 'finding out for oneself' sounds at first as if it would be likely to be chosen by an Interpretation teacher, yet here it occurs in an undeniably Transmission category. We can offer only guesses by way of explanation. It does seem that many of these responses interpret 'finding out for oneself' as obtaining ready made information from books. This may indicate that Transmission teachers take over the current 'liberal' phrases about 'finding out for oneself' but reinterpret them in a Transmission manner, so that the finding out does not involve the pupil in using language to reinterpret for himself whatever it is he does find out. If this is a fair interpretation, it throws light upon one way in which teachers reinterpret curricular innovations in the light of their existing conceptions of knowledge and learning, and thereby confound the innovators' intentions.

6. The Remaining Categories

Those categories of response which do not appear in Groups One and Two (Sections 3 and 4 of this article) are those which any teacher is equally likely to make. These require only brief summary.

Abilities. Responses in this category express teachers' concern to relate written tasks to pupils' abilities.

Supplementary Teaching. These responses refer to lessons in which pupils' writings act as the focus for continued work on the same topics.

Acquisition of Skills. The development of abilities and skills such as 'the writing of a report'.

Relation to Oral Discussion. This includes responses which indicate concern that written work should be related to other activities, especially to preceding discussions. (When discussion was mentioned as the exploring of possible options in writing this was categorized as 'Context'.)

Objectives. The subject set fits in with the teacher's purposes.

Feedback. Written work was set in order to obtain information about the success of a lesson, or about pupils' progress and understanding.

Errors. Responses indicated that teachers took 'marking' to include the indication or correction of errors in content or in the use of the conventions.

No reader will be surprised at the presence of the Feedback category amongst these general categories: the satisfaction of teaching depends largely on gaining from pupils some impression of how well they are learning. The three categories 'Abilities', 'Objectives' and 'Relationship to Oral Discussion' are equally easy to account for, since they all appear to relate to the teacher's pride in the efficient planning of his work.

The presence here of three other categories however is not quite so obvious and therefore deserves consideration.

'Acquisition of Skills' and 'Supplementary Teaching' may well be represented here partly because of the difficulties inherent in categorizing replies to an open-ended questionnaire. Over a third of the teachers indicated an interest in writing as a means of improving pupils' control of language, but this could mean widely different kinds of learning.

The last of these general categories to call for attention is 'Errors'; three-quarters of the teachers thought that it was their responsibility to correct mistakes in their pupils' writings, although only a third of these wrote that they made corrections as a follow-up with the full class. Three-quarters is a very large proportion and represents a great deal of teachers' time. One wonders whether such an expenditure of time contributes proportionately to pupils' learning, or whether teachers should put more emphasis on Comments and Replies, which only a fifth of the teachers thought important enough to mention.

7. Assumptions about Classroom Communication

The following diagram summarizes what has been presented so far.

TRANSMISSION   INTERPRETATION

<-->

Recording	} *Function*	{ Cognitive Development
Acquisition of Information		Personal Development
Product	} *Awareness*	{ Context
Task		Concern for Pupil's Attitude
Assessment	} *Responses*	{ Replies and Comments
No or Minimal Follow-up		Future Teaching
Corrections		Publish

Contrary beliefs about knowledge, and about what constitutes teaching and learning, seem to underlie these views of classroom communication. The following is a hypothetical reconstruction of these beliefs:

The Transmission teacher . . .

(1) believes knowledge to exist in the form of public disciplines which include content and criteria of performance;

(2) values the learners' performances insofar as they conform to the criteria of the discipline;

(3) perceives the teacher's task to be the evaluation and correction of the learner's performance, according to criteria of which he is the guardian;

(4) perceives the learner as an uninformed acolyte for whom access to knowledge will be difficult since he must qualify himself through tests of appropriate performance.

The Interpretation teacher . . .

(1) believes knowledge to exist in the knower's ability to organize thought and action;

(2) values the learners' commitment to interpreting reality, so that criteria arise as much from the learner as from the teacher;

(3) perceives the teacher's task to be the setting up of a dialogue in which the learner can reshape his knowledge through interaction with others;

(4) perceives the learner as already possessing systematic and relevant knowledge, and the means of reshaping that knowledge.

This interpretation seems to bear some relationship to Bernstein's theoretical constructs, 'classification' and 'framing'. It suggests that a Transmission teacher's view of his subject matter as public, and as clearly differentiated from everyday knowledge and from other subjects, will tend to accompany the relative exclusion of pupils from the power to formulate knowledge. Similarly it suggests that an Interpretation teacher, who perceives little or no barrier between school knowledge and everyday knowledge, will tend to allow his pupils to have some part in determining what counts as knowledge in his lessons. Thus teachers' assumptions about classroom communication provide a framework in which we can understand how beliefs about knowledge relate to the role assigned to pupils in learning.

Who then were the teachers who leaned towards an Interpretation or a Transmission view of classroom communication? Each teacher's responses were reduced to a single index which indicated where the teacher stood upon the Transmission-Interpretation dimension. A positive index represented an Interpretation view, and a negative index represented a Transmission view. (This constitutes the vertical scale of Fig. 2.) The teachers were then grouped according to the subject they taught; this made it possible to see whether teachers of the same subject tended to have similar views. The pattern of scores in the subject groups is displayed in Fig. 2.

The block for each subject represents not the full range of indices, but an estimate of where the central two-thirds of those teachers fall. To take Biology as an example, there is a two-to-one chance that any particular Biology teacher will fall within the narrow range of indices shown by the Biology block. It is clear from Fig. 2 that the Biology teachers in this sample were very alike in their views, and that the Physics teachers too were like one another. There was a little wider range amongst teachers of Languages and of Chemistry. Geography teachers were the least homogeneous, but teachers of History, R.E. and English showed almost as wide a scatter. Thus we have here a measure of the extent to which different subjects tend to constrain teachers' views: the Sciences and Languages place stronger constraints upon their teachers than do most arts subjects. One might guess that the exceptionally wide latitude amongst Geography teachers is related to the fact that in some colleges and universities Geography is treated as a science and in others as an arts subject.

If instead of looking at the dispersal within each subject, we compare the mean indices for the different subjects, a different pattern emerges. The means for most subjects (from Biology to History in Fig. 2) lie within a relatively narrow range in the Transmission half of the dimension, whereas the mean for

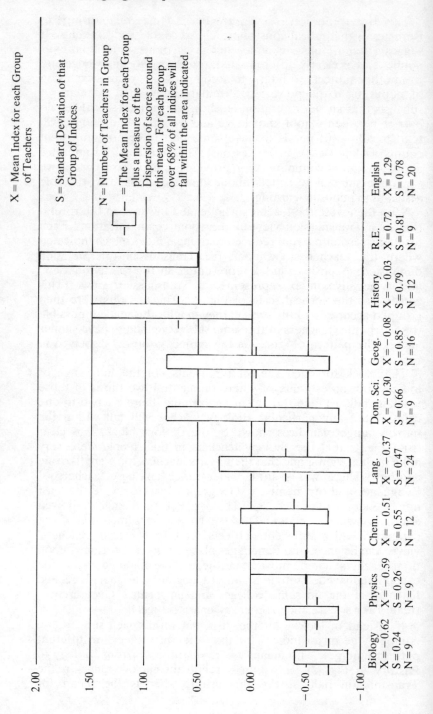

Fig. 2. Indices on Interpretation – Transmission Dimension

X = Mean Index for each Group of Teachers

S = Standard Deviation of that Group of Indices

N = Number of Teachers in Group

⊢—⊣ = The Mean Index for each Group plus a measure of the Dispersion of scores around this mean. For each group over 68% of all indices will fall within the area indicated.

English	R.E.	History	Geog.	Dom. Sci.	Lang.	Chem.	Physics	Biology
X = 1.29	X = 0.72	X = -0.03	X = -0.08	X = -0.30	X = -0.37	X = -0.51	X = -0.59	X = -0.62
S = 0.78	S = 0.81	S = 0.79	S = 0.85	S = 0.66	S = 0.47	S = 0.55	S = 0.26	S = 0.24
N = 20	N = 9	N = 12	N = 16	N = 9	N = 24	N = 12	N = 9	N = 9

Religious Education, and still more the mean for English, shows these two subjects to lie well out on the Interpretation end of the dimension.

Representing the indices in this way, however, may over-emphasize the effect of subject commitments upon teachers' attitudes to communication. The blocks in Fig. 2 are mere indications of dispersion, not the limits of dispersion. A third of the teachers in the sample do *not* fall within the block for their subject, so that we may have Interpretation scientists and Transmission English teachers. In fact, only 49 per cent of the variance in the factor scores is accounted for by the subject taught; the other half must be accounted for by the values and beliefs that teachers have brought with them from other aspects of their personal histories. Teachers are not mere puppets of an academic discipline. (This figure, and the indices represented in Fig. 2, have been shown to be significant at $< p.01$.)

One of the most notable overall findings is the large proportion of teachers who made responses which fell in certain of the Transmission categories:

Task	54%
Acquisition of information	44%
Assessment	41%
No follow up	69%
Corrections	37%

Let us add to these two general categories which received responses from the largest proportion of teachers:

Feedback	54%
Errors	76%

A substantial body of teachers thus see writing more as a task set to their pupils than as either a communication between two human beings or an opportunity for the learner to explore new material. They value it highly as a means of memorizing information and as a source of feedback about how much their pupils remember and understand. They believe that their task when they receive pupils' work is primarily to correct errors and assess it, and they tend thereafter to hand the work back without further comment.

We wish to question whether this complex of attitudes deserves its popularity; it may be that some teachers hold these opinions without full awareness of their implications for pupils' learning. On the basis of our own educational values we doubt whether the acquisition of information should be valued so highly as it seems to be. We ourselves would put greater emphasis on helping pupils to think for themselves. For us, the major surprise in our results was the presence of 'Cognitive Development' at the Interpretation end of the dimension: we should have expected all teachers to value thinking highly, and not only the minority of Interpretation teachers. It is possible that some teachers see thinking as determined by inherited intelligence, and not in terms of strategies which it is their business to develop within the framework of their subjects. Musgrove and Taylor in their book *Society and the Teacher's Role* surmise that current educational theories 'have removed the emphasis in teaching from intellectual exchange to social relationship'. Our evidence would seem to lead in a contrary direction. It is precisely those teachers in our sample who value social relationships who also value intellectual exchange. What the Transmission teachers, on the other hand, value is the memorizing of established knowledge.

Next let us put beside the 30 per cent who mentioned Cognitive Development the 24 per cent of teachers who thought that writing contributed to their pupils' personal development. If half of our teachers do not understand that writing is a means by which pupils can make sense of the world, and see it only as a source of feedback or a means of recording and memorizing information, this shows a radical ignorance of the nature of language and its functioning in learning. We regard this as a serious inadequacy in teachers' understanding of the means available for carrying out their teaching tasks, so serious that it merits urgent action by those responsible for initial and in-service training.

The use of language is not a skill like swimming which once learnt can be applied wherever there is water. Writing is a social activity, and depends on our sense of the social relationships we are taking part in. Thus it is important for teachers to see to it that pupils perceive the topic for writing as being within their competence, that they envisage various real audiences for their writing, and that they understand its purpose. Writing to be an effective tool of learning needs to be more than a routine exercise, and to become an act of communication. In analysing our results we interpreted the category called 'Context' very liberally, including in it references to preliminary discussions and to the physical environment for writing. In spite of this liberality only 22 per cent of teachers made responses in this category. Similarly only 21 per cent made responses in the 'Comments and Replies' category; this is relevant because an important part of making classroom writing into an act of communication is to see to it that communications are replied to. Of similar significance is the group of 22 per cent who utilized pupils' writing as a springboard for later lessons. It seems that about a fifth of our teachers understood how much can be gained by making written work into a dialogue.

By now we have betrayed our own bias: we are clearly Interpretation teachers. While we respect Transmission teachers' regard for their specialist subject and emphasis on its proper standards, we think it misguided to be so aware of one's final academic goals as to underrate the part to be played by pupils in reaching them.

ACKNOWLEDGEMENT
We are indebted to members of H.M. Inspectorate for engaging the help of appropriate schools.

Teaching English as a Foreign Language and Mother Tongue Teaching: Some Parallels

By J. E. McDonough and S. H. McDonough

Editor's Introduction

The perspectives on language contained in the contents of this book demonstrate the importance of language in education in two main respects. Firstly, language is seen as an important means by which a learner makes sense of experience, orders, and reorganizes his world. Secondly, attention is drawn to the communicative function of language with implications for helping learners to communicate meaning in talk and writing and to understand others through listening and reading.

The teaching of English as a mother tongue and the teaching of English as a foreign language have both been guided by these perspectives; however, there is sometimes a tendency to see these areas of activity as entirely separate.

The McDonoughs, in the paper which follows, accept that there are specific problems and methods which relate to particular teaching situations, but their main concern is to explore those aspects of both fields where it would be profitable to share approaches, methods, materials, and philosophies. They examine historical and psychological parallels and the functional approach to language which has influenced both mother-tongue teaching and foreign language learning. There is indeed a similarity between the 'Language Across the Curriculum' approach which considers the role of English in secondary school subjects and the analysis of required study skills on which a good deal of English as a foreign language teaching is based.

It may be wise to assume as the McDonoughs do that differences are ones of degree rather than of kind until (and if) it can be shown that the processes of learning for the two categories of student are significantly different. Their paper then contains implications for the teaching of language to both native and foreign speakers and for the teaching of English throughout the world.

B.W.

Abstract

This article discusses current parallel developments in the teaching of English as a foreign language and as a mother tongue. The authors suggest that, while each teaching situation has its own unique problems and procedures, concern for the communicative function of language has come to be central to both, and that therefore philosophies, problems and in some cases materials can be shared with profit. The paper discusses the use of communicative function, as an integrating principle for syllabus design, and the related issue of study skills and their general ability across the curriculum. Some problems encountered by practitioners in both fields are compared, such as the possibility that different psychological processes are used by the two types of learner, and the conflicts inherent in the teacher's role.

A T first glance the teaching of English as the mother tongue in schools (MTT) (as well as, more recently, in the context of adult literacy), and programmes in English as a foreign language (TEFL), particularly at tertiary level, have little in common. It is the aim of this article, however, to suggest that this lack of mutual relevance is only apparent. An examination of developments in each field reveals considerable areas of overlap at various levels of decision, from very general patterns of thinking, to aspects of methodological principle and procedure, to the design of materials and views of language on which this depends. It will also be suggested here that there are more concrete implications for actual materials and pedagogical techniques. To assume that there is not overlap would be to regard each of these two pedagogical 'disciplines' as running along its own separate tracks, and thus to subscribe at least implicitly to the view that the different areas of language teaching/learning should be compartmentalized.

Three notes of caution should be sounded at the outset. Firstly, we wish only to set out some of our perceptions as to developments in each field, and not to prescribe the procedures of one as a remedy for the other. However, we write from professional involvement in TEFL and only peripheral involvement in MTT, and this fact is obviously liable to bias the nature of our perceptions. Secondly, 'TEFL' and 'MTT' are obviously not monolithic concepts; each has its internal distinctions and tensions, and there are important senses in which questions of overlap and relevance are also significant within each field. Thirdly, although the aim here is to emphasize similarities, it is not the intention to claim that there are no differences requiring entirely independent sets of decisions and based on different types of constraints.

1. Historical Parallels

Historically, though not necessarily simultaneously and with identical emphasis, TEFL and MTT have had many preoccupations in common, and have gone through rather similar stages of acceptance and rejection of various approaches. This process sometimes gives the appearance of being built up on sets of polarizations and oppositions. Most practitioners in each area know that the situation is considerably more subtle than this; however, representation in these terms is probably valid to a certain extent, and is helpful in highlighting parallels.

Macmillan (1976), for example, categorizes the major influences on TEFL chronologically as:

(a) literature,
(b) logic,
(c) linguistics (by which he means structural linguistics, in the first instance),
(d) language in use.

Firstly, with reference to, (a) Strevens (1971), in a contribution to the debate in that area of TEFL labelled 'English for Special Purposes' (ESP), similarly points out the invalidity of the claim of the primacy of literary studies in many areas of language teaching. In TEFL, the case for the demotion of literature has largely been made – outside the domain of specialist literary courses – but is still being hotly debated in MTT. (This point will be taken up in a different context below.) Secondly, and with reference to (c) above, any claims that the teaching of grammar in either TEFL or MTT should have primacy, and should constitute the defining factor in a syllabus, are losing ground, though this almost certainly happened earlier in MTT than in TEFL. Thirdly, MTT has since been through a period where the emphasis was placed firmly on the freedom of creativity as opposed to the prescriptiveness of formal grammatical knowledge. This view clearly still holds, but a new polarization appears to be crystallizing from criticisms of 'creativity' in some quarters. Doughty (1974), for instance, tends to prefer the concept of 'ordered' over that of 'creative' (though it is important to note that by 'ordered' he does not mean 'structured' in any traditional grammatical sense), and states: 'There is no doubt in my mind that the effective development of the progressive consensus approach [non-prescriptive; creative] is hindered by its lack of a properly linguistic perspective on language' (p. 25). Again, it will be seen later that he is not referring to knowledge of a formal grammatical system, but to the communicative properties of language systematically investigated. Moreover, the *Bullock Report* (1975) is likewise unsympathetic not only to the teaching of grammar exercises, but also to 'creativity', if this means that 'the forms of language can be left to look after themselves' (Chapter 11). Finally, TEFL has not really been through a phase emphasizing the importance of 'creativity' in quite the same way, though some research has been carried out on programmes which minimize teacher interference. This research, however, is relatively peripheral; it is, rather, the current functional perspective mentioned above that is particularly crucial in all aspects of TEFL at the moment. (One should not, of course, overlook the close parallels with work in foreign language teaching, though discussion of these parallels is outside the scope of the present article.)

The aim of this section has been to show, albeit superficially and with considerable oversimplification, that the developments and changes enumerated above in orientation to both major areas of language teaching under discussion raise questions both as to the nature of language, pedagogically speaking, and the nature of curricula and syllabuses. We will now turn in more detail to some of those aspects that are currently most under scrutiny.

2. Language Teaching and Language Function

It has already been indicated that, in both TEFL and MTT, there is a move towards functional analyses of language and their pedagogical implications. This move is particularly strong in TEFL at the present time, and the bandwagon effect naturally brings with it the danger that the 'functional approach' will be regarded as a universal panacea. Some attempts are being made to redress the balance (see, e.g. Johnson, 1977), and the point is only raised as a caveat.

Initially set out in the context of the Council of Europe's (1973) Unit Credit Scheme for foreign language teaching, Wilkins' proposals for 'notional – functional' syllabuses have had considerable influence in the planning of programmes and the development of teaching materials. His basic tenet is that grammatical syllabuses do not adequately take account of language in its social context, and of the purposes for which the language is being learnt; hence we should, as teachers and programme planners, pay more attention to developing our learners' '*communicative* competence'. The 'categories of communicative function' proposed by Wilkins are not formless, but quite highly structured and include, for example, the use of language to inform/persuade/warn/suggest/request. (A much fuller list, with discussion, can be found in Wilkins, 1976, Chapter 2.). He further draws a distinction between synthetic and analytic approaches. The former gives rise to a syllabus where language is learnt as a set of discrete, usually structural, items; this is relatively inefficient and incomplete since the learner will not necessarily know anything of the functional interdependence of the items learnt. The analytic approach, as will be seen from the very short list of examples above, is based in the first instance on an analysis of behaviour; thus grammatical items are in no way deleted from a syllabus, but they become dependent on a prior analysis of communicative categories. More realistically, too, it can be shown that there is not a one : one relation between form and function.

The 'notional approach', then (and it must be stated that labels tend to be used differently according to the writer), contains the centrally important point that it is, in the first instance, non-linguistic in any narrow sense. It is concerned with what a speaker of any language 'knows' (consciously or unconsciously) about how to use his language. For example, speakers of English/Japanese/Arabic/Spanish all know that they can use their language to request information, or to refuse to do something. By taking account of this, the programme designer/teacher is capitalizing on shared knowledge, and it is only then that he looks at the structural realization of the communicative category for whatever language he is dealing with. Hence, the approach has considerable powers of generalizability. One important development has been by researchers working in the field of teaching English to non-native speakers learning for specific purposes (ESP), particularly for science and technology. Widdowson (1975a), for instance, claims that we are being less than fair to our learners if we seek to teach them only a list of the structural items of English most commonly found in scientific writing. It is very likely that learners in an ESP situation will have some knowledge of the methodology of science in their own language. They will know, for example, that science tends to proceed by the use of such concepts as definition, classification, hypothesis-formation, all of which have a number of structural realizations. It would therefore be more realistic, and economical of time, to make such categories the defining feature of syllabuses.

The arguments are, of course, far more complex than has been represented here; we have simply tried to indicate the nature of the trend in current developments in TEFL. There seems to be an interesting convergence with some aspects of the debate surrounding MTT. It is clear that the impetus for the developments in TEFL has been provided to a large extent by a disenchantment with structural syllabuses, and that the starting point for MTT is rather obviously somewhat different and more diverse. However, it is the convergence and its implications that we will concentrate on here. One of Doughty's (1974) basic tenets is that linguistics, as concerned particularly with functional analyses of language, should have much more of a place in the school curriculum, not to be learnt as just another set of neutralized language categories, but in the sense that 'There must be at the centre of the idea of the discipline a concept of language that sees it as fundamentally a variety of human behaviour' (p. 30). He therefore develops a concept of 'Language Study' (which might also legitimately be referred to as 'Applied Linguistics') which has the function 'of mediating between the insights of linguistics and the linguistic needs of teachers and pupils.' (p. 34). To this end, the compilers of *Language in Use* (1971) have developed a number of basic functional categories of language, each containing a set of topics, so that pupils might become more aware of the range of uses of their own language. *Language in Use* is based fairly heavily on the functional study of language set out by Halliday (e.g. Halliday, 1970, 1973), and is grouped around Halliday's three major general functions: the 'interpersonal' function, which is concerned with language as a vehicle of social interaction; the 'ideational' function, which revolves around the individual's expression of experience; and the 'textual' function, which takes account of the structure and nature of language in itself and its internal cohesiveness.

Whilst it is true to say that functional syllabuses and materials for TEFL have a more diffuse base and tend less to espouse one particular theory of language, the fundamental conceptual overlap between MTT and TEFL is clear, at least as far as developments described here are concerned. It is significant that, in all cases, the learner is regarded as a competent native speaker of *a* language, and the 'knowledge' that he possesses can be turned to good effect when he learns another language and/or develops more consciously his command of his own.

One final point needs to be made with reference to functional approaches to syllabus design. A functional view mitigates against the piecemeal and allows greater comprehensiveness in an interesting way, because it can have a kind of 'umbrella' effect in showing the interrelatedness both within and between different areas of language teaching. For instance, the following 'compartments', listed randomly, might be found to be linked to a certain extent under such an umbrella, and insights from one might then be more easily relatable to another:

(1) General TEFL.
(2) Special-purpose language teaching.
(3) English as the mother tongue.
(4) Teaching of literature (which might be reinstated with more respect if integrated into a more general view of language).
(5) Teaching of science and other subjects in the native language.
(6) Teaching of modern languages.
(7) Adult literacy.

Greater interrelatedness might then support the proposals made, for example, by Hawkins (1974) and Doughty (1974), that 'language' be a legitimate area of study in schools, since it would presumably have the power to link a variety of interests and study areas within the school curriculum.

3(a). Study Skills

Mention of the whole curriculum raises the important question, implicit in (2) and (5) in the above list, of the relation of language to subjects outside 'the English lesson'. In MTT this relation is commonly discussed under the heading of 'Language across the Curriculum', and in TEFL/ESP under the rubric 'study skills', but the very different labels once again obscure significant similarities. Both are concerned with the (necessary and realistic) breaking down in relevant contexts of the hard and fast contours that identify 'English' (as the mother tongue or as a foreign language) as a subject. The *Bullock Report*, for instance, comes out against the full compartmentalizing of subjects within the school, which has tended to result in the severing of English from the rest of the curriculum. A similar point is made, likewise with suggestions for rectifying the situation, by Creber (1972); Britton (1974), too, propounds an 'operational' view. (These points of view, by implication at least, suggest to some extent a more fruitful overlap between mother-tongue English and other subjects than between English and foreign languages in the school.) The 'study skills' approach (as set out, e.g. by Candlin, Kirkwood and Moore, 1975) is concerned to 'minimize situational randomness' (p. 9) by analysing carefully the study situations in which students need to operate in language; language is then logically dependent on a prior analysis of study activities. Such an analysis, for both TEFL and MTT, is likely to reveal a fairly large number of different skills – writing essays, reports, outlines, answering examination questions, making notes, referring to non-verbal data, reading for different purposes, for example – all of which will give rise to finely differentiated language work.

The cross-curricular/study skills approach briefly expounded here implies that 'the subject English' has a clear service role to perform. For both TEFL and MTT, however, there is potentially a conflict. As Doughty (1974) puts it, one problem is:

> the fact that [subject] teachers' views of English . . . are dominated by their concern for its fundamental importance as a service, as the provider of 'language for learning', while teachers of English seem to them to be most concerned with things that appear irrelevant to this service function. (p. 59).

It is undeniable and understandable that language teachers, the majority of whom have been trained in a literary/humanities tradition, are likely to put up some resistance to, and even feel threatened by, the breaking down of what they see as the boundaries of their subject, and the more positive realization, that language teaching has in a sense been liberated to probe into many more areas than were traditionally open to it, is only likely to proceed rather slowly. The role of the teacher is bound to undergo some changes as a consequence, since it is more than likely that his/her pupils will know more about other subjects in the curriculum than the English teacher does. To quote an EFL perspective: the teacher

> must be prepared to stand down from the central role . . . and let the specialized knowledge and experience of the students generate specialized interaction of which he personally is not capable. Having established the conditions for such interaction, his role will be one of observer, adviser and corrector of errors. A specialized class is soon frustrated if the level of expert discussion is constantly limited to the level of expertise of the language teacher. (Webb, 1976, p. 130)

3(b). Study Skills – Generalizability of Skills

The product of an analysis of language needs in all the subject areas in a school would presumably be a classification of the competent uses of language expected by subject teachers. As such, it is the raw data for two types of decisions, which are nevertheless interdependent. The first is an evaluation, perhaps in the context of a whole school language policy, of various demands made on the pupils. A critical appraisal of what pupils are being expected to do 'across the curriculum' might reveal unsuspected (or uncomfortable) imbalances in, for example, the proportion of class time devoted to reading rather than answering written questions (*cf.* Harrison and Gardner in Marland, 1977, p. 146); the proportion of time spent taking dictation (*cf.* Martin, 1977, p. 146) or the proportion of writing tasks associated exclusively with assessment (*cf.* Martin, *op. cit.*, p. 147), to take three examples that have received some investigation, principally by the Schools Council Projects on the 'Effective Use of Reading', and 'Writing Research'. The difficulty of instituting such a policy of evaluation cannot be exaggerated, but movements are in train in various schools to set up whole school language policies and committees in which such discussions can take place (e.g. Appendices 2–5, Marland, 1977).

The second type of decision is a breakdown of reading texts, writing assignments and possibly talk situations, into components that can be taught. Paralleling the developments in study skills in TEFL, it is natural to suggest that these components should be defined in terms of communicative function. The advantage of this approach, we argue, is that functions which are used or required in several subject areas can be isolated for teaching purposes; this would have the desirable consequence of economizing teaching time and, somewhat more abstractly, of (perhaps) sharpening the students' perceptions of the generalizability of the communicative skills they are learning.

With reference to reading, this second type of decision involves an analysis of what the *Bullock Report* called 'the active interrogation of a text'. The work of Smith (1971) and Goodman (1967) on the use of prediction as a strategy for decoding text, embodied in the phrase 'the psycholinguistic guessing game', complemented by the more abstract theories current in psycholinguistic research on comprehension strategies in both listening and reading (e.g. Clark and Clark, 1977) have shown that competent reading is an active process involving not only guessing on the basis of recognition of transitional probabilities between words, but also considerable intellectual effort in using different strategies for discovering the message encoded in the printed symbols. But reading is more than decoding the literal meaning of a text; the work of Widdowson (1975b) has made explicit the competent reader's use of interpretive techniques for discovering the author's communicative intent. Decoding strategies and interpretive techniques, such as prediction, questioning, examination of syntactic and lexical cues, repeated examination of subtexts in relation to the whole, identification of discourse markers, and the recognition of rhetorical function of items within sentences, sentences within paragraphs, and paragraphs within the whole text (for a summary, see Marland, 1977, 'Subject reading strategies', pp. 104–128) can be identified and taught to pupils. Such strategies and techniques are useful for approaching any sort of written text, such as poems, novels, historical surveys, experimental reports, economic surveys or political arguments. This is not, of course, to deny that each of these genres may have special characteristics (for example, the probable addressee, the relation of the text to objective reality, its presuppositions about shared knowledge) of which the reader also needs to be aware.

With reference to writing, the second type of decision also implies a breakdown of assignments into teachable units. In this case, there might be summarizing, opening an argument, presenting evidence for an argument, describing a chronological sequence exemplifying an argument, presenting a dilemma, describing causal and other relations, deriving and presenting conclusions, and so forth, rather than restricting attention to superficial features such as spelling and punctuation. Each of these could be made the end point of a set of graded activities of various sorts, and in turn they can be gradually integrated into high-level activities such as essay writing, according to the demands made on the pupil by the various uses of English he is required to command in various categories. In EFL, an example of a widely used text-book using these techniques is *Writing as a Thinking Process* by Mary Lawrence. In terms of one popular classification of writing tasks, that of the London University Writing Research Unit, many of the above examples of sub-skills would be included under the term 'transactional writing'. However, it seems that an analysis in terms of a study skills approach and one in terms of the concept of transactional writing (Transactional = 1. Informative (record, report, generalized narrative, analogic, speculative, tautologic). 2. Conative (regulative, persuasive) (from Britton, in Davies, 1975)) are not so much in opposition as complementary. Where the sub-divisions of the 'transactional' concept emphasize the distinctive-ness of these styles of writing, the study skills approach builds upon those elements of organization and communicative function which they share. It should be noted that this feature of the overlap between TEFL and MTT developments is in no sense in opposition to an approach emphasizing 'expressive' or 'poetic' writing, for it appears to be self-evident that both approaches should coexist and benefit each other. (In fact, this coexistence is usual in both TEFL and MTT situations.) However, in passing, it has yet to be demonstrated that creative or 'expressive' writing is a necessary prerequisite for transactional writing, at least where equally well-elaborated justifications and schemes of work exist for both (*cf.* Gatherer's comment as formal discussant on Britton's paper, in Davies, 1975).

However, in arguing that it is possible to generalize the effective-ness of most teaching activities across subject area, we do not ignore the point that a tidy scheme of generalizable strategies and learning activities at the level of the syllabus is spurious and useless unless the learners themselves perceive its value. Unless the pupils realize that these approaches and techniques can be used in circumstances other than the English lesson, the sense is lost. This raises the question of the extent to which it is desirable either to introduce into the English class text and discussion material from other subjects upon which to base study skills activities, or to assume that work on general or literary texts and subjects will generalize to other subjects because teaching activities and functional skills will have been chosen on the basis of a needs analysis in those subjects. Any individual teacher's solution to this problem, both in TEFL and MTT, largely depends on his/her conception of his/her role, as mentioned above (Section 3a).

4. Language Learning Processes

It might be objected that the arguments we have put forward about the parallels between TEFL and MTT rest on a prior assumption that the processes of language acquisition are similar in the two situations, which may not be warranted. Despite the current research interest in second language learning (for reviews, see McLaughlin, 1977, or Cook, 1978) there is as yet very little hard evidence on the similarity or dissimilarity of the processes of learning one's first language and subsequent languages. The area of greatest controversy is at present the comparison of the processes used by the pre-school child in puzzling out the structure of the language of its environment and those used by children of primary school age and secondary school age in learning additional languages, in or out of school. While it is becoming clear that both sets of processes are characterized by 'creative construction' (Dulay and Burt, 1974), there is disagreement on the exact nature of the parallels, and about the importance, to a discussion of processes, of the obvious differences in the circumstances of learning; for example, age, maturity, knowledge of writing. Furthermore, the comparison tends to emphasize artefacts such as the supposed 'childlike' state of the second language learner in not having enough language to express mature opinions, whereas this state of sometimes acute frustration is unlikely to be analogous with that of a child acquiring the first language. In general, the extant research supports the claim that the processes of language acquisition in these different circumstances are much more similar than was previously thought, especially in relation to the acquisition of communication function (Hatch, 1976). However, the comparison most relevant to the topic of this paper would be between speakers of English as a foreign language using English to learn other subjects and native speakers of English in (mainly) secondary education. In fact, very little research has been conducted on this comparison. There is no evidence to support or refute the idea that foreign and native speakers use qualitatively different processes in tasks such as extracting meaning from a spoken or written text. Until evidence that refutes this claim is produced it is reasonable to assume that, for both, the processes in competent performance of listening and reading skills as they are being slowly revealed by psycholinguistic research are qualitatively similar. It is very unlikely that the reading process is different in kind if you choose to read your own language rather than an additional language. Of course, the speed and the amount that is comprehended may be different, because the accessibility of the syntax and lexicon may be different in the foreign language. In writing, it is known that non-native speakers use strategies of avoidance of syntactic construction they find difficult (Schachter, 1974); it is not clear whether anything similar happens in native writing in schools. There are no objections, therefore, from extant psychological research on the processes of acquisition of languages, to the claim that the differences between the two populations of major interest in this paper are differences of degree rather than kind.

5. Conclusions

We have argued that developments in TEFL and MTT have been converging to a point at which to continue regarding the philosophies and methodologies of each as quite separate and independent is counter-productive. This thesis has been elaborated principally by reference to historical antecedents, the 'functional umbrella', the issue of study skills across the curriculum, and psychological processes.

At several points the changing role of the English teacher has been mentioned. It is clear that the question of the English teacher's responsibility for the language skills of his pupils in other subject areas is a vexed one, but one that is equally familiar to teachers of EFL and MT. In discussing whole school language policies, Marland (1977) makes the point that there are two modes of procedure, which he labels 'specialized' and 'disseminated'. A 'specialized' procedure employs specialists for each component of the curriculum, a 'disseminated' procedure exhorts all teachers to contribute in certain areas. A similar opposition has been current in TEFL circles; for some, the English teacher is solely responsible for the students' language, for others, the subject specialists should also take responsibility for, and therefore training in, language teaching. Marland also makes the point that a language policy across the curriculum does not choose between the alternatives, but has to choose a suitable combination for that particular school; similarly, subject specialists and language teachers in TEFL programmes need to collaborate, and a needs analysis is a frequent starting point. However, there is a particular and interesting potential role conflict for the language specialist in both these situations. If it is true that language and thinking are as closely interwoven as some believe (Bruner, 1975), then the possibility exists that the different styles of writing, for example, demanded in different subjects reflect different expectations as to the nature of intellectual processes. That is to say, different subject specialists may be demanding different varieties of thinking. If this is so, then the language specialist may be in a state of conflict in deciding how best to fulfil the language needs of the pupils, without appearing to pull them in several directions at once. It is in the spirit of this paper to suggest that an approach based on communalities of language function across the curriculum provides both a pedagogic solution, and an integrating role for the language teacher. While the adoption of such an approach presents this challenge, it does not of itself prescribe or preclude the choice of any particular pedagogic techniques for the classroom.

Of course, there are differences between the TEFL and MTT situation. At the level of the comparison between college age and postgraduate non-native speakers and secondary school age native speakers, we have argued that these undoubted differences are mainly ones of degree rather than kind. These groups of students differ in the depth of their knowledge of the language, the breadth of their knowledge of the subject areas, their experience of the particular teaching situation, and sometimes in their preconceptions of the learning task, to say nothing of their emotional development and personal discipline. Students learning English to further their studies of another subject approach the language learning task with different personal aims, and different background knowledge to pupils who are learning both the subject matter and the new uses of language for the first time. These differences are, however, ones of degree. As regards the organization of teaching, it is not often that the TEFL teacher is in the fortunate position of the MT teacher of being able to participate in decision-making across the curriculum in the context of a 'language policy'. More frequently, the EFL teacher is only able to take decisions immediately affecting his own classes.

Nevertheless, we have argued that teaching in either situation is showing remarkable and important parallels with the other. These parallels have come about from a variety of developments in each field and have centred on the usefulness of a conception of language as a set of expressive devices for a range of cognitive and social functions.

References

A Language for Life (1975) Report of the Bullock Committee (London: HMSO).

Atkinson, D. and Wilkinson, A. M. (1966) 'A Test of Listening Comprehension', *Educational Review*, Vol. 18, No. 3.

Bailey, Beryl (1964) 'Some Problems Involved in the Language Teaching Situation – Jamaica', *in* Shuy, R. (ed.) *Social Dialects and Language Learning* (Illinois: National Council of Teachers of English).

Baratz, J. C. (1968) *A Bidialectual Task for Determining Language Proficiency in Economically Disadvantaged Negro Children*. Washington D.C.: Report from the Center for Applied Linguistics.

Baratz, S. S. and Baratz, J. C. (1970) 'Early Childhood Intervention: the Social Science Base of Institutional Racism', *Harvard Educational Review*, 40. 1, pp. 29–50.

Barnes, D., Britton, J. and Rosen, H. (1969) *Language, Learner and the School* (Harmondsworth: Penguin).

Barnes, D. (1971) 'Language and Learning in the Classroom', *Journal of Curriculum Studies*, 3. 1, pp. 27–38.

Barnes, D. (1975) *From Communication to Curriculum* (Harmondsworth: Penguin).

Bereiter, C. and Engelmann, S. (1966) *Teaching Disadvantaged Children in Pre-School* (Prentice Hall).

Berko, J. (1961) 'The Child's Learning of English Morphology', *in* Saporta, S. (ed.) *Psycholinguistics: A Book of Readings* (New York: Holt, Rinehart and Winston).

Bernstein, B. (1959) 'A Public Language: Some Sociological Implications of a Linguistic Form', *British Journal of Sociology*, 10.

Bernstein, B. (1967) 'The Role of Speech in the Development and Transmission of Culture', *in* Klopf, G. J. and Hohman, W. A. (eds.) *Perspectives on Learning* (New York: Mental Health Materials Center).

Bernstein, B. (1970) 'A Socio-linguistic Approach to Socialization: With Some Reference to Educability', *in* Gumperz, J. J. and Hymes, D. H. (eds.) *Directions in Sociolinguistics* (New York: Holt, Rinehart and Winston).

Bernstein, B. (1970) 'Education Cannot Compensate for Society', *New Society*, 26 Feb.

Bernstein, B. (1970) 'A Critique of the Concept "Compensatory Education"', *in* Williams, S. (ed.) *Language and Poverty: Perspectives on a Theme* (Madison, Wisconsin: University of Wisconsin Press).

Bernstein, B. (1971) 'On the Classification and Framing of Educational Knowledge', *in* Young, M. F. D. (ed.) *Knowledge and Control* (Collier-Macmillan).

Bernstein, B. (1971) *Class, Codes and Control,* Volume I (London: Routledge and Kegan Paul).

Blank, M. and Solomon, F. (1969) *Child Development,* 40. 1, pp. 47–61.

Bloom, B. S. *et al.* (1956) *Taxonomy of Educational Objectives* (London: Longman).

Britton, James (1970) *Language and Learning* (London: Allen Lane, The Penguin Press).

Britton, J. L. (1971) 'What's the Use?' *in* 'The Context of Language', *Educational Review,* Vol. 23, No. 3.

Britton, J. (1974) 'English in the Curriculum', *in: CILT Reports and Papers,* No. 10.

Britton, J. (1975) 'Teaching Writing', *in* Davies, A. (ed.) *Problems of Language and Learning* (London: Heinemann).

Britton, J. *et al.* (1975) *The Development of Writing Abilities 11–18* (London: Schools Council, Macmillan Education).

Brown, R. (1973) *A First Language: the Early Stages* (London: Allen and Unwin).

Brown, R. (1974) *A First Language* (London: Allen and Unwin).

Bruner, J. S. (1975) 'Language as an Instrument of Thought', *in* Davies, A. (ed.) *Problems of Language and Learning* (London: Heinemann).

Bruner, J. S. (1975) 'The Ontogenesis of Speech Acts', *Journal of Child Language,* 1, No. 2, pp. 1–19.

Bullock Report (1975) *A Language for Life* (HMSO).

Candlin, C. N., Kirkwood, J. M. and Moore, H. M. (1975) 'Developing Study Skills in English', *in* ETIC. The British Council: *English for Academic Purposes: Problems and Perspectives.*

Carroll, J. B. (1968) *Development of Native Language Skills beyond the Early Years* (New Jersey: Princeton, ETS).

Cassidy, F. G. (1967) *Jamaica Talk* (Cambridge: Cambridge University Press).

Cassirer, Ernst (1946) (transl. Susanne K. Langer) *Language and Myth* (New York: Dover Publications).

Cazden, C. B. (1970) 'The Neglected Situation in Child Language Research and Education', *in* Wolfson, J. (1976, pp. 145–164).

Centre for Information on Language Teaching (1974) *The Space Between,* Reports and Papers, No. 10.

Chomsky, Carol (1969) *The Acquisition of Syntax from 5 to 10,* M.I.T. Research Monographs No. 57 (Massachusetts: M.I.T. Press).

Chomsky, Noam (1975) *Aspects of the Theory of Syntax* (Massachusetts: MIT Press).

Clark, H. and Clark, E. (1977) *Psychology and Language* (New York: Harcourt Brace Jovanovich).

Cole, M. and Bruner, J. S. (1971) 'Cultural Differences and Inferences about Psychological Processes', *in* Wolfson, J. (1976, pp. 165–180).

Cook, V. J. (1978) 'Second Language Learning: a Psycholinguistic Approach', *in: Language Teaching and Linguistics: Abstracts* (in press).
Council of Europe (1973) *Systems Development in Adult Learning.*
Creber, J. W. P. (1972) *Lost for Words* (Harmondsworth: Penguin).
Crystal, David (1976) *Child Language, Learning and Linguistics* (London: Edward Arnold).
Crystal, D. and Davy, D. (1969) *Investigating English Style* (London: Longman).
Danes, F. (1964) 'A Three-level Approach to Syntax', *Travaux Linguistiques, de Prague*, I, 225–240.
Davie, R. *et al.* (1972) *From Birth to Seven* (London: Longman).
Davies, A. (ed.) (1975) *Problems in Language and Learning* (London: Heinemann).
Department of Education and Science (1971) Education Survey 13, *The Education of Immigrants* (HMSO).
DeSilva, W. A. (1969) 'Concept Formation in Adolescence Through Contextual Cues with Special Reference to History Material', *Ph.D. Thesis*, Birmingham.
Dixon, John (1965) *Growth through English* (London: Oxford University Press).
Doughty, P. S. (1969) 'Current Practice in English Teaching', *paper presented to Conference of Teachers in Approved Schools*, Language, Life and Learning (Sunningdale).
Doughty, P. (1974) *Language, 'English' and the Curriculum* (London: Edward Arnold).
Doughty, P., Pearce, J. and Thornton, G. (1971) *Language in Use* (London: Edward Arnold).
Dulay, H. and Burt, M. (1974) 'A New Perspective on the "Creative Construction" Process in Child Second Language Acquisition', *in Language Learning*, 24, pp. 253–278.
English Teaching Information Centre (1975) *English for Academic Purposes: Problems and Perspectives* (The British Council).
Erikson, Erik H. (1965) *Childhood and Society* (Harmondsworth: Penguin).
Firth, J. R. (1935) 'The Technique of Semantics', *Transactions of the Philological Society*. Reprinted in Firth, J. R. *Papers in Linguistics 1934–51* (London: O.U.P. 1957).
Firth, J. R. (1958) *Papers in Linguistics, 1934–1951* (London: O.U.P.).
Firth, J. R. (1964) 'The Tongues of Men' (originally printed 1937) in *The Tongues of Men and Speech* (London: O.U.P.).
Firth, J. R. (1968) 'Linguistic Analysis as a Study of Meaning', *in* Palmer, F. R. (ed.) *Selected Papers of J. R. Firth 1952–59* (London: Longman Linguistics Library).
Foley, J. P. and Cofer, C. N. (1945) 'Mediated Generalization and the Interpretation of Verbal Behaviour II', *in* Experimental Study of Certain Homophone and Synonym Gradients, *Journal of Experimental Psychology*, 32, 169–75.
Geach, Peter (1969) 'Should Traditional Grammar be Ended or Mended?' *in* 'The State of Language', *Educational Review*, 22. 1, pp. 18–25.
Giles, H. (1970) 'Evaluative Reactions to Accents', *Educational Review*, 22, pp. 211–27.

Goldman-Eisler, F. (1961a) 'A Comparative Study of Two Hesitation Phenomena', *in: Language and Speech*, 4, pp. 18–26.

Goldman-Eisler, F. (1961b) 'Significance of Changes in Rate of Articulation', *in: Language and Speech*, pp. 171–4.

Goldman-Eisler, F. (1961c) 'Continuity of Speech Utterance', *in: Language and Speech*, 4, pp. 220–31.

Goodman, K. S. (1967) 'Reading: A Psycholinguistic Guessing Game', *Journal of the Reading Specialist*, May.

Greenfield, P. M. (1966) 'On Culture and Conservation', *in* Bruner, J. S. *et al.* (eds.) *Studies in Cognitive Growth*, pp. 225–56 (New York: Wiley).

Halliday, M. A. K. (1965) 'Speech and Situation', *in: Some Aspects of Oracy* (N.A.T.E.).

Halliday, M. A. K. (1969) 'Relevant Models of Language', *in* 'The State of Language', *Educational Review*, 22. 1, pp. 26–37.

Halliday, M. A. K. (1970) 'On Functional Grammars'. Paper read to seminar *The Construction of Complex Grammars* (Boston: Massachusetts (mimeographed)).

Halliday, M. A. K. (1970) 'Language Structure and Language Function', *in* Lyons, J. (ed.) *New Horizons in Linguistics* (Harmondsworth: Penguin).

Halliday, M. A. K. (1973) *Explorations in the Functions of Language* (London: Edward Arnold).

Halliday, M. A. K. (1975) 'Learning to Mean', *in* Lenneberg, E. and E. *Foundations of Language Development* (U.N.E.S.C.O. and I.B.R.O.).

Halliday, M. A. K., McIntosh, Angus and Strevens, Peter (1964) *The Linguistic Sciences and Language Teaching* (London: Longman Linguistics Library).

Harding, D. W. (1937) 'The Role of the Onlooker', *in: Scrutiny*, VI(3), pp. 247–58 (Cambridge: Deighton Bell).

Harding, D. W. (1962) 'Psychological Processes in the Reading of Fiction', *in: British Journal of Aesthetics*, II(2), pp. 133–47 (London: Thames and Hudson).

Harpin, W. S. *et al.* (1973) *Social and Educational Influences on Children's Acquisition of Grammar* (University of Nottingham School of Education).

Harrison, Bernard (1976) *The Literate Response* (unpublished Ph.D. thesis, University of Exeter).

Harrison, C. and Gardner, K. (1977) 'The Place of Reading', *in* Marland, M. (ed.) *Language Across the Curriculum* (London: Heinemann).

Hartog, P. and Rhodes, E. C. (1936) *An Examination of Examinations* (London: Macmillan).

Hasan, Ruqaiya (1969) 'Code, Register and Social Dialect', paper presented to London School of Economics Seminar *Language and Society* (London, May).

Hasan, Ruqaiya (1971) 'Syntax and Semantics', *in* Morton, J. (ed.) *Biological and Social Factors in Psycholinguistics* (London: Logos Press).

Hasan, Ruqaiya (1973) 'Code, Register and Social Dialect', *in* Bernstein, B. (ed.) *Class, Codes and Control: Applied Studies in the Sociology of Language* (London: Routledge and Kegan Paul).

Hatch, E. (1976) 'Discourse Analysis and Second Language Acquisition', *in: Workpapers in TESL* (UCLA).

Hawkins, E. (1974) 'Modern Languages in the Curriculum', *in: CILT Reports and Papers*, No. 10.

Hawkins, P. R. (1969) 'Social Class: The Nominal Group and Reference', *Language and Speech*, 12, Part 2.

Hitchman, P. J. (1966) *Examining Oral English in Schools* (London: Methuen).

HMSO (1964) *Half our Future* (The Newsom Report).

Holbrook, D. (1961) *English for Maturity* (Cambridge: Cambridge University Press).

Hudson, W. (1960) 'Pictorial Depth Perception in Sub-cultural Groups in Africa', *Journal of Social Psychology*, 52, pp. 183–208.

Hudson, W. (1967) 'The Study of the Problem of Pictorial Perception among Unacculturated Groups', *International Journal of Psychology*, 2, pp. 90–107.

Humphrey, G. (1951) *Thinking* (London: Methuen).

Hull, C. H. (1952) *A Behaviour System* (New Haven: Y.U.P.).

Hymes, D. H. (1970) 'On Communicative Competence', *in* Gumperz, J. J. and Hymes, D. H. (eds.) *Directions in Sociolinguistics* (New York: Holt, Rinehart and Winston).

Inhelder, B. and Piaget, J. (1959) *The Growth of Thinking* (London: Routledge and Kegan Paul).

Jackson, G. H. (1932) *Selected Writings,* Volume 2 (London: Hodder).

Johnson, K. (1977) 'Adult Beginners: a Functional, or Just a Communicative Approach?' Paper delivered at B.A.A.L. Annual General Meeting, September 1977.

Katz, J. J. and Fodor, J. A. (1963) 'The Structure of a Semantic Theory', *Language*, 39, pp. 170–210.

Keislar, E. and Stern, C. (1968) 'Effects of Dialect and Instructional Procedures on Children's Oral Language Production and Conception Acquisition', *in: Urban Education*, 3 (3), pp. 169–176.

Knight, R. (1977) 'Examiners' English', *in: English in Education*, 11. 2, pp. 24–32.

Labov, W. (1967) 'Some Sources of Reading Problems for Negro Speakers of Non-standard English', *in: New Directions in Elementary English* (Illinois: National Council of Teachers of English).

Labov, W. (1968) 'The Reflection of Social Processes in Linguistic Structures', *in* Fishman, J. (ed.) *Readings in the Sociology of Language* (The Hague: Mouton).

Labov, W. (1969) 'The Logic of Non-standard English', *in: Language in Education*, pp. 198–212 (London: Routledge and Kegan Paul).

Labov, W. (1970) 'The Logic of Non-standard English', *in: Language and Poverty*, Williams, F. (ed.) (Chicago: Markham).

Lamb, S. M. (1966) *Outline of Stratificational Grammar* (Washington, D.C.: Georgetown U.P.).

Lane, M. (1970) (ed.) *Introduction to Structuralism* (New York: Basic Books Inc.).

Langer, Susanne K. (1960) *Philosophy in a New Key* (3rd edn.) (Cambridge, Mass.: Harvard University Press).

La Priere, R. T. (1934) 'Attitudes Versus Actions', *in: Social Forces,* Volume 13, pp. 230–37.

Lawrence, M. (1972) *Writing as a Thinking Process* (Michigan: University of Michigan Press).

Lawton, D. (1966) 'A Study of Linguistic Differences . . . in Working Class and Middle Class Boys . . .' *unpublished thesis* (University of London).

Lewis, M. M. (1963) *Language, Thought and Personality in Infancy and Childhood* (London: Harrap).

Littlewood, W. T. (1974) 'Communicative Competence and Grammatical Accuracy in Foreign Language Learning', *in: Educational Review*, Vol. 27, No. 1, pp. 34–44.

Loban, Walter (1963) *The Language of Elementary School Children* (Champaign, Illinois: NCTE).

Luckman, A. W. (1964) 'The Meaningful Learning of German Vocabulary by Eleven-Year-Old Pupils in a Selective Secondary Technical School in Birmingham', *unpublished M.Ed. thesis* (Birmingham).

Lyons, John (1963) *Structural Semantics* (Oxford: Blackwell).

Mackay, David and Thompson, Brian (1968) *The Initial Teaching of Reading and Writing,* Programme in Linguistics and English Teaching, Paper 3 (London: Longman).

Macmillan, M. (1976) 'A Survey of Recent Trends in the Development of English Courses for Students of Science and Technology', *in* Wilson, G. (ed.) *Curriculum Development and Syllabus Design for English Teaching,* RELC/SEAMEO (Singapore University Press).

Malinowski, B. (1923) 'The Problem of Meaning in Primitive Languages', Supplement I to Ogden, C. K. and Richards, I. A. *The Meaning of Meaning* (London: Routledge and Kegan Paul).

Malinowski, B. (1935) *Coral Gardens and their Magic,* Volume II (London: Allen and Unwin).

Manchester School of Education (1966) C.S.E. Research Project: English Panel – Interim Report.

Marland, M. (ed.) (1977) *Language Across the Curriculum* (London: Heinemann).

Martin, M. (1977) 'Writing', *in* Marland, M. (ed.).

Martin, N. *et al.* (1976) *Writing and Learning across the Curriculum* Schools Council (London: Ward Lock).

McCarthy, D. A. (1954) 'Language Development in Children', *in* Carmichael, L. (ed.) *A Manual of Child Psychology*, pp. 492–630 (New York: John Wiley).

McLaughlin, B. (1977) 'Second Language Learning in Children', *Psychological Bulletin*, 84, pp. 438–59.

McNeill, D. (1976) *The Acquisition of Language* (New York: Harper and Row).

Midwinter, E. (1969) *Educational Priority Areas: the Philosophical Question*. The Liverpool E.P.A. Project. Occasional Paper, 1.

Moffett, James (1968) *Teaching the Universe of Discourse* (Boston: Houghton and Mifflin Company).

Mohan, B. A. (1969) 'An Investigation of the Relationship between Language and Situational Factors in Card Games, with Specific

Attention to the Language of Instructions', *Ph.D. thesis* (University of London).

Mordecai, J. (1966) 'West Indian Children's Language Study', *Dissertation* (University of Birmingham, School of Education).

Morris, C. (1956) *Signs, Language and Behaviour* (New York: Prentice Hall).

Morris, J. M. (1966) *Standards and Progress in Reading* (N.F.E.R.).

Muehl, Lois and Siegnar (1970) 'One Way to Extract the "Square" Root from Opera', *The Journal of Negro Education,* Volume XXXIX, Number 1 (Washington, DC: Bureau of Educational Research, The Howard University Press).

Musgrove, F. and Taylor, P. H. (1969) *Society and the Teacher's Role* (London: Routledge and Kegan Paul).

Osgood, C. E., Suci, G. J. and Tannenbaum, P. H. (1957) *The Measurement of Meaning* (Urbana).

Peel, E. A. (1962) 'Meaning and Learning', *B.P.S. Bulletin,* Number 48, July.

Peel, E. A. (1972) 'The Quality of Thinking in Second School Subjects', *Educational Review,* Vol. 24, No. 3.

Piaget, J. (1926) *The Language and Thought of the Child.* Revised edn. 1959 (London: Routledge and Kegan Paul).

Piaget, J. (1970) *Structuralism* (New York: Basic Books Inc.).

Pike, K. L. (1967) 'Language in Relation to a Unified Theory of the Structure of Human Behaviour', 2nd revised edn. (The Hague: Mouton, Janua Linguarum Series Major 24).

Pope, Alexander (1709) *Essay on Criticism.*

Postman, N. and Weingartner, C. (1966) *Linguistics: A Revolution in Teaching* (Los Angeles: Dell Publishing Co.).

Raph, J. (1967) 'Language and Speech Defects in Culturally Disadvantaged Children', *Journal of Speech and Hearing Disorders,* 32, pp. 203–14.

Roberts, R. (1971) *The Classic Slum* (Harmondsworth: Penguin).

Sapir, E. (1921) *Language* (New York: Harcourt, Brace and World, repr. Rupert Hart-Davis).

Schachter, J. (1974) 'An Error in Error Analysis', *Language Learning,* 24, pp. 205–14.

Sebeok, Thomas A. (ed.) (1960) *Style in Language* (New York: Wiley) (for Jakobson, Roman, *Linguistics and Poetics*).

Smith, F. (1971) *Understanding Reading* (New York: Holt, Rinehart and Winston).

Southampton Institute of Education (1966) *C.S.E. Trial Examinations: Oral English,* Schools Council Examination Bulletin 11 (London: HMSO).

Stratta, L., Dixon, J. and Wilkinson, A. (1973) *Patterns of Language* (London: Heinemann).

Strevens, P. (1971) 'Alternatives to Daffodils', *in* CILT Reports and Papers No. 7, *Science and Technology in a Second Language.*

Thorndike, E. L. (1944) *Teachers Word Book of 30,000 Words* (New York: Bureau of Publications, Teachers College, Columbia University).

Tough, Joan (1969) 'Language and Environment: An Interim Report on Longitudinal Study', *unpublished report* (Leeds University, Institute of Education).

Tough, Joan (1973) 'The Language of Young Children: The Implications for the Education of the Young Disadvantaged Child', *in* Chazan, Maurice (ed.) *Education in the Early Years* (University College of Swansea).

Tough, Joan (1976) *Listening to Children Talking* (London: Ward Lock Educational).

Turner, G. J. (1969) 'Social Class Differences in Regulatory Language', *report prepared for Sociological Research Unit* (University of London Institute of Education).

Turner, G. J. (1973) 'Social Class and Children's Language of Control', *in* Bernstein, B. (ed.) *Class, Codes and Control: applied studies in the Sociology of Language* (London: Routledge and Kegan Paul).

Turner, G. J. and Pickvance, R. E. (1969) 'Social Class Differences in the Expression of Uncertainty in Five-year-old Children', *Language and Speech*.

Vernon, P. E. (1969) *Intelligence and Cultural Environment* (London: Methuen).

Vygotsky, L. S. (1962) *Thought and Language* (Cambridge, Mass: M.I.T. Press).

Wade, B. (1978) 'The Assessment of Oral Competence at 16 + ', *English in Education*, June.

Wax, M. L. and Wax, R. H. (1971) 'Cultural Deprivation as an Educational Ideology', *in* Leacock, E. B. (ed.) *The Culture of Poverty: A Critique* (New York: Simon and Schuster).

Webb, J. (1976) 'Reflections on Practical Experience in Designing and Counting ESP Courses at the Colchester English Study Centre', *in* Wilson, G. (ed.).

Wells, G. (1974) 'Learning to Code Experience through Language', *Journal of Child Language*, 1. 2, November.

Whorf, B. L. (1966 reprint) *Language, Thought and Reality* (Cambridge, Mass: M.I.T. Press).

Widdowson, H. G. (1975a) 'EST in Theory and Practice', *in* ETIC.

Widdowson, H. G. (1975b) *Stylistics and the Teaching of Literature* (London: Longman).

Wight, J. and Norris, R. A. (1970) *Teaching English to West Indian Children: the Research Stage of the Project*. Schools Council Working Paper 29, (London: Evans Methuen Educational).

Wight, J. (1971) 'Language Deprivation and Remedial Teaching Techniques', *in: The Selected Proceedings of the Second International Congress of Applied Linguistics* (Cambridge University Press).

Wight, J. (1971) 'Dialect in School', *Educational Review* 24, pp. 47–58.

Wilkins, D. (1976) *National Syllabuses* (Oxford University Press).

Wilkinson, A. *et al.* (1965) *Spoken English* (University of Birmingham).

Wilkinson, A. (1966 2nd ed.) *Spoken English* with contributions by Alan Davies and Dorothy Atkinson (University of Birmingham Faculty of Education).

Wilkinson, A. (ed.) (1969) *The State of Language* (University of Birmingham, Faculty of Education).

Wilkinson, A. (1971) *The Foundations of Language* (London: Oxford University Press).

Williams, J. T. (1977) *Learning to Write, or Writing to Learn?* (N.F.E.R.).

Wilson, G. (ed.) (1976) *Curriculum Development and Syllabus Design for English Teaching*, RELC/SEAMEO (Singapore University Press).

Wiseman, S. (1949) 'The Marking of English Composition in Grammar School Selection', *British Journal of Educational Psychology*, 19, pp. 200–209.

Witkin, R. (1974) *The Intelligence of Feeling* (London: Heinemann).

Wolfson, J. (1976) *Personality and Learning 2* (London: Hodder and Stoughton).

Yarlott, G. (1972) *Education and Children's Emotions* (London: Weidenfeld and Nicolson).

Yerrill, K. A. J. (1977) 'A consideration of the later development of children's syntax in speech, and writing: a study of parenthetical, appositional and related items'. *Unpublished Ph.D. thesis* (Newcastle University).